FROM STAR WARS TO SUPERMAN:

CONVERSATIONS WITH MAKEUP LEGEND

Stuart Freeborn

BY JOE NAZZARO

From *Star Wars* to *Superman*:
Ten Years of Interviews with Makeup Legend Stuart Freeborn
By Joe Nazzaro
First Edition
Copyright © 2025 Joe Nazzaro

Published in the USA by:
BearManor Media
1317 Edgewater Dr #110
Orlando, FL 32804
www.bearmanormedia.com

Perfect ISBN 979-8-88771-631-2
Case ISBN 979-8-88771-632-9
BearManor Media, Orlando, Florida
Printed in the United States of America
Book design by Robbie Adkins, www.adkinsconsult.com

*Dedication: For my wife Sheelagh,
my collaborator and confidante, always*

Table of Contents

Introduction: My Dinner with Yoda and Other Adventures

Back in the mid-nineties, my wife Sheelagh and I sold Virgin Books our idea for a project that would spotlight a small group of film/television makeup pioneers and their protégés. The list of pioneers was easy to put together: Dick Smith, the 'godfather of makeup.' John Chambers, who won an honorary Oscar for Planet of the Apes (there wasn't an official category until 1981). Michael Westmore, a veteran of numerous Star Trek TV shows and an Oscar-winner himself. Christopher Tucker, the creative genius behind the Elephant Man. And of course, Stuart Freeborn, whose work on such films as Star Wars and 2001 made him a legend in the industry. I had already met Freeborn a couple of years earlier and knew he was a born storyteller; in fact, it would be easy to write an entire book on Stuart alone, with a career that spanned more than half a century of the British film industry.

Over the next several months, Sheelagh and I began lining up interviews in New York, Los Angeles and the UK. The latter usually involved a short drive to Freeborn's Esher home, which also encompassed the sprawling workshop used to build countless creatures from aliens to apes. As I had already discovered from my first visit, a trip to Freeborn-Land generally lasted the better part of a day, ending only when the supply of audio tape and batteries ran out.

After doing a number of interviews, I got a call from our editor at Virgin Books. A new publisher had taken over, and he didn't think our pioneers and protégés idea was 'sexy' enough (yes, that was the word he used). We did some poking around, but nobody else was interested. I was eventually able to re-purpose some of that interview material over the years, but nothing with all those Freeborn interviews, and believe me, there were a lot of them. I think at some point I added it all up and figured we had nearly 24 hours on tape.

For many years, even after Stuart's passing in 2013 at the impressive age of 98, I tried to figure out how that wealth of material could be shared; eventually deciding I would publish it myself. But how do you stitch together a series of random conversations into a cohesive whole? The answer: you don't.

While I was sorting out my disorganized library one day, I came across a book called Eisner/Miller, a full-length interview between comic book legends Will Eisner and Frank Miller. Presented in Q&A format, the sprawling conversation ran more than 300 pages. That's when I realized I could use a similar structure: run all of the interviews as one giant freewheeling conversation, breaking things up with additional background information.

The end result, I hope, is that reader will get a real feeling what it was like to sit on the Freeborn living room couch or in their beautiful back yard (albeit without the airplane noise), leaf through his photo albums, or tour his workshop.

Joe Nazzaro
New Jersey, 2023

Stuart Freeborn Interview Part I

In the pre-Internet days, information wasn't as readily available as it is today, which meant a journalist often had to do a bit of detective work. In the case of Stuart Freeborn, I discovered he and his wife lived in Esher, maybe ten miles from our flat in Brentford. Even better, his number was in the phone book, so I called Stuart, who immediately agreed to do an interview. It was a short trip by train, and Stuart offered to pick me up at the station. 'I'm easy to spot,' he told me, 'just look for somebody who looks like Yoda!'

The Freeborns turned out to be wonderful hosts, and that trip turned out to be a precursor of all future visits, where a one-hour interview usually ended up taking half a day or maybe longer. And I quickly learned that a conversation rarely went in a straight line, instead meandering in all manner of different directions.

Unfortunately, when I got home that afternoon, I discovered that my tape recorder batteries had run down, rendering much of the tape utterly useless. I subsequently invested in a new tape recorder that showed the amount of battery charge, but the damage was done. I ended up spending far too much time reconstructing bits of conversation from memory, but it wasn't long before I made a return trip to Esher…

Tell me about your early career. What made you want to get into the entertainment business at the time?

I actually got in at the age of 36, but I had been trying since I left school at age 14. I was at a boarding school, and in my last year, we did a lot of concerts, and I was in all of them, but I also became the makeup man. What I really wanted to be at that time was an actor, which was why I enjoyed being in those concerts; I enjoyed *acting*, but I kept waiting for those heavier characters to come up, because I liked all the makeup involved. They eventually said, 'Hey, we can't be doing all that stuff as well; you'd better be our makeup man!' so I ended up making everyone else up, including myself, and the more I did it, the more I enjoyed it. It was fun, and that's how the first conception came to me before I left school.

I then went around all the agencies up and down Wardour Street, trying to put my name down as a crowd artist, because I had already gone to the studios and tried to get in, but no, so I wrote to them, expecting to get some sort of answer even if it was only a 'no,' but I didn't even get that. I got nothing, so 1 thought, 'Well, I'll actually go to the studios, and talk to the chief makeup person there!' Having written to them and not gotten any answer, I thought I would just try, even though it was a long way for me to even get to the studios. I didn't have a car or anything, so I cycled all the way, and it was a *very* long way, in an area I didn't know. This was in the old Elstree days, before even EMI, so I went to go in, and there was a commissionaire standing at the gate- there was a big car park on the high street, and you had to go through the car park, and there was a commissionaire at the studio so I parked my bike around the corner, and walked around, saw the commissionaire, and went to walk in with the other people, but he saw me and said, 'Come here, where are you going?' He recognized I wasn't a regular you see, so I said, 'I'm going in to see the chief makeup man!'

He asked if I had an appointment, and I said, 'I've written to him,' and he said [in a very loud voice,] 'Have you got an appointment?' I said, 'Well… no,' and he said, 'Get out!' I walked out and hid around the corner, thinking, 'I haven't cycled all this way to be told to get out!' so I went around the other side, came up from the other direction, waiting until there were some more cars, and a lot of people, and then I got in closer to them on the opposite side to where he was standing and got in quite a way. But, suddenly, I heard a voice say, 'Oi, come 'ere!' I pretended I hadn't heard him, and I was still going in, and he said again, "Oi, you pretending not to hear me! Come 'ere!" so it was no good, I had to go back. He said, "I thought I told you to get out," so that was it. I tried to get into other studios, but I didn't even get through the gates not even a few yards before getting dragged out.

So then I thought, 'Maybe if I did photographs of a few makeups…' I had to get some money to buy the makeup, and I had an office job, strangely enough, for the Dunlop Rubber Company as an office boy, so I learned a lot about rubber. I was interested in rubber because it was new, and I used it later after I was in films, with latex.

Anyway, I then thought 'Well, I should let them see what I can do,' so I bought hair, spirit gum; all that stuff, and I went home, and fixed up a whole lot of lights connected to a rack: of switches. I used to play the violin in those days, so I still had a music stand, and I bought an old camera, a wooden one- for about two shillings, and stuck it on top of the music stand. It didn't have a shutter- it wasn't an expensive camera, so what I did was get a bit of cardboard, put a bit of black velvet around it, made a hole in it, and fixed it up with a rod, so if I turned it a certain way, it would take a picture.

I also had a mirror on a piece of wire, and I balanced it so if I put it just between where the plate was in the camera and me, I knew that what I saw in the mirror was exactly what was on the plate. And I knew that if I touched it, it would swing round, and it would stay at the back, so first of all, I'd be looking in the mirror with all my makeup on, then I would get the lights right, then I would get what I thought was the appropriate expression, then I touched the mirror so it swung around the back, and then took my own picture on this portaplate thing.

I did lots of those, and I also did a lot of photos of the make-up in process where I was doing an aging, because I was still in my teens at the time, so I was making myself up as an old man:

bald head, and beards and wrinkles and all those things. I tried to get it all in, but in stages.

Then I'd go into the bathroom, and process them all. I couldn't afford an enlarger but I had as a kid, an old magic lantern, so I'd set that up and use that as an enlarger. I had a picture frame where I pinned the prints and turned all these portaplate plates into 10 by 8s until I'd got a nice collection. I parceled them all up, and sent them off to the different studios thinking, 'Well, at least they can see what I'm doing!'

So I waited and waited and waited- nothing, nothing, nothing from anybody, not even 'Thank you for sending the pictures, but they're not good enough!' Just nothing, so I thought, 'Obviously I'm not doing the right thing!' The only books I could get on makeup were on theatre makeup which was quite different from film makeup, but I realized that, and tried to adapt my approach to a more natural makeup than theatre makeup, which like scenery you painted very coarsely and contrast-y so you could see it from the back of the theatre, and as I said, it was pretty crude, so I thought it's not good enough.

Because there were no books on film makeup, the only thing to do was actually put the makeups on film. I had read about a local chap who was interested in setting up a 16 mil cine-society. People were just beginning to buy cine-cameras, so I sold my bike and a few other things and bought a cine-camera, and I contacted this chap. We both went into this together, and got a lot of other people, including one chap, whose name was Maurice Denham, who was a bank clerk who wanted to be an actor, and who became a buddy of mine. You've heard of him of course.

I used to write the scripts for these projects we were doing, and I used to write in all kinds of aging and turning normal English people into Chinese; all sorts of things. It meant me doing makeups full-time, and I got quite good at it. We all operated the cameras- well, we all did everything, the actors and everything, and we got a lot of know-how on how to make a better film. I was getting on with makeup, so when I saw the film, I realized it didn't need much improving; just a touch here and there, and I was getting to the point where I didn't know how to make it any better, so I thought, 'Now's the time to maybe do some photographs and send them out again, and maybe I can improve!' which I did, but nothing ever happened. I didn't get anywhere, so I thought, 'Well, that's the finisher!' but I also realized that perhaps I could pull some stunts to get a bit of attention.

In those days, there was a war with Ethiopia going on. Haile Sellasie was sort of rescued and living in London, and I noticed there were many photographs of him in the newspaper, but you only saw him with his pith helmet on. You never saw him without that helmet, so I got a pith helmet, because when I was buying the makeup and doing the film business, I used to go around all the stores in London buying all sorts of bits and pieces; hats, any odd thing. I used to buy them as part of my makeup equipment, so one of the chaps in our society, his father was in the car hire business, so I said to him, 'Do you ever drive any of your fathers cars?' and he said, 'Yes I do, I've got a peaked cap and everything!'

I said, 'Oh good!' and told him what I had in mind, and he loved the idea. I said what I needed to do, because I lived in Beckenham at that time, 'On a Saturday afternoon when it's really busy, and the streets are full of people, I'll make myself up as Haile Sellasie, I'll put on the nose, and darken myself down, put a black beard on and pith helmet, and it will be great fun!' so this was one of the stunts I pulled. I sat in the back of this Daimler [luxury car] and he drove many times through Beckenham High Street on a Saturday afternoon when everybody was out shopping.

So I thought, 'Well I'll see what happens after that!' and there it was in the paper: lots of people were convinced they had seen Haile Sellasie driving through Beckenham High Street, and they would all very much like to know what he was doing in Beckenham. Why did he come to Beckenham, and where was he going?

The next week, a lot more people had written to say they were very positive they had seen Haile Sellasie 'and we have been inquiring, but we can't get anywhere.' This went on week after week, and they never did solve the problem. I rushed out and bought copies of all these papers, hoping that this and the other stunts I had pulled would actually do something.

We also used to show our films every Saturday afternoon in the ballroom of the Regal Cinema, where we had our own little screen and projector, so relations and friends would come and buy tickets for one and sixpence and we made just enough money to buy more film and carry on regardless. And people were very interested in somebody with a camera moving and somebody acting, so they would come along and stop, very interested in what was going on, so I provided scenes we could do in Beckenham High Street on a Saturday afternoon. Even if it wasn't anything in the film, we would have the artists on the curb, camera at the back, with the people around, then we would say "Action!" and stop, and they'd go on and wait on the other side, and say, 'Right, cut, that's it!' and the people would come up and say, 'Am I in the film?' and we'd say yes.

They said, 'Where can I see this?' because all they wanted to do was see themselves. 'Well, as a matter of fact, in the Regal Cinema over there, every Saturday afternoon! 'Where do I get a ticket?' 'Well, we just happen to have some here- they cost one and sixpence!' So we got a lot of people interested.

Part II: 4/13/96

After that first interview, I wanted to talk to Stuart about his work on the various Star Wars films. This was the first of many times I got 'the tour,' in which a visitor got a first person-narrated walk-through of the workshop, where exhibits included a skin-less skeleton of the singing horse from Top Secret, scale-model flying doubles created for Superman, and the crown jewel of any visit: a series of original alien Star Wars heads, still in pristine condition. No matter how many times I got 'the tour' over the next several years, it was always exciting.

An interesting Star Wars side-note: I did raise the question on several occasions about the first film's iconic, alien-filled cantina sequence and why so much of it was later done as 'pick-ups' with contributions from a young Rick Baker and his team. I had heard several versions over the years, notably that Stuart fell ill due to the pressures of working on Star Wars; or that George Lucas felt the original scene looked a bit sparse and ordered additional, more crowded shots, but for some reason I never got a straight answer from Stuart. The full story will remain a mystery…

You originally got involved with *Star Wars* because of a character created for a series of TV commercials?

That's right, and I've still got him. It was for a Bird's Eye Pea advert, where one of their publicity artists had got the idea of little green men from Mars. He had this vision of a little green man with a head that looked just like a pea, so what they wanted was it to be a blank face with two eyes, which they decided would be like fly eyes, a tiny 'V' nose, and just a slit for a mouth. The rest would be smooth like a pea, so if you turned it around, it would look like a pea head. It was only when you came around that you could see this little bit.

Of course my problem was that the costume was also going to be smooth all over, and I had to blend the edge, which then had to be very thin, so the problem was getting a foam rubber that was fine enough, but also strong enough to stretch over the circumference of the head and close up tightly around the neck. Of course there were two of them, so I cast these two guys and really refined my foam rubber to get this quality. I'd never really needed it before, to improve the quality to get that strength.

I made these two heads, which were very simple, and not long after that, I was doing another film that needed a lot of special FX. I had my lab in the studio, and I was developing something or other because I got involved in quite a few films that needed that type of work, and I saw this youngish chap walking around. There was nobody else there, just me and my lads working away on something, and this chap was walking around, picking things up and looking at them, and I thought, 'Who the hell is he?'

Then he came over and said, 'Excuse me, but my name is George Lucas-' and I thought to myself, 'Yeah, who the hell is George Lucas? I've never heard of you, mate!' He said, 'I've written this script called *Star Wars* and it's got a sequence in it which is this cantina sequence, and I've got people coming from lots of differ-ent planets, assembling like you would go to a pub, and all drink-ing away. It's a futuristic, outer space film, but all the other films are very clean and precise and perfect, and I think there's going to be ugliness in my film, so I want the aliens as ugly as possible, with yellowy goo coming out their nostrils or the corners of their mouth- real nasty!' I thought, 'Oh my God, what is he on about?'

Anyway, I thought it had to be true, and then he said, 'So I'm looking for somebody who I think could do this, and I've been told you've done things like this, so they told me to come up and see what you've done.' I didn't really have anything there that I had done before, just the stuff I was working on at the time, but he said, 'Have you go any other things that you've done in the past, heads and things like that?' I said, 'Yeah, I've got loads of them back home, stuffed up in the attic.'

He said, 'Well, could you bring them down?' I said okay fine, so I brought all the odd things I had made before, including these little green-headed men, and I thought he wasn't going to be interested in them because they were so plain.

But he started looking at everything and saying, 'Oh, that's not bad, I like that, that's good- oh I like that!' and he started looking at the plain green head. I said, 'Oh, I'm afraid we couldn't use it like that, because the Bird's Eye Pea company own that design, so I wouldn't dare use it as it is, but I could disguise it a little bit, so you'd still have the same thing but they wouldn't even recognize it.'

He said, 'Fine,' so I added this Mohawk thing over the top, and put a different mouth on it, which was a working mouth because he had to talk, and I put ears on it and little scabby things all over it, so instead of being smooth, I broke up the surface. It still had the same eyes, because George loved these big fly eyes, and it became the character that gets blown up in the cantina. I had to hurriedly make two or three special ones to be blown to bits, because unfortunately they never do it in one take.

How did you go from working on that one character to doing the whole film?

Well, just the normal makeup is a full-time job, but we had all these things as well. Anyway, I modeled another head and added all these bits on, and called George and told him I had something for him to see, so he came back and saw it and loved it. He used it in several of the films; different versions with different colored eyes I'd made for it, so we used a number of them, even after he'd blown the original one up. I wasn't doing *Star Wars* at that point, and then I was suddenly doing *Star Wars, Superman, Star Wars, Superman* with one or two other films in-between. This other film I was doing involved a lot of specialized lab work, so that's how I got involved. I still had several months still to go on it, but I think *Star Wars* might have been the next one.

That's when I went up to Elstree Studios, got a lab set up over there and started modeling. It was the cantina creatures that George needed for the first film; those were the most important ones, and then a few others. We were halfway through it when George said, 'I've been thinking, and I want to add something...I've added a few scenes with a new character called Chewbacca, because I've got a dog named Chewbacca, and I was looking at him, and I thought maybe it should look something like a dog.' I said, 'Okay, I'll model you up something by tomorrow morning.' He said, 'Not quite a dog, but it's got to look eight foot tall,' and I thought, 'My God, that's going to be a problem, because if it's that tall, a natural human being likes to use his own natural arms, but they won't be high enough, so we'll have to strap his arms down and find another way of making false arms and I don't want to do that, so I've got to get the tallest person I can.'

Anyway, I modeled the head slightly like a dog, but he wanted it big and cuddly. He didn't want it fearsome, only when he wanted to be, because he was a goody, and the kids were going to love him anyway, however big and ferocious he was. So I made him kind of cuddly-looking and furry, and George came in and looked at it and said, 'Yes, yes...but I was looking at my cat last night; perhaps if it could look something like a cat.' I said, 'I know exactly what you mean; I'll have it ready for you in the morning!' so I did something slightly like a dog, slightly like a cat, with my own vision on top of that, and he came in and said, 'That's it!' so that's how Chewbacca came about.

I laid on all the hair myself. Alec Guinness wouldn't wear a lace beard, so I had to lay that hair on every day, comb it out, trim it and iron it and make it look the same every day; all loose hair. You can't do that on foam rubber, because it kills it stone dead. I had to find special glue that I invented and experimented with, and it was half-latex blended with glue, and they were miscible. I kept trying until I found two things that worked; a glue that was miscible with a latex, so I still got the elasticity, and it was still sufficiently sticky enough to hold the hair as I laid it on- you spread it with your fingers and tap it with your scissors and spread it, then you change the color and whatnot, and you comb it and iron it. So I put all the hair on and got Chewbacca.

And then the wardrobe people said they had got animal costumes, but they didn't work because a fur that's a real skin goes rigid, but it wouldn't fit a human being anyway, so they said, 'Look, this is not costume, it's makeup. The makeup doesn't finish on the face, so whatever Stuart Freeborn is doing on the head, he's got to do all over the body; it's nothing to do with us!' so I now had to find a way of putting fur all over an actor to match what I'd done on the head. I thought, what looks like animal fur, and I got a jumper made of a certain type of animal fur, and it was fine, because it covered the knitting. It was knotted, but you could also rough it so it looked like fur, so I thought that was good for the basic suit. I found by making it like a wig and knotting hair into it- I found all different animals have different textures on different parts of the body, so it's courser down the back of the spine and different colors too, so by having human hair, yak hair and horse hair which was the coarsest- I always had bundles of all of it, and I'd do plans for the girls who were going to knot it for me and draw exactly what type and texture of hair and to use and what color, I'd give it to them and they'd knot it accordingly, like making a wig.

I made rigid urethane casts of all the bodies and they actually made it on that body. I did hundreds of body casts, and knitted to that measurement of the body cast, and then the girls came along and knotted the hair in, and it worked, so we could make any kind of animal without making costumes- you'd just knit and knot.

That costume must have been very uncomfortable to wear.

It depends on the knitting. You can set it for different coarseness of knitting, whether it's got big holes in it or very tight- the higher the number, the coarser it is, so we settled for about nine, where it was reasonably close, but we varied that according to how much hair was going to be on a particular area and how short it was going to be, for two reasons. One is the shorter and thinner the hair, the more you could see through it, therefore it had to be a little bit tighter, but at the same time, you'd make it as loose as you can for the artist to breath and be comfortable in, and we never had any problems, because there were other areas where I had to make it a bit tighter; it depended on the weight and length of the hair, then I'd have to say the tension of this area has got to be different from the other one, because it's got to be a little closer. It's got to be 11 or 12 because that is the longest hair is, according to the length. I had to work all this out by trial and error, and it worked, and the artists seemed happy.

What was the understructure made of?

There were various kinds of wool to do that, but in the end, I thought it would be marvelous if I could use something that was stretchier, and it was a combination of the two. I tried cottoned elastic, getting samples of the thinnest cottoned elastic and tried it on one of the three knitting machines I'd bought to do this. My wife knew how to handle these things, and we had other knitting ladies in who were experts at it, but the knitting machines wouldn't take it because it was too heavy, so I contacted a firm up in the Midlands that made all this stuff. I told them what I required was a cottoned elastic that was fine enough to be used on a knitting machine- was this possible?

They said, 'Strange you should say that; but we've had this problem before and it's been requested, and we've now made one!' I explained what I wanted it for, and they sent me a big carton of it, which worked beautifully. And then we could have other fur in the machine that was automatically knitted into it, so it was knitting it, and also as it knitted it, the fur was on it. Of course they had to be able to spend pennies throughout the day, so they had to be able to undo something themselves. I learned this on the monkey suits for *2001*, which gave me the clue. I had special gauntlets specially made that went right to the top, and that was my base on the plaster moulds I'd made of all the arms, and we modeled the foam rubber fingers that much longer, which they could operate using their own fingers to grip things with. Then, as the fur went up this way, I could put Velcro around the base of this bit coming down and Velcro on the bit coming up, and a little split bit that they could undo and slide the whole thing off themselves with the hands still on.

How did you apply some of the techniques you learned from *2001*?

George Lucas was amazed that I was able to bring Chewbacca in within a couple of weeks, but I knew what I was going to do with the mechanisms, because I'd worked all of it out on *2001*. I also had lots of little bits and pieces in my lab that I was able to use without having to make them. All I had to do was cast Peter Mayhew's body and model the face I wanted, make it into foam rubber and put the mechanisms in. It's a not a question of the foam rubber going straight onto his face; I had a lightweight rigid urethane mask underneath, shaped in depth so I could vary the depth of the foam rubber, which I needed to be different thicknesses in certain areas- there were certain areas where it had to be thin where it's got to stretch a lot when he opens the jaw, and other areas where I wanted to maintain the muscle shapes had to be thicker, so I would give myself a bit more room by giving myself more of a hollow in the surface of the urethane.

I knew all this thanks to four months of trial and error on *2001*, because I had said to Kubrick, 'If you want all these monkeys, we've got to shoot it at the end not at the beginning,' so I could spend whatever time I could working on them, and by the end of that year and a half, I had developed the monkeys sufficiently.

With Chewbacca, I had done all the research, so all I had to do was do it again, and of course a lot of my bits and pieces and toggles were already made. Once George Lucas said that was the shape he wanted, I just went ahead and did it, without wasting time with trial and error, trying to figure out mechanisms.

Say you have an actor with cables going up his trouser legs- well, with 35 actors as monkeys, fighting and rolling around, there's no way you can have cables running up their trouser legs, so it kills that idea stone dead, and radio control doesn't always work with all the amplifiers and electrical equipment, so *that* idea doesn't work, so it had to come from the artist themselves, and I still believe that. It's much more subtle to have an artist's own movements transmitted to the surface from his own muscles than you can do by other means.

How many mechanisms did Peter Mayhew have?

I was lucky, because you've got different film unions of dwarves, ugly people, tall people; all sorts of weird people who because of what they are put themselves in the film books. So I went through the book of tall-ies and the tallest person I could find was six-foot eight. That wasn't enough, because I couldn't get him up to eight feet, and George was insisting, 'He's got to be eight feet!' and you don't ever say no to George, you just give him what he wants somehow, but I didn't have anyone tall enough and I didn't want to have to use mechanical arms.

I went around looking for some time, asking everybody, and one day when I was finally starting to despair because I didn't have anyone tall enough, I went into the canteen, which was the place I seemed to get my best inspiration, and I saw a continuity girl I'd worked with some years ago. We hadn't seen each other for some time, so we sat together and she said, 'You look worried.' Well, that was me, I'd always got something to worry about, and I said my problem was trying to find someone taller than six-foot eight; had she ever come across anybody that tall or taller?

She said, 'As a matter of fact, I have. I was in Croyden Hospital for a while, and there was a porter that was the tallest person I've ever seen.' I dashed over to the telephone and called them and said, 'I hear you have a porter there who's very tall.' They said yes, and I said, 'You probably know how tall he is' and they said, 'He's seven-foot four,' I thought, 'That's fine, that will do me great!' so I told them who I was and what I wanted him for, and said, 'Can you spare him to make a film?' They said they'd talk to him and see if they could do without him for a while, and they came back and said, 'Yes, under the circumstances, you can have him.'

I told George this, and said, 'We'll get him up there, and you see if he's any good for what you want to do,' so Peter came up, and he was a lovely fellow. I explained what I had to do, life-casting him and so forth, which he'd never have done to him before of course, and he was all for it.

So George sent his assistant down to pick him up, and after a while, the phone rang again and it was George- 'He's perfect, he can take direction very well; carry on with what you have to do!' so that's how it happened. Of course seven-foot four to eight feet left me eight inches, so when I modeled his face, I modeled another four inches on the top, and put another four inches on his feet, so I actually got him to eight feet high and George loved it.

Do you remember shooting the film on some difficult locations?

Oh yes, we were shooting in the desert, and we had several camera units, so while one lot was shooting in one place, another unit would be shooting somewhere else. They both might want Chewbacca at the same time, so I had to find a double for him that was as tall as possible and make everything fit, which was very difficult.

We had one scene where he was supposed to be coming down some stairs, and they were using a stunt double, and George said, 'That's all right, we're not coming in that close, so you'll be all right!' Fortunately, I happened to be on the unit where they were using the double for Chewbacca, and this guy started coming down the stairs. Well, the real Chewbacca's knees touched all the time; Peter was quite skinny, and when he walked, he was very knock-kneed.

The stunt double was just the opposite: he was muscly, and his legs were bow-legged, and when he came down the stairs, he was walking all bow-legged, and I said, 'Cut, you can't have that, it's terrible!' I forget who the assistant director was, but I said, 'That's no good, it won't match!' so I had to go up to the stunt guy and say, 'Whatever you do, you can't walk like that; you've got to come down knocking your knees together!' He said, 'Oh, okay,' so from there on in, he was okay. It's just as well I was there, because it looked terrible.

Did you delegate all of the straight makeup on the film?

I still took two or three of the principle actors and actresses. Quite often, I used to hand over the leading ladies to my wife, and the rest of the crew would be allocated accordingly. We were very conscious of the artists, especially the principal ladies. I would say two-thirds of the actors and actresses we worked with were from Hollywood, and I know only too well that if an actress had never been to England before, and I knew she had done a lot of films, because I made a point of seeing all the films and taking notes on the kind of makeups I'd see them wearing. I knew that they would say, 'Miss So and So will be coming over on this plane,' and I knew I've got to make her up, and what would be going through her mind, because she's never been to England before, and she had a regular makeup artist with her from film to film that she's always insisting on, but they won't allow that makeup artist to come with her. Some still do, but there are many times when that didn't happen and I was aware of that, so I know her background, and I know she was on the plane thinking, 'I'm used to my own makeup man and only he knows these special things; how good are they in England?' and when she gets to England, she instinctively feels the worst, so there are all these subtle currents going on.

So I would say, 'Come in, sit down,' and immediately say, 'I'm aware that you have a makeup artist, and he's very good, so you've probably got very comfortable, knowing that he's with you. I think it's only fair to both of us if you explain to me the things that he does especially for you, that you like, and things that by trial and error you've decided to do; which shape of the eyebrows and what shadowing above and beneath the eyelids, and the lips; all these little touches. You tell me about them, so I have some idea, and we can catch up much quicker.' I'm not going to say, 'I'm doing it my way!' and plonk it on, which is what they're terrified of.

So they'll tell me all these things and I'll agree, and we'll happily go on for a few days like that, and then maybe I'd say, 'Because of the shape of that little bit there, have you ever tried doing it like this? Think about it!' and she'll say, 'Yeah, let's try that' and after a while, I'm doing a lot of the things I want to do, as well as what she's used to. And at the end of the picture, she might say, 'Can you make me a chart of everything you did?' and I'm thinking, 'Oh my God, that poor makeup man on the other end is going to be handed this list!'

Luckily, you had a number of young untried actors on *Star Wars*.

That's right, so we really didn't have those sorts of problems.

Kath Freeborn: Carrie Fisher came in with all her own makeup, from this fantastically expensive clinic in the States, and it was absolutely useless for filming. For a start, it was all liquid, but you humor them when they first come in, so you don't say, 'You can't use that.' The thing against it was you couldn't re-touch it up. Because it's liquid, it's like paint, so you can't blend it at all. I didn't like the color anyway; I thought it was much too pale. It was all right for society use, but much too pale for filming, so when [producer] Gary Kurtz came in one morning, I said, 'I'm not at all happy with this makeup she's brought over; it's got no color and you can't blend it at all!'

He said, 'it is rather pale, isn't it?' so eventually I said, 'let's try this makeup; it's a little bit darker, and you need a little more bounce,' so I eventually got her using something else, and we abandoned the original makeup and went over to the other one. You have to give over for a little while though, don't you?

Stuart: It's all about getting their confidence first, and then you can do that because they're interested in what you have to say. There's something else that some cameramen don't realize: if you photograph human skin without any makeup at all, it might look fine to the eye but what comes out on that emulsion is quite different to what you see with the eye, because it has the power of penetrating the skin and picking up the redness underneath, and any little blotches and things come through and register. That's why for this technical reason, we have to put on a base anyway, something fairly opaque, with a certain amount of resistance to being penetrated. At least you start with a smooth base, and you're not getting the pigments under the skin that only the emulsion will pick up. There are times when we'll do a complete naked body for instance, and I'll say, 'I'm sorry, but this lady has got to be made up all over!' The director will ask the cameraman, 'Is this true?' and he'll say, 'Oh, it will be fine,' but on film it looks dreadful, so we put some makeup on and she was fine.

Did Alec Guinness fall to you?

Stuart: Oh yes, there were quite a few main artists like that. We'd worked together with David Lean, so Guinness knew I'd gone further than most as a makeup artist, but we also had all the characters that had special needs, so I really had to do them all. On *Oliver Twist*, there were very few people around who could do straight makeups, but anything beyond that, a lot of them were okay with glamour and ladies makeups, but to do old ageing and false noses and eye bags, wrinkled lips and bald heads. So few did that, and I knew that, so I had to all those characters like Bumble the work-house boss man.

So you already knew Guinness...

Yes, but in actual fact I didn't make him up in *Star Wars*; my son did. He was very good at hair work, especially beards, so my son made him up and put on the beard. Guinness would say, 'You'd better watch out, because you son is pretty damned good; he's going to pinch your job any time now!' so we had a bit of a laugh about that. But he was quite happy about it, and I had enough to do anyway.

Didn't production bring in an additional team of people to do some of the cantina aliens?

I did it all on *Star Wars*, which was a huge success, and I knew Lucas figured he could make a lot of toys out of the creatures we designed, and he made a lot of money out of the toys, so when he came up with *The Empire Strikes Back*, he'd written in a whole lot more interesting characters that would make good toys, as well as being interesting characters in the film.

Anyway, there was so much more in the way of creatures, and I went through the script, and made notes and went to George and said, 'George, I love it, but there are so many creatures, and I only have a certain number of people on hand that I've trained that are available to do this kind of work, and with that number of people running this thing, I'm only going to be able to do about half of these creatures. I've timed it out and I know how long it will take, and I know I won't have time to do all these creatures.'

I knew Phil Tippett quite well- I'd visited all the studios in Hollywood and got to know them all, so I said, 'Why don't you get somebody like Phil Tippett who would be only too pleased to make these sort of things,' so that's what he did, so Phil Tippett took over half the creatures, so he did his half and I did the other half.

So who did the cantina creatures for the original *Star Wars*?

I think it was only the Bird's Eye Pea ones that we had, and I changed them around so they couldn't be recognized. For the others, Ralph McQuarrie did drawings for some of them, but sometimes George would say, 'I like that one and that one; that's a good idea, but I don't want it quite like that,' so it would be up to me to change it to how he wanted it.

What was Lucas like as a director?

He was all right, and I think it all worked fine, so we were all a bit surprised when we found out he wasn't going to direct the second one.

Did anyone have an idea how big the first one was going to be?

None whatsoever. I don't think even George knew it would be so big, but he had a lot of confidence in it, obviously. They sent me the script, and I sat here reading it, and I was halfway through it, and I thought, 'I don't know that I want to do this film; I don't think I can bother to read the rest of it. I can't get the feel of it, and I don't think it will be very successful,' but I carried on, and the next third of it changed completely somehow, and I said to Kath, 'I changed my mind; I think it's going to be great, and I'm going to do it!' When I read the second half, I could see what the first half was leading up to, and I suddenly got the feeling for it, so George must have known that it was going to be something.

Was it a foregone conclusion that there would be a sequel?

We knew there was going to be a second. I had talked to George about this, and he said, 'I have two prequels.' After the second one, he was thinking about doing one of the prequels and then he changed his mind and said, 'No, I think I'll do the third one first and then I'll think about the prequels; I may or may not decide to do them. Maybe people will be getting fed up with them by then. You can only take so much of things and suddenly they lose interest, so you can't go on and on.'

I had a word with him on the very last day when we were on location in the desert I think it was, on the last one, I said, 'George, how about your next film- are you going to do a prequel, or are you writing another one to follow this?' He said, 'Interesting question, at the moment, it all depends on how this third one goes. Maybe people will be fed up with it and the audience might drop a lot, so it depends on that. If it's still popular enough, I'll make up my mind on whether or not I will go on to the one after, or we do one of the prequels.'

So that's what happened, but he started working with Spielberg, because they were buddies and started together, so he was with him for a while, and he used a lot of the money he got from *Star Wars* to back Spielberg because they were in it together, but he took a back seat for a while. And eventually there were rumors that he was going to come back, and at one point, I spent some time in Hollywood; that's when I saw Dick Smith at first and then flew over to Hollywood, because I knew quite a lot of people there and somebody said, I think it was]*'Empire'* director] Kershner who invited me to dinner in Van Nuys and there was this girl I knew from one of the films and she said, 'I'm going too,' so she came around and picked us up and drove us up into the mountains and we had a lovely meal with

How did you end up working on Yoda?

They said, 'You turned people into monkeys for *2001*; if you can turn them into monkeys, you can turn them into anything, as long as they're human beings, and that's down to you, there's no other department for it.' I said, 'Okay, but Yoda is a puppet; you can't a human being inside; you can get a hand in-' and they said, 'Well, that's good enough, isn't it? There isn't anyone else who knows the anatomy and the movements from those muscle shapes and flesh and that combination that makes the expressions just right. There isn't anybody else in a department that can do this kind of thing, so you'll have to forget about being a makeup man.' I said, 'Well all right, but technically is it right?' and they said, 'Don't worry about it, just do it!' so I did.

Which is not as easy as it sounds.

No, it isn't, but I did it anyway. I thought, 'I'm out of bounds here, but I'm going to do it!' so that's how it happened.

You've gone on record as saying the funny-looking bits of Yoda were taken from your own face, and the intelligent parts were taken from Einstein?

The very first time George saw it, he said, 'That's it, *that's* the way I want it.' And from there on, I didn't change anything else.

Did you have to work it all of out, or were there people who could help you?

I had to work out all the mechanisms, because nobody else was into it in those days. It was engineering, but fortunately there was a time in my life during the war- I volunteered for the Air Force, to fly, and then I was invalided out of that, and they said, 'Now you can go back into the studio!' and I said no, I couldn't do that while there was a war on, so I thought perhaps I could work in a factory and make things as a draughtsman for whatever was needed, whether it was machinery or tools or whatever.

They said, 'Well yes, we don't have that many places for draughtsman, and if you're going to want to do it, you'll have to spend six months on the bench to know enough about engineering to know what to draw.' I said okay, fine, and this was the best thing that ever happened to me, because I went on the bench and specialized in things that were very fine, and we had to take tests to determine our aptitude, so up on a stand they had a square bit of steel one-eighth of an inch thick and in it was a small slot that was cut out, and then you got a piece of metal pushed into the metal and a light behind it and you should not be able to see the light through any of the cracks; that was the test, and I did it, drilled the pieces, filed them down and put my name on it and handed it in with all the others.

A couple of days later, I was passing the place, and the other guy's work had been taken down and mine was put up! So I knew I could do this very fine work. It was the same as make-up in a way, losing the edges of false noses, which I had been doing for a long time, and it had to be very exacting, and I had been doing it for a long time, so I went on to engineering. They had this huge radar machine that was in the early days, and it was enormous with dozens of screens and god knows what and they said, 'This has got to be in the corner of a gun field where they've got four guns in the field to concentrate on one plane coming in, so the guns will automatically point to this one spot where the controller of the machine points it,' so I was put on to the task of miniaturizing this machine.

They said, 'Listen, we can see what you can do, so how badly did you want to be a draughtsman?' I said, 'Well, I really don't care; I love doing this work,' and they said, 'We would rather you stayed, because we don't often get people with this kind of ability to do such fine work and we can see you're obviously good at it, so you would be much more useful to us doing this, because we can always find draughtsman easily!'

I said fine, I don't mind, so they said, 'You seem to know a lot of the people here, so you pick the people you think will be useful to you, so you design it all and get them to help you,' so that's what I did; I miniaturized it down to something very simple and it worked even more efficiently. I also used to make my own tools, tempering the steel according to the hardness I needed, so I knew how to handle metal and make little gadgets, so when it came to *2001* and I needed all these little mechanisms, I still had all my tools. As you can see, there's are loads of them down here and boxes or every engineering tool I could want, so I was able to design and make Yoda, as well as the little creatures like the Ewoks and I was able to make all the mechanisms for the movements of the eyes and the eyelids. So you've got all the blinking done in tandem, but then you've got the squinting and little Yoda of course was good at that. And then you've got the frowning, which is the bit in the middle, which is important, and that's where I knew I was going to have a problem.

I said to Gary Kurtz, I wasn't going to have time to sit there and operate Yoda, so I had to have somebody who did that. He said, 'Well, who would you like?' and I told him the best person for my money was Frank Oz, who was very good at it and he also had a good voice. So they talked to the Henson Company and they said, 'Yes, Frank Oz will do it!' so I cast his hand in one position and put clay over the top of his fingers and thumbs and worked backwards from there.

Frank has a very double-jointed thumb, so I cast his hand in that position, so for opening the mouth he does that, and then for the movement of the bottom lip, he does that and for the movement of the top lip, he had to use these two fingers, but he didn't use that one, so I cast his hand in plaster in that position. And I worked backwards when I modeled him, because those fingers were key to the movements of the lips, so they had to fit absolutely in position. From that position, I modeled the lips and from the lips, I did the rest of it.

Because Yoda was only going to be a couple of feet high, keeping the head in the exact proportion was out of the question, so I had to cheat the head so it was a bit out of proportion because I had to get Frank Oz's hand in there plus the mechanisms to operate everything and that was cutting it right down to the minimum, so I thought, well, it's a creature from outer space; so what does it matter? You can have a bigger head, so having done that, inside the urethane skull that goes under the foam rubber, I used his little finger that he wasn't using and put a rigid loop inside, so as he put his finger through it, his hand is connected to the entire skull so it's not slipping about. There had to be a connection that he could make by putting his hand inside, so I used his little finger for that. This finger wasn't doing anything, so I had my own controls that operated the ears up and down, backwards and forwards, the eyebrows and eyelids and the movement of the eyeballs; I did all that, but I wanted a frown in the middle, but Frank's finger was in the way of where I wanted another mechanism.

I said to Frank, 'You're not using that finger, are you?" He said no, and I said, 'Well, I want a frown, so what I'm going to do is cut a slot in the urethane and stick a thimble inside the foam rubber so you can put the tip of that finger in the thimble and when we want him to frown, you can move that finger in the thimble.' He said, 'No way!' and I said, 'I'm sorry, Frank, but your finger is in the way, so I'll have to cut it off, because there's no room for another mechanism!' and he said, 'Oh… all right.'

Were you on set to work the mechanisms, or was that delegated to somebody else?

Later I did, because there was so much to do especially in the second film. When we were doing the first half, I worked together with Frank, so we were both down in that hole together. Mark Hamill was standing on the grass, while we were down in a big hole, along with our four-inch monitors to see what was happening, so we each had one for that so we could see what the camera was looking at and we could then see the movements we were doing. So it was Frank Oz and me together; Frank with his arm up there and I was sitting next to him doing my controls and movements.

We did that together for quite some time, and after that, I had to get to get somebody else, because there was just no way. I just didn't have time to do it as well as all the other creatures I was involved in.

On the second film, I delegated a lot of that work to Phil Tippett, so he did half the creatures while I was still operating Yoda with Frank Oz. On the third one, we got another puppeteer to work with Frank Oz to do all the movements.

What other creatures did you have to do for '*Empire*?'

I had Yoda to do, plus a lot of other new creatures. We had the big snow creature to work out, so I modeled the horns for it and everything else and worked it all out. I didn't go up there myself so I put it in the hands of other people to look after it and operate it, because I still had so much to do in the studio for when they came back that I couldn't go up there on that location, so we got him all fixed up and I never saw him again. I stayed in Elstree and carried on producing more things, so I couldn't afford the time to go up, but I got it going and it worked all right.

With the big gap between *The Empire Strikes Back* and *Return of the Jedi*, did you end up doing another *Superman* film in-between?

I did *Superman II* in-between, and as it happened, they all worked out successfully.

There was a real industry boom at the time, wasn't there?

I got one of my boys Tom Smith to work on the first *Indiana Jones* film, but something happened and he was on another film when they came to do the second one. Oh no, they wanted to do a lot of retakes and he wasn't available so I finished it for him, so I did get to work with Spielberg on some extra scenes on *Indiana Jones*.

With *Return of the Jedi*, you split up the aliens again?

Absolutely. Jabba the Hutt was nearly 20 feet high, so first of all to construct him, I had to get wooden struts and chicken wire and then I used four tons of clay to model Jabba the Hutt over the chicken wire. It was cast in seven sections of plaster molds, and then I had to have one of the big rooms, the 'money room,' where they had the big safes in the studio. I had all the safes taken out and we turned the room into a giant oven. I had to use the entire room, because there wasn't an oven big enough to put it in. We then put each heavy section on a little trolley and put it all together- it all had to be wheeled into this room and then I had the controls outside the room to get the heat up for the right amount of time, so I had to work out how long it would take the heat to penetrate the different thicknesses of foam rubber.

That was the big problem, because it had to be much hotter to cure the center. It's no good having nice soft foam on the outside and the rubber is uncooked on the inside. It's got to be cooked all the way through, so you've to change the thickness of the plaster on those areas. On the thicker bits of foam rubber, you might have thinner plaster, so you've got to work out the thicknesses of the plaster molds so they're just right for helping you to control the temperature of curing the foam rubber of varying thicknesses, from very thin to quite thick. You can't overheat the thin edges and destroy them, so you work all of this out by trial and error about how long you've got to keep it at a lower temperature until it's all heated up, and gradually turn it up so the extra heat is getting in to where you want it without destroying the thin edges.

Jabba the Hutt was all about solving these problems. They were the same as they were with smaller characters, but they were much more significant when they're that much bigger. Having done that, and successfully got to the point where we could take out the foam rubber, I knew we were going to have further problems because of the tail. Although they didn't use it all in the end, Jabba originally had to lift up its tail and bend it back and knock people over, so there had to be a mechanism inside this huge tail.

Actually, it was about 18 feet high so nine feet of it was tail. I had to work out how I was going to put this mechanism in, so I chose one of my little dwarves who I knew was very strong- he used to tell he he'd got a black belt, but I knew he was strong and he was very bright so I said, 'I need somebody about four feet high, and I'll make a little seat for you inside the thick part of the tail and it will be down to you to operate the movement of the tail. I'm going to make it as light as I possibly can,' so I had to make the foam rubber as thin as I could, and then I had four rings going every now and again down to the tip, and four wires attached to several saucepan lids with the wires coming through them so one didn't foul up the other. They were all on a fixed rod so he could move them around, and by tipping one, the top wire would lift it, or if he pulled it sideways, the side wire pulled it to the left or right, but when it turned into an 'S,' it meant the top one was now the bottom one, so he had to use the bottom one for the opposite movement, so I couldn't just use the gravity for the down movement.

To take the weight away, I was going to have a big heavy weight from a rigid post coming up with this weight pivoting so it would almost be balanced, so he could move the thing but it wouldn't have the weight against it. I would balance it with a counterweight so at the slightest touch, it would lift up of its own accord. It might be slightly heavier than the weights, but it was easy for him to move it and then make separate movements, so I fixed up this thing, but then I got another idea.

Because there were supposed to be certain movements in the rest of the body, I thought it would be nice if I could get other movements in the flesh going down the tail, so I turned that weight into an electric motor with a speed control and an on/off control, which my little friend could put his feet on and control. I knew he was bright enough to do those things, and at the same time, his hands were operating the controls.

The big problem was, when we got the foam rubber stretched over the outside of the tail, you could just see the rings through the rubber, so as light as I could get it was still not enough so it showed the rings and I thought, 'What do I do?' And then I remembered in my younger days, my grandmother had a big shop of materials she used to sell; all kinds of materials for dressmaking and that sort of thing; masses of it, and when I was five or six years old, I was taken up there and I loved it. It was fascinating to see all these colors and materials, and down in basement where they had masses of it, there was a netting made of monofilament and woven so when the girls were wearing their skirts, the crinoline, this was shaped around it so it held the crinoline out but was lightweight, so it would bend around but it still held the shape. I remembered that and thought, 'That's what I need!'

So I had this rigid urethane shape of the tail itself and measured it all out and I got the girls to pin the monofilament- I had rolls and rolls of it specially made- and pin them across and then seal them at the crossway, so when that was taken off, I had a cone shaped stocking to pull over the rings and the foam rubber went over that. It still had to be very flexible to waggle the tail but it worked, so I must say, I got lucky; I just got the right ideas that somehow worked. There were so many times I was near to disaster, and when I think back, I think, 'My God, how lucky I was!' but these ideas all seemed to work. It was uncanny.

How many people did it take to operate the creature?

Two things happened, the day they were going to shoot on Jabba. For weeks, I had two guys that I called 'the astronauts,' sitting side by side in the top. The guy on the right hand side, his arm operated one of the little arms. The arms of the creatures are half the size of humans in comparison to the bottom, so I thought, if I've got two guys using their arms and I just put the foam rubber hands on them, they would be the right length in proportion to the rest of it and the width with two arms side by side will give the shoulder width which is twice the amount than it would be on these creatures, so that put me on the right proportions.

Now, I had two problems. We had spent a lot of time and money sending somebody to Central Africa to find the right kind of big frogs that were in the fishbowl. Every now and again, he would put his hand in the bowl, and you could see them so they had to be alive, but we only had so many of them, and he would put them in his mouth, so I thought, well, the guy on the right hand side will put his hand in, so the fishbowl has got to be on that side, so he could put his hand in, pull out one of these frogs, and with his left-hand inside the head, he could open up the mouth- he had the controls to open the mouth- and put the frog in.

The thing was, I had to make two separate throats, because on the other side, the other guy would use the hookah and put in all sorts of rubbish to eat that went down the other throat, but the throat on the right hand side would only allow the frogs to go down because that one was full of water, and after each shot, the prop guys had to take them out alive and put them back in the bowl for the next shot, so I mustn't kill any of them off, so I had to make this special throat and fill it with water so our guy on the right only would coordinate his movements to make sure that frog went down the right throat.

I had two more guys in the belly; one was smoking a cigar and when they saw him pick up the hookah and put it in his mouth, the chap on the left at the top would blow through this tube and the smoke would come out of the corner of Jabba's mouth. The other guy in the belly, when Jabba would laugh, he would push the belly in and out so the belly would move as he was doing the laugh, and my little dwarf fellow would wiggle the tail, so that was five people in total inside to work it including the tongue and the eyes. And the two guys at the top would squeeze little bags to make all the nasty, sticky stuff to run out of the eyes and the nostrils and the corner of the mouth; different colored gooey muck to make it look really horrible, so that was their job as well as open the mouth and do other things. If you remember that scene when they were all there, including lots of lovely little creatures, we had to put Jabba on a big trolley, wheel it over to the stage, take it off and put it where he's supposed to be.

They rehearsed with Richard Marquand the director, and this time they're going to shoot it! Okay, 'Action… and then cut, cut, cut! 'I think I would like to see that bowl of frogs on that side!' so Marquand came up and moved it to the other side, and I said, 'No, you ruddy well won't; put it back there!' He looked at me and said, 'What do you mean?' I said, 'I'm sorry, but you shook me so much when you did that, but you obviously don't know,' so I had to do a quick explanation that 'He's got to be on *that* side, because only this guy is made to put it in the throat with the water in it; otherwise, they're all going to be dead in the first take!' After all these weeks of rehearsal and getting it all moving just right and the coordination of the whole thing and he was going to screw it all up! Anyway, Richard put it back, so he just made that little mistake, which shook me for a bit.

So that was one thing that happened, and then we had been shooting for several days on it, and there's a scene where Princess Leia throws a rope around his neck and tries to choke him, so we were doing it and she's got high heeled shoes on and George Lucas said, 'I'd like you to jump up on him and do it. It would be more realistic,' and I thought, 'Oh, I don't like this!' because just underneath there was my little dwarf's head, so George decided to do this on the spur of the moment, and she got up there and it all started sinking in and I heard this guy inside it, 'Owww!' and I said, 'No, no, you can't do that!' He asked 'Why not, what's the problem?'

I said, 'Look, I've got this little fellow in there, and you're hitting the top of his head. It's all right, we'll make it so you can still do that, but you've got to give me time, because I've got to fix it a little bit. It will still go down a certain extent, but not that much, so I can put a wooden frame in there, so when she does get back up there, it will go so far but no further. That way, he'll be safe under there but you can still get the effect of soft flesh going in.' So that's how we did it, but we almost killed off my little dwarf who was doing an extraordinarily good job and it all worked really well.

Considering all the pitfalls involved.

Oh, God, yes!

Were the Ewoks your responsibility?

Ralph McQuarrie did a lot of drawings for individual designs of faces, so there were the young ones and older ones and the lady ones and the warrior types. We made them all look quite different and specially modeled each one and added the costumes. But yes, we designed and made them all.

You couldn't put in too many mechanisms, could you?

Oh no, they were fairly straightforward. I would have liked to get more mechanisms in there, because those were their own eyes, but I wanted more of something else. I had to spend so much time up in Crescent City, that place where all the trees were, and we also spent time in the desert because George wanted something there, so I wasn't able to do certain things. When we came back, I did a few extra mechanisms on one or two of them, but very little in the way of mechanisms. They're mostly just costume, so we just had to get all the suits made but we really didn't have time to get into any mechanisms for them.

So you didn't have to worry about facial expressions.

Not very much. There wasn't the urethane underneath; it was just a foam rubber face that went on to their own faces, so it was a simplified version. And of course they were all furry anyway, so you weren't going to see much and so we were able to get away with quite a bit without too much work. There were one or two extra bits and pieces I put in at the last minute when George said, 'Would it be possible to get this extra movement in?' so I would do it for the odd one or two.

Looking back, what was your proudest achievement from the Star Wars films?

I suppose Yoda, really. Chewbacca was simple for me, because I already had all the headaches with the monkeys on *2001*, so he was fairly easy for me, and it was a nice character, but Yoda was completely different, because it was a combination of me and Frank Oz both working on him at first before handing it over to other people. That was such a different character.

And an important one.

Oh yes, exactly. He was such an important part of the story. And because he talked so much and conveyed so much of the story, a lot depended on him, so he had to be lovable but believable and still able to do these things; similar in a way to Chewbacca: that was the kind of reaction you wanted to have from the audience. Yoda wasn't easy, and I had a lot of headaches getting him to that stage where it all worked, and there were certain persistent things that wouldn't work right, so George said, 'Right, tomorrow morning, we shoot on him!' and I still hadn't got him going right.

Everybody had already left for the day at that point, and I stayed all night long; I never went home that night and finally, about five in the morning, he was doing what I wanted him to do. Nobody knew about that, but that's how close it was for me. At five in the morning, he suddenly started working right, so I had over-come whatever problems I was having with its movements and it worked and we carried on, but nobody had a clue about how close it was. It was the same with the monkeys in *2001*.

Did I tell you the story about the fur? I always pushed the fur in with the top of the needle broken so you got a fork, so you pushed it in the foam rubber and it worked. But Kubrick said he wanted to shoot in a couple of days, and I said I only had a little beard work still to do on the foam rubber faces, but when I came to do it, fine, I bent down to get the comb and scissors and there was no hair in it. It had all popped out, because of the strength of the hair! I had to use real hair to make it look right, but there wasn't enough strength in the foam rubber to hold a bent hair, which was a little technical fact that I hadn't thought of!

I stayed awake all night wondering how I was going to do it. he next morning, I got a hypodermic needle and pushed the hair through and it worked, so once again, I don't know how but it worked and we got everything ready on time, but Kubrick never knew, nor did anybody else. Only I knew what had happened.

When you hear about the new *Star Wars* films, do you wish you were involved, or do you feel you've done them already?

In some ways, I'd love to go back and be involved again, but I have to admit, I don't know whether I could sustain it. I seem to have excessive energy, and I can go with very little sleep. If I have seven hours of sleep, that's fantastic, but I hardly ever got more than six hours of sleep and often far less than that, and we still carried on working, but I don't think I would like to subject myself to that again. I don't think it would be wise. I'm not far off 82 now, believe it or not, so it makes sense to say, 'Forget it!' I hate the word and I could never say I was retired; It's just so foreign to me, and I'm still doing enough, but to actually be working in a studio again and to have to be there at that time of the morning and take on all the sweat and worries of a job and things not working out and how to make them work; I probably wouldn't be able to do that. I don't know, I feel everything is still in me ready to do it again, but I've got a funny feeling that maybe I would regret doing it. I think I'd better leave it to the young boys now and let them come up with their own things.

But if anybody has any questions, you're ready to answer them.

Well, exactly. I would be only too pleased to do that, but I think that's enough. I've got to retire sometime and I did work for close to 60 years, so I can't really go on much longer than that!

Part III: 1/9/97

The first of our book-related interviews, and this time Sheelagh came along. Stuart and Kath loved her, so our visits took on a much more social element. And because she was a makeup artist herself, Stuart would also test her knowledge, interrupting a line of discussion by abruptly saying, 'Okay, girl, how would you do this…?' which is why this particular conversation started with the two of them swapping techniques for applying bald caps.

This time, Stuart also brought out his photo albums, which invariably would raise a whole series of questions. Add the usual digressions, as well as two people asking questions now, and the interview pretty much found its own directions now. All you could do was hold on for dear life…

[Conversation is already in progress; Stuart is showing Sheelagh the photo of a bald cap done for a film]

Sheelagh: Did you punch hair into the cap, or was that a separate wig?

No, because I used a new cap every day for the 52 days I did it. It was a toupee piece on the top, and I couldn't have a new one every day. It took long enough as it was; it took me a good three hours, and I had to make it so I could cut out things that were unnecessary. The quickest way of doing it rather than putting hair in anywhere; it just had to be a toupee that went straight on. I don't know if I mentioned the problems when the camera boys came in very close: if you've got a bald cap on and then put a toupee on it, you stick it of course around here and in certain areas, but where the lace is sitting on it, you have to stick it down on the cap; otherwise it moves and you can see it, so although you can see through it, it's very fine hair, you've got to have the hair on it, but you've got to stick it down and then it kind of disappears, but you can't put glue all over the bald cap and press it down, so the answer I found, was to put my glue, the spirit gum underneath the lace itself and then leave it overnight .

On the day when you put it on I just put on a little solvent, a mixture of acetone and alcohol. You just put it on with a little brush and run it down over the lace from the top of the wig and that just melts it enough to stick and then you just press it. You don't get the glue in between the little holes and it solves the problem.

Sheelagh: So you're activating the glue the following day.

That's right. It's dry, but you activate it by putting a little solvent on the lace after it's on. Otherwise it's impossible to know exactly where the lace is going to fall. And you can't really put wet glue on the lace and less there's spirit gum on the lace itself. To put a mustache on, you've got to put the glue on the skin, don't you? It's just a little thing from a makeup artist to another makeup artist, a little point of interest.

Looking at these Oliver Twist photos, I didn't realize Robert Donat had tried out for the part of Sykes and you did a makeup test, even though the role was taken by Robert Newton. You can't see anybody else playing that part now.

No, you can't. Robert Newton fitted that part very well. He was perfect for it. A lovely man, but of course he was hitting the bottle all the time. I had just done him up all nicely, and I was frantically trying to get him out. Our makeup room was upstairs so we had to get down the steps, and I would say, 'Please, Mr. Newton, we are all on the set waiting for you; please come down!'

When we got to the bottom of the steps, there was a corridor, and there was a char lady about to scrub the floor. She had just got down on her knees with a bucket of water and a scrubbing brush, and was obviously going to scrub the floor, and just as they're trying to get Robert Newton down to the set because he's already late, he turns around and says, 'Oh, I scrubbed the decks on my boat- I'll show you how to do it!'

She said, 'Oh, no, Mr. Newton!' He said, 'No, no, my dear!' and got down on his knees and gets the scrubbing brush and he starts scrubbing the floor.' The assistant said, 'Please, Mr. Newton, we're waiting for you!' and he said, 'No, go away!' and insisted on scrubbing the whole floor before he went to the set! I had just put a beard on him, which takes time to do.

Another time, I made him up and he want to set, so I quickly packed up my box to look after him- I generally had assistants there- but these characters were my own makeups, and they were a bit tricky, so I had to be on the ball all day long with them. I came down the long corridor, and there were the fire buckets of sand all the way down the corridor, and there was Robert Newton with his makeup on, upside down with his head all in the sand bucket. He had somehow put his head in it, so there he was, up against the wall upside down, and he said, 'Here, you didn't know I could do that, did you?'

They had a guy to look after him so he didn't have any smuggled bottles, who had to sit with him on the set all day and watch him. And then he wasn't in a shot, so they were shooting away and he was supposed to be sitting there with this guy looking after him, and they said, 'Right, Robert, it's your turn now! Oh, he's not there! Where's he gone?' The guy said, 'Oh my God, he's gone! I just went out for a moment and when I came back, he was gone. I didn't see him go; he just disappeared; where is he?' They couldn't find him anywhere.

So we go to another set and shoot something else. That was early in the morning. In the afternoon, they were shooting away and said, 'Right, that's it, up with the big doors!' because they wanted to change the scenery, so the big doors went up, and there was Bobby Newton, sitting on a cart horse and saying, 'Hiya, folks!' He was sitting on this horse and nobody knew where he got this raggedy horse from. We never did find out. He really was an incredible character. He was lovely in every way, but he did these mad things.

Sheelagh: Was it due to alcohol, or was he a crazy character any-way?

It was coming up to Christmas on this job and we were going right through to Christmas. One morning he said, 'I've met a very pretty young girl and I want to marry her. I asked if she'd marry me and she said yes, but only if you give up the booze.' He said, 'I've been thinking hard about it, and I love her so much, I'm going to give it up.'

I said, 'That's great if you can; that's wonderful,' but it was a couple of weeks before Christmas and he was working every day and as each day went by, he was off the booze but he got worse and worse and worse. He was just impossible and we were thinking, 'We can't handle him anymore; it's having a terrible effect on him! Christmas is coming, maybe he'll get back on it!' and he did, actually, he got back on it and he was fine, but unfortunately he didn't marry this girl, so that was too bad, but apart from those things, he was a lovely fellow.

Sheelagh: So it was a genuine addiction.

It was an addiction, yes.

Did you have to make up the dog as well? Considering the other strange jobs you've done over the years…

I probably did, because I've been involved in so many animals-dogs, horses, elephants-

Sheelagh: Elephants.

We did several films all over India and one of them was a comedy in which they had a few problems with elephants. We were in Mysore to start with, where they had two fantastic elephants; one was almost black and the other was almost white. The black one had pink ears and we used these elephants a lot, so there had to be some continuity. They then said, 'We're going down south, so we have to get the elephants in a van and take them down,' but the elephant boys said, 'No way, not possible. You can't put an elephant in a van!' They said, 'How long would it take to walk them?' I forget what they said, but it was going to take so many hours a day and they had to feed them on route all the way, so it would take several weeks before they could get there, so that was no good at all, because we had to keep shooting. We couldn't afford to lose three weeks, so they looked at me and said, 'Stuart, we're going to drive you down there, so you look around and select two elephants that you can make up to look like these two elephants we've already seen!'

I got in a jeep with this Indian boy who was my driver and we started driving down there, quite a long way. It wasn't a road, just a track with woods all around it; way out in the wild. The tigers there were 15 feet long from nose to tail, and I had learned this before we went on the trip. We were halfway there and they said, 'Whatever you do, if you see any tigers, don't stop, just keep going!' And lo and behold, there was a tiger who saw us coming and came right up to the track and was standing in front of us.

My little driver was about to pull up, otherwise he would have hit him, and I said, 'Keep driving, keep driving!' The little boy didn't speak much English, so he didn't really understand me, but I shouted 'Keep driving!' and fortunately, he kept going and at the last moment, the tiger jumped out of the way, because we wouldn't be here any more. We would have been gobbled up in no time at all, and I thought, 'I believe it now that I've seen this one!' He was at least 15 feet long, maybe more.

So we kept going, and finally got to this little village. We were told, 'When you get to this little village, turn to the left and there's a little junction. You'll see a big wooden hut, and there you'll find the logging master there, so see him and do a deal with him. He'll show you all the elephants, and you pick the two you think you'll be able to make up to look like these two.'

When we got to this little village, there was nobody there, absolutely nobody in the streets whatsoever. I said, 'Just turn left here,' and there was this little wooden hut as they described it, but there was nobody there. I thought, 'That's strange!' but I got out and knocked on the door and somebody said, 'Come in, come in!' They pulled the little driver in too, and they said, 'We've got an elephant here in musk,' which meant it was getting sexy, and some of them go mad. They said, 'He's already killed six people,' so if there were any villagers out there, it would kill them. I'd seen a few more like that since then, and you have to have respect for them.

I explained what this was about, and he said, 'All of our elephants here are logging elephants. Each of them has half of their tusks broken off, because their tusks would break otherwise, so we have to cut them off,' so they used the short half to lift the logs. I thought, 'Oh my god, that's another problem!' This was not an ordinary everyday makeup job; but that's what I love about it: it doesn't ever get boring.

Anyway, I walked all the way around the elephants and I had my camera so I took pictures and the two I had, one was ten feet high and the other was 11 feet, but the highest one I could find was nine feet and the others were closer to eight feet, but none of them were the right color, because their colors were unique. There were all sorts of variations of gray and not one had pink ears!

I took photographs of the tallest elephants I could find, and a couple of them were around nine feet and I thought I could leave it to the camera boys in the way they shot it so we could get away with it, so I took various pictures of them and eventually got back and thought, I had to be aware of what kind of paint I could use on an elephant, so it didn't harm the skin in any way, so I said, 'Can we get somebody who knows about that sort of thing to advise me?'

I looked at various paints of all kinds to see what was available and talked to this person about it and he said, 'I think this water-based paint will be all right and you don't have any problems,' so I got so many gallons of it and a team of little Indian boys with brushes to paint these elephants the right color. They tested it and said, 'Yes, that will do fine!' We had to do pink on the ears, so I thought I would have do that part, because there were certain shapes and things on them, and I had seen naked girls at circuses on the backs of elephants running around and I thought, if they can do it, I can, but god almighty, the hairs on the elephants were spikes like needles, so I had to get off the elephant very quickly. They didn't tell me that they had to shave the elephants first before you could sit on their necks and it was impossible to get them shaved, but in the end, they did put something over them.

So there I was, painting the ears of elephants, but I still had a problem, and what was I going to do? We were miles away from anywhere, in this location we were going to shoot and I still hadn't solved this problem. If I was home with my lab, it would be no problem at all, but here I was, without a lab and without anything at all, so how did I put the tusks on?

I got the boys to paint the elephants because they wanted to shoot with them the next morning, and I saw the Indian boys sitting at the tables with all their food. They had these big bags of red plastic cups they had started putting out, so I went up to them and said, 'Could you spare a bag of these cups? I've got a little problem with the elephants and I need these for the tusks!' They said okay, but I still didn't know what I was going to do with them.

Anyway, I got all these plastic cups and put one inside the other to extend them and twist them a little bit, so I got that slight curve in it, and I got quite lucky in that they fit on the cut-off end just right. I went to the camera boys and said, 'Look, how many spare rolls of camera tape have you got?' they asked why, and I said, 'I've got a problem with these tusks!'

I modeled a bit to get the point on the end, but I put these tape all the way up and down around it and got it nice and smooth and then painted it to look like bone with little brown streaks and bits of white. We put them on and the director said, 'Fine, great, let's shoot them!' The elephant got down on its knees in the middle of the mud with the elephant boy, who grew up with the elephants; they never leave that elephant; they spend their lifetime with it, so they start them very young, almost the same age and as they both grow up, they stay together and they can speak to each other, as it were, so whatever he says, the elephant knows, so the boy will grab an ear and shout into it and the elephant knows exactly what he's saying, so it's quite extraordinary. So the elephant was going to be sitting down and then get up and then charge across into the scene.

So we've got him all made up and he's got his tusks all ready and they say, 'Action!' so the boys shouts in his ear and jumps on his back, and up the elephant goes and the boy says [chanting] which means 'Go fast!' and off they go, so this elephant was charging up, but he saw the trees and he wasn't too happy with the bits we had put on him, so he went over to the trees, and boom, the tusks went flying. They said, 'Cut!' and I thought 'Oh, God, no!' so they got the elephant back again and the boy shouted at him and really told him off that he mustn't do that so I had to put it all back on again, so they shot something else while I was getting ready and then we had another go and up came the elephant, and this time it doesn't towards the tree so they got the shot. All in a day's work.

And then they wanted a tiger to jump on to the stunt guy. He's standing on the rocks and the tiger jumps on him, but he said, 'I'm not going to do it with a tiger, but I wouldn't mind if it was a leopard,' so they got a leopard, but as you know, a tiger has stripes and a leopard has spots, so once again they said, 'Right, makeup!' The stuntman said, 'I'll take the chance but even a leopard can be pretty fierce. Perhaps Stuart can fix his mouth, so it doesn't open!' so I had *two* jobs on this leopard; to paint him *and* change his spots to stripes; and I also got a couple of the animal boys to try and force his mouth shut, so I put this tape all the way around and then I had to get some similar hair to match his fur and put it all over to disguise it so you didn't see the tape.

So now I've turned the leopard into a tiger, as well as making it impossible to eat anybody, so we shot it and it's still in the film. The leopard wasn't pleased, but it did what they wanted it to do, which was to jump on the stunt guy. You would have thought he wouldn't do anything until he got rid of the tape, but it worked somehow, so the animal guys managed to talk him out of it.

Sheelagh: Which film was this?

It was aß Tarzan film [*Tarzan Goes to India*].

[We begin looking through a book of photos]

Oh yes, the *2001* monkeys. That was a last-minute thing, because the wardrobe people decided that it wasn't wardrobe. They told Kubrick, 'It's not costume, and makeup doesn't necessarily finish on the face, does it?' so that was it, we had to make everything, including practical breasts so they could feed the real baby chimps.

Sheelagh: I see you have the most important item, which is the whiskey bottle.

Oh yes, that is necessary; it reminds me of everything that happened.

Sheelagh: [Looking at makeup room photo] You didn't have lights on your mirrors?

No, we didn't have them all around the mirrors in those days. I think we did put them in eventually.

Going back to the elephants, they were for *Tarzan* and not *Elephant Boy*?

That was for *Tarzan*. But I did several films with Sabu as well.

Sheelagh: What happened to him in the end?

He got onto drugs and that, and died. When they saw him in Hollywood, they loved him and thought they could use him, so he was making films there for two or three years and then got into drugs. He had been fine, but there must have had some misfortune about certain parts, like everybody in Hollywood at some point where you get the element of 'We've got just as many of you, maybe more.' I think there was that elements sooner than it was here, and it was even worse at that time when he got involved, so that was sad, because he was a lovely fellow. It was a terrible waste. [Looking at the book again] *The Yangtze Incident* was based on a true story in the Yangtze when the war started. The whole thing took place on a boat, and we actually got the original boat. My makeup room was the boat's first aid room and we could see where the hull had been all patched up where a shell had come through it from the Chinese who were on the land on one side, so we patched it up and that became our makeup room.

I had one of these [stations] for each artist, so if a film went for several months and you come back again, I would look at this, so I would have a photograph of my makeup table and exactly what it is that I used, so that was always useful.

[Seeing a photo of Christopher Lee] I did two more movies with Christopher Lee in Rio de Janeiro, which was nice. Having spent two years on *2001* and knocked ourselves out 12-18 hours a day, seven days a week with one Sunday off in three, so we did two years of that and Kath was with me, so we thought, 'This is it, we're going to give things up altogether for a few months and have a long holiday!' We were planning to go to somewhere like the Bahamas and just take it easy, and then Christopher Lee phoned up and said, 'I'm going to Rio de Janeiro, because I've got two films to do over there, and I want you to come over and make me up.'

I said, 'I'm sorry, Chris, but we just knocked ourselves out on this film and we've got to take a rest!' He said, 'You can make it a rest, because you're only going to be making me up and I've already made the condition that I only work half a day each day, and you've got nobody else to worry about, so you've got half a day off every day, and if I don't work, you don't work, but you will be paid for the entire film.'

I said, 'What about my wife?' and he said, 'We'll pay your fares over and your wife's,' so I thought we might as well do it, because we had talked about Rio de Janeiro before, so we went and did this film there and it worked out fine. So he was in the first one and then the company said, 'Look, we're going to make another film here in five week's time, a different film and not with Christopher Lee. We're going back to England right now, but we would like to pay your hotel to stay here, because we'd like you to be here for the film. Shirley Eaton is in it.' She was the girl in gold paint from James Bond, but we did a film together in Hong Kong where they had a Chinese makeup man and she hated him and refused point blank to do the film unless she could select her own makeup man.

Fortunately I had made her up on a few other films so I didn't know her that well but she remembered me, so they said, 'We've got Stuart Freeborn out there already,' and she said, 'That's fine, as long as you've got him; otherwise I'm not making the film!' So they told me, 'We'd like you to stay, and we'll pay everything!' so we had five weeks in Rio before she came over, and another four months with Shirley Eaton.

Was that the Dracula film with Christopher Lee?

I did one in Spain, which was the Dracula film, but this was a Fu Manchu one in Rio de Janeiro.

Did you do some work on *The Wicker Man*? I've just seen a note in one of your books.

There was *something* I did in *Wicker Man* that was an interesting makeup, but I didn't work on the whole film. I'm sure I did *The Wicker Man*. That was with Edward Woodward? We did *Kidnapped* together, the Disney film and another one like that, and I think *Wicker Man*. I know I did something, but maybe it was just for one actress or something like that. I did quite a bit of that, where I just go in for one artist.

[Looking at photo of a beauty makeup] In-between films, I would be inundated by commercial people, and I tried to do some of them, because maybe you had picked up some useful information or tricks and hadn't had a chance to use them yet, so for this one, I made a special colored lipstick to match the nails and earrings, so they all had to match. I painted over them by hand so I could put the lacquer over the top. I made all my own nails, modeling the shapes and pressing them out. But I got inundated by companies from Paris and all over Europe and they had seen it all and said, 'Can you supply us with so many thousand sets?' and I had to say, 'Sorry, no way, but there's no way; that was a one-off!'

Oh What a Lovely War, all the 'sirs.' I've got a lot of stories to tell about that- I must tell you about them! But first, Mia Farrow. She was married to Andre Previn the conductor fellow, and refused to do this film, *Blind Terror* [also called *See No Evil*] about all the murders. She and her boyfriend in the film loved horse riding so they go out riding and she has an accident on the horse, hits her head and she's all right now, but she's blind. While she's in the hospital, he takes a spare horse with him, because she still wants to be able to ride horses, so they come back to the big house where the family is living and they get off the horses and he says he'll help, but she says, 'No, I've got to learn; I've got to find my own way about, and the family is in there anyway, so I'd rather do it on my own!' He says, 'I understand,' and goes off.

She goes up to the door and goes in, finds her way up the stairs and goes into a bedroom and says, 'I think I'll take a bath!' and goes into the bathroom and turns the water on. It takes a while for the bath to fill up, so she goes down to the kitchen and as she walks across the kitchen, we see a broken whisky bottle with jagged edges sticking up and the camera is on the floor and as she walks across the kitchen, she doesn't know it's there but as it happens, she misses it and carries on and goes up the stairs and goes into the bathroom and puts her hand in the bath. Being blind she doesn't realize that her father or somebody like that is dead in the bath with his eyes gouged out, so it's a horrible mess , in the bath and she puts her hand right on his face so this is the first bit of blind terror.

She runs back into the bedroom and her sister is naked on the bed murdered, her throat cut, so she hits her hand on it and realizes her sister is dead as well. She can't run, but she's got to go as fast as she can and she comes down the stairs and finds a body, which is the gardener, now dead on the floor in the hallway. And she goes into another room and finds her mother dead in the armchair. She goes back in the kitchen and hears a noise and she realizes the murderer is still in the house and she runs across the kitchen and steps on this jagged piece of glass, and the foot comes up and you see all the blood running out, so I had to make this false piece of foot.

The glass was too heavy, so I got a piece of Perspex that was the same thickness, sawed it up and put it in boiling water and bent it around so that it was the same shape as the bottle and made it the same shape as the piece of glass, so that was very much lighter and it worked, so I was able to push it in and added the blood capsules so it all worked fine.

She also has to run across a frozen lake, as well as this forest, which is in the winter and has all these leaves that have sharp things on them. She was supposed to run across them in bare feet, and then the lake is frozen solid and it cracks, so this is all part of the blind terror with the murderer, who's after her the whole time.

When we were in the pre-production meeting, Mia Farrow said, 'Oh no, I couldn't do all of that!' It had to be done in the real winter because they had to have the breath showing, so I was going to have the same problem I had with David Lean on *Oliver Twist* in the winter, where I had to do this double for Henry Stephenson, because he said it would kill him if he stayed there for so many months and couldn't do it, so David Lean said, 'Stu, you've got to sort yourself out a double,' which I did. He had quite big earlobes, and I had to make them the same for the double.

So what was I saying? Oh yes, Mia Farrow. She said, 'No, I couldn't do that, running through those woods in my bare feet, with all those needles in the leaves,' and with the ice, she said, 'No way!' She didn't want to do it, so they said, 'Well, if you're not going to do it, we've got to find somebody else, and if you won't do it, there's not going to be anybody else who wants to do it, so they looked at me and said, 'Stu?'

I said, 'What am I supposed to do about it?' But I said, 'All right, I'll try,' so first of all, I made a cast of Mia's leg. I went to where she lived with Previn and did it in the kitchen because she didn't live too far away, and she said, 'I would love to do the film, but I can't do it unless I've got physical protection against these things!' I said, 'I think I can do it, I've got an idea,' so I went down there and cast her legs and brought them back here, using the long oven in the shop, which I converted specially for hanging up her legs. I duplicated six pair of legs and I bought some warm tights and put them over the plaster cast and cut the toes out and made toenails and glued them in to the tights.

I then stippled latex on, put it into the oven, took one out and put another one in and take the other pair out. I had photographs of her legs, so I was able to add all the freckles and veins and all the colored markings using colored latex and building it up until I got the right kind of thickness so you could still get it on her legs and peel it off but at the same time make it thick as possible to keep her warm, so I made the fake legs with the toenails and everything. Basically all I had to do was pull them on. She actually wore very little makeup, because she had to look worn and ragged, so it certainly wasn't a glamour makeup; just the opposite, really, so

I still had to make her up but do very little. I put it on her thinking, 'I remember the time in the film business when I used to make up people's faces, but now I'm making up their feet!'

Sheelagh: How long did it take to make the legs?

A couple of weeks or so; stippling them and letting them dry. I had to make quite a few pairs, so I was doing them all day long. I had three pairs; six legs hanging up in the oven and taking them out one by one, so there were always five cooking, as it were. I got them just right backwards and forwards and got them just right, and then put on the feet with the pieces of Perspex that went in them. I made a special set for that scene, and the other sets were extra-thick for running over the leaves and through the ice, and she was quite happy with them. All she had to do was pull on those stockings, so it sounds strange, but it's true.

You never did a lot of gruesome movies, did you? Apart from _The Omen_, as a notable example. Are those effects written in the script from the start?

Those things are usually in the script, so you've got to try and match up to what they want. You might say, 'Look, it can't be done quite like that but I can do this…' and make a slight variation. As long as it conveys what they want, you don't have to necessarily stick to what's in the script.

So David Warner's' head getting cut off by a sheet of glass was in the script?

It was. The head had to look properly translucent, with all the veins underneath and the blood just right. That shot was partially dependent on what the wind was going to be like at the time, and I think the director was pleased to let me say 'Action.' He said, 'Go ahead, rehearse it and when you're ready to shoot, just nod to me and I'll say 'Action' when you feel it's right,' so we went ahead and it worked.

You can just imagine that huge sheet of glass coming through the air and hitting David Warner right _there_. I had maybe a tolerance of an inch or so and that was about all where it would still be all right; further off than that would be a disaster. He was supposed to be standing a certain way and he's then got to spin, so there were many things connected to it when the glass hits him and then the body falls down, and all in one take. The camera then pans in on the body, but it's all in one take, but we got it all on the first go. I didn't have a second chance.

Sheelagh: If you avoided the gruesome stuff, why did you want to do *The Omen*?

There was so much in *The Omen* and to a certain extent, just a certain amount of gruesomeness, so it was interesting to do and I loved the artists working on it.

I understand your work on the scene where Gregory Peck stabs the nanny was so successful; it was too scary to use.

Some of it was in the original film, and what we did looked great but it was a bit on the scary side, so they toned it down a little, so one of the best shots is gone, but it was also cut so much for TV, I couldn't believe it. That effect was quite a problem to do, because of the wig and the piece. I took advantage of the fact that it wasn't three-dimensional so as a makeup artist, you've got to remember that it's flat, whereas if it's going to be seen on film three-dimensionally, you've got to think twice about it. But it was a full-face shot and I explained to the cameraman, 'Don't shoot it straight on, because I'm going to take advantage of the fact that I'm going to build half of the face up but you won't see it on screen because you don't have the depth,' so I could get away with it, as long as she doesn't turn around, so if you could help me with this in mind,' and he understood.

I built up one whole side of her face and got the tubes coming across underneath the wig and coming across for the blood to come out where I wanted it to come out, and it looked horrifying; it was almost too realistic, so I had given them what I wanted but it was up to them to decide whether or not they could use it. But I got away with it because she didn't turn around. In the version I saw, you didn't even see him use the knife. A lot of it was cut for TV, so it lost a lot of its punch, that time they showed it.

So you generally avoided doing that kind of movie?

When I became known for doing those sorts of thing, people who specialized in horror films were on to me, but I thought, 'I don't want to get involved in nothing but horror films!' I already had plenty of films to do, but would get calls in-between other films I was doing and they would explain what it was and I'd say, 'I'm sorry, I'm not available.' I didn't do any purely horror films, but with films like *The Omen*, there were bits of horror in it, which is different, because you've got good artists in it, and it's an interesting film. I like doing complicated makeups, and I've always been fascinated by things that perhaps haven't been done before, so that was what interested me most.

Sheelagh: Not the graphic stuff.

I wasn't interested, so I always turned them down, but if it had something like David Warner's' head, it fitted in and it was okay; that was permissible and I would fit it in.

In some ways, a film like *10 Rillington Place* was more horrifying.

Oh yes, Dicky Attenborough at his worst. That was interesting in terms of how far we could go. It was called *10 Rillington Place*, because seven prostitutes had been murdered there and stuffed up a chimney. We were going to use the original house but there were other people living in it, so it was actually the next door but one, so there was the original drain thing in the middle of the road where he put the bodies down, so they hadn't changed the name of the road when they took the bones out. That was an interesting job.

There's a note in this book that you used a new kind of plastic for the first time?

That was in the early days when we hadn't got into things like that. PVC had only just come out. Foam rubber wasn't even used for that kind of makeup, so I had a few interesting jobs to do on that film.

Changing the subject for a moment, here's a picture of Peter Sellers from *Dr. Strangelove*.

He was originally going to play the part of Slim Pickens the pilot, who looked completely different from the other characters. Instead of just putting a bald cap on him, I made a foam bump underneath to make him look more intelligent, subconsciously a bigger brain bump. I also did that with Dicky Attenborough as the murderer in *10 Rillington Place*, because I had a death mask of him. The thing is, when you read these books about shapes of heads, they can almost tell when you're a murderer or not to that degree and maybe you'd better not get too close to that person. The thing is, it's almost an ape head with little hollows in it, and when I read about that being a part of a murderer, I made the foam rubber piece and then put the cap on to get that similar shape, so it worked out all right.

Here's a picture from a 1970's production of *Alice in Wonderland* that featured Sellers.

These were all big-name people. They wanted me to create a look enough like a creature [Sellers played the March Hare] but still keep it so we could see the actor underneath, so you were caught between the two, as it were. Dudley Moore played the Dormouse, Michael Crawford was the White Rabbit and Robert Helpmann as the Mad Hatter. Fiona Fullerton played Alice. Did I tell you about her? That was an interesting thing. They're all dancing around the Pool of Tears, so you've got to see tears to make the pool; there's no pool unless she cries. That means you've got to see a lot of tears coming down off the face to make the pool, but if you know elementary chemistry, you know that two molecules of water have the greatest affinity for each other of anything else, so when they originally made cigarettes without cork tips, they would absorb the moisture from the lips, and if you took the cigarette out of your mouth, it would peel the skin off your lip. That's why they put cork tips on them. For the same reason, if you've got tears running down here, it would never fall off; it would go underneath straight down in front, like perspiration and I knew they didn't understand this and didn't know their chemistry, but I did at that time, and I knew I had a problem, so I wracked my brain but nothing came up.

I used to watch all these things on telly about new inventions for the future and I got lucky again. I've gotten quite lucky quite often but in this case, I had a problem for which I didn't have an answer, so I was sitting there watching this thing about thee two guys out in the country at this little river, where they made a boat out of brown paper, exactly the same way you would make a paper hat, so they folder it the same way and you can either use it as a ht or a boat. They put it on the water and they both got in and it sank as the water came through the paper, so I watched these two guys, who then powdered it all over with some white powder, they put it back on the water and both got in and sailed down the river.

I thought, 'Aha, that's the answer to my problem!' so I made some investigations and contacted the company, who said it was a material they make in Central America somewhere, but they finally got me the address so I sent a cable to them. I said I was very interested in the program and told them the reasons why I would very like to be in possession of some of their materials, so they sent me a big carton of it and I've used it ever since for all sorts of things. The wardrobe people can't thank me enough because they were able to use it on their costumes and didn't have to wait for them to dry, so it changed their lives completely, so I gave them something to start with and then they've been able to get it too. I can't remember the name of it, but it's a kind of silicone powder, but exactly it is, I'm not sure.

So if you powdered a face with it…

I only powdered it underneath, but the trouble is, it was opaque white and I had quite a problem finding the right kind and color of material to blend with it that didn't destroy it, but I finally found one and got it down to a sufficiently pink color that you didn't notice it anymore, so I tested it with the tears, and of course a lot depended on how I made the tears. I had made different tears for different reasons, so that was quite a science in itself. The consistency of the tears was quite different for this was different from what I used on many other occasions.

The interesting thing is, tears don't necessarily appear straight away. It might be a long scene without a cut, and the tears have to appear somewhere, so you've got to make these tears appear and make her look like she's crying naturally, so I developed a technique for that as well without putting tears there. I found that different artists had entirely different sensitivities for their eyes, so if we had a crying scene I would say, 'Look, before we do makeup, I want to make it easy for you when the time comes for you to cry, so I've got to do a test on top of the makeup with a little bit of menthol down there and see how long it takes for the tears to come up.' With some of them, I had to put it quite far down because they were quite sensitive, and others I had to put it right up because they weren't sensitive at all, but in gauging that, I knew exactly where I should put it so when the time was right, they cried at the right time. So that was an interesting makeup thing.

I did a religious film where this girl had to cry. I started things off enough to get them going, and from there on everything goes right for them, but they had a lot of action going on first, so it had to be very much delayed, and then you see her boyfriend coning from the distance and come up to her. The tears start to run down, so I had to have things planted, but they mustn't run down for quite a long time. You don't see it right away, because we're more or less behind her, but as they warm up, you see the tears coming down quite heavily, so the menthol wouldn't have been enough, so I had to have a mixture of glycerin with a little touch of gelatin to get the consistency right to gauge the amount of time that it would take to melt, so I had different mixtures worked out until I found exactly the one I wanted.

After rehearsal, I figured out how long it was going to be, because they didn't quite know, but after rehearsal, they could say, 'That's how we're going to did it!' so I timed it out with my watch so I could select the right mixture, which I had made up already and it worked, so that was another interesting little thing that I did.

[We continue looking at pictures] That was with Dom DeLuise, a lovely guy; we did a few films together. Gene Wilder was a lovely man. And Gilda Radner.

That was *Haunted Honeymoon*?

It was in one of them. We did two films with him, this one and *Sherlock Holmes Smarter Brother*.

[Looking at another photo] This is Finlay Currie. He was playing the part of Peter in *Quo Vadis*. They said, 'And now we want to go back to the Last Supper, when he was only 24 years old,' and he was pretty old then, and I said, 'Can I pick the actor that I think I can make up to look a very young edition of him?' And they said, 'But it won't be Finlay Currie, would it?' I said no, but I had so many other artists to make up, I didn't have any spare time, so I said 'Surely it would be better to have a different actor,' because I didn't know how the hell I was going to make him look that young, so the director said, 'I'll tell you what, we'll do both! So you make the young boy up and you can also de-age Finlay.' I said, 'What's the point of that? I haven't got time with all the other actors; I'll be here until four in the morning.

Anyway, I did it and it was so frantic. They were rehearsing on the back lot and I had made up the other artists, and he was supposed to be with me, but he wasn't there and I couldn't see an assistant, so I ran out on the back lot and there were all these people from the crowd, hundreds of them, so I just couldn't find him. I had the Jesus Christ actor to do as well, which is one of the reasons I was so frantic, because he hadn't turned up either, and I had to get him out of the way so I could make up Finlay Currie. But I couldn't remember his name, so I just yelled out, 'Jesus Christ!' and all of these people looked at me. We were in Italy of course, so they were all Italians and I thought, 'They're going to murder me!' so I ran back inside quick. Anyway, they did choose the real de-aged Finlay Currie and used him in the end, but I still had to do the other one as well.

[Leafing through the photos] Robert Taylor, Peter Ustinov, Buddy Baer, he was a character, oh Patricia Laffan. I had to use real gold leaf, not gold plate for her fingernails [as Poppaea], because apparently that's what they used to use in those days to put on the fingernails and toenails, and they wanted real gold leaf not gold paint, so it was a real time factor thing, because I had these other people to do as well, so I had to get it all down and I had to find a quick way of sticking on this gold leaf and cutting it. And she had a cheetah with her as well, so they said, 'The way to get it used to her before we start filming is to be with her all the time,' so it was with her in the makeup room, so there it was, behind the makeup chair! I daren't tell it to get out of the way or tread on its tail or its foot or it would have my leg off at any moment, so it was terrifying, having to walk around the damn thing. Anyway, I had to do all of this with that damn cheetah around there. Dear me, that was a nightmare.

Let's see, oh, Peter Ustinov. He was quite young at the time, as Nero, and the director was giving him hell. He really went crazy directing Peter Ustinov, and would shout at him time and time again. He was never happy with anything they did, and suddenly, Peter Ustinov got up in front of the camera and started doing his own act, copying the director and all of his dialogue. He did the whole thing perfectly, because he's a great actor, so he did the whole thing and everybody clapped and cheered. The poor director wanted to walk off the set, because it was just incredible. I've always admired Peter, who was a perfect mimic, with a great sense of humor. He would go to wardrobe and they would put him in all these robes, and before I could get him in the chair to make him up, he would do a whole act of a Brighton Boarding house lady, with a cockney accent and he did everything perfectly, wearing all these robes.

You started to tell us before about working with the 'Sirs' on *Oh, What a Lovely War.*

I made them all up as actors and they got to know each other and become chums, so they all knew each other. When Dicky Attenborough decided he wanted to direct, obviously he was going to use all of his the actor friends in the film to help him out. They weren't asking too much money, but were helping him along on his first film because they were pals. It was a wartime film, a musical, and Dicky Attenborough had seen it and thought he would like to make a film of it. It was all about the slightly risqué songs that they sang during the war.

In order to give himself a little bit of experience with directing and setting things up, for the first week, we were shooting without the big boys, all the Sirs, just to get his hand in, so we did the stage scenes in a little theater on Brighton Pier, where they used the actual stage. For the audience, we were away from London, so they couldn't suddenly call upon the crowd artist union, so they used the crew and put them in, so we were all sitting in the chairs in front of the stage with the camera at the back, so we were the audience and you could see the back of our heads. Maggie Smith as the leading singer comes on and it's all to do with the beginning of the war and trying to talk the boys into joining up, so the song is specially written so Maggie Smith and all the dancing girls- one of them was Jane Seymour, and it was the first time she had done anything in films, so she was one of the dancers. She had got married to Dicky Attenborough's son for a while and then she was on to other things.

Maggie Smith's song went on and on about joining up 'And if you're willing, we'll give you shilling.' That was the last line, and the front row of the audience was the wardrobe department, which consisted of the wardrobe ladies, who were very nice ladies and her crew of five who were all queer. They used a lot of queer boys because they had great costumes so it was normal and they were lovely fellows. Anyway, Dicky Attenborough was rehearsing and this was his first time directing anything, so he rehearsed it about five times and suddenly he said, 'This time, we're going to shoot. And... action!' so the dancing girls came out and Maggie Smith sings her song. And they go to the line, 'If you are willing, we'll give you the shilling and make a man out of you!' and one of the little queer boys suddenly stood up and said, 'It'll take more than a shilling to make a man out of me!' and 'Cut! Who said that?' Poor old Dicky. Anyway, that was the first week.

Before they came down, I knew all the artists and what they wanted and got them to up to the wig-makers, because we had to have toupees and wigs made- this was all the big boys, and of course they were all well known characters, so everybody knew what these generals looked like, the French and English and German generals, so I knew exactly what they looked like, and they all had hairpieces, whether it was the Kaiser with his pointed moustache and all of that, so Larry Olivier was going to be the Kaiser and the other boys were all playing well-known characters that people knew, so I had to get him to look as realistic as possible, so I got him all fitted up, because once I was down there, I wasn't going to have time to deal with that as well, so I had to have them all set, with the beards and moustaches and toupees all in boxes and ready to fit the artists, so it was done before I went in.

We finished the first week of shooting, without the big boys and we knew the next day was going to be the day when we were going to use all the well-known actors, all the Sirs, so I went in my makeup room where I got the makeup and whiskers and everything in line for the different artists, knowing what time they were coming in. Anyway, I had to get up early in the morning so I went to bed and the phone rang beside my bed. It was Dicky Attenborough, who said, 'Stu, I've been in the bar with Larry (that's Sir Laurence Olivier, of course) and he's changed his mind about playing the part of the Kaiser. He wants to play the French general instead; that will be all right, won't it?' I said, 'No, it won't because it means I won't have a toupee for him as the French general!' He said, 'Oh, you'll think of something!' and put the phone down. So what do I do?

I went to my makeup room the next morning and started to sort things out. I had a few artists come in, and then Olivier came in, who I've known for many years- when he first started in 1936, I was working with him and Vivian Leigh; they were both married but having an affair, which I knew about, because I was making up the artists on all the pictures so I would just finish up with Vivian Leigh- I've told you about this- Larry would come in early and I had just got her lipstick on beautifully and boom, he would kiss her and spread it all over, so he would try it every morning and I had to kick him out.

Anyway, I worked with him on many films after that, so when he came in, he would normally be full of jokes and we would have a laugh, but on this morning, he came in knowing that he wasn't going to play the Kaiser anymore. He wanted to play the French general, so now he was going to deal with me. He didn't know what happened between Dicky and me, so he came in and said, 'Good morning.' I said, 'Morning,' which was not my usual way, so I didn't speak to him and he sat down and looking at me in the makeup mirror.

I put the ordinary makeup on him and I said to him, 'Larry, we've worked together for years now,' and he looked at me and I said, 'So you won't be at all surprised at anything I might do!' He didn't know if I was genuinely very angry at him or not, because I was putting on an act all the way through. So he sat there, wondering what the hell was going to happen to him. So I thought this French general had a nice big blonde moustache, so I stuck this moustache on, and of course I had a box full of them as spares, as I always had on a job like that, so I didn't smile or anything, I just got another blonde moustache out and stuck it on his forehead.

I walked away and let him look at it and he didn't know what to say or think. He knew I was very angry at him by now, because I hadn't said anything at all. Anyway, I got a whole row of moustaches and put them over the top of his head, and it was all moustaches, and I combed them in and it all worked fine. I didn't know if it was going to work, but it did, so he got up and smiled at me, and he was going out the door and turned around and said, 'I won't tell a soul!' We went down to set and that was it, it was fine. I said, 'You'd better not tell anyone you're wearing a head full of moustaches!' It was only when they finished shooting late in the afternoon when I told Dicky and he fell apart and we all had a good laugh.

Is it true when you get a bunch of 'Sirs' together, they can be big kids?

Well, yes, exactly that. The most mischievous out of that lot? Quite a few were mischievous in different ways. The very last thing Larry ever did a year before he died was the show *Time*. They had a 15-foot plaster head of Larry Olivier for this show and he was using a walking stick and he could hardly walk even with the walking stick, so he had this makeup done in the cellar of a building nearby the BBC and they could get him there but they couldn't get him up the stairs. What we had do was sit him in this seat and set up the camera, so all he had to do was long speeches, but film him so you got this head, which was a three-dimensional screen, because the big head was seen in depth and they didn't use a normal lens, which is made to have a very shallow focus, so the tip of the nose and the ears were slightly out of focus, because you had 45 times magnification in a close-up on a big screen, so they always used this shallow focus lens for normal work, but here, we had to use a very deep focus lens, a special lens for deep focus, because they wanted it sharp with that great depth for most of it.

Being projected on to that screen, he couldn't move his head side to side, because there was no way to move the camera. It had to be absolutely rigid, but as these speeches were so long, being the actor that he is, once he got into the speech, he instinctively starts to forget about movement and just does what he feels he has to do as far as what's involved in that speech, so he just couldn't do it. He would start all right, but in order to concentrate and get the whole thing out, he would forget what he had been told about not moving his head a fraction of an inch left or right. We did it for two or three days and never got a shot, so they looked at me and said, 'Can you do anything to help us out?'

I said, 'There is, but you've got to give me a day or so to do it,' so I cast the back of his head and made a rigid shell so when he got his head in it, it would go in as deep as possible on the sides, but his hair would cover the edge of it so there was enough to cover his head but he couldn't move it sideways, so I thought I might get away with it, and it worked: he got his head in it and couldn't move his head, He was quite happy about that, and said, 'I don't have to think about it now so I can just come out with my speech!' so he was very pleased about it.

We've talked about *Top Secret* before, but Peter Cushing talked about his scene in his biography, saying he had some kind of eye infection after this was done. Was he just making a joke, because of the magnifying glass gag in the film?

I don't remember anything about that. That was the only thing he did in the film, and he was very happy about it. I don't know what he was suggesting, because it never bothered him at all. He wasn't on it very long and it was only that one take. I even cleared his eyelashes because the first problem was, when I tried it on myself, it was quite uncomfortable because of your own eyelashes, so I made sure I had enough distance between the false eye over it so his eyelashes didn't have to touch, and they didn't when I asked him. I said, 'Look, I'm trying to make this so your eyelashes don't touch it,' so he could blink normally and he said it was no problem at all. It wasn't on him long anyway. I don't see anything that could have hurt his eye.

Kath: It's amazing the number of people that remember that scene.

Was it a fun film to do? You created a lot of the gags.

Ninety percent of the gags were done in that shed down here. We even had the real horse here and cast him. It took seven of us to operate that horse. We also had the other scene I've talked about before, where Omar Sharif was the little dwarf, so I cast his face and put it on one of our *Star Wars* dwarves, who was about three foot eight and put the mask on him, so when he comes in and they say, 'Oh, what happened to you?' it's the silliest thing ever and gets a real laugh. We made the entire squashed car for that gag. I think Kenny Baker played Omar. Have I told you any of those stories?

We used up all of the dwarves that were on the list as available for film work when I needed that many more, so I advertised for dwarves and we had a lot of new people coming in, the dwarves that is, who would just come in for a few day's work and go back to their normal jobs. This isn't really about Kenny Baker, but I was looking around and saw this little chap, so I said, 'What do you normally when you're not working in films?' and he said, 'This is the first time I've done any film work,' and I asked what he normally did and he said, 'I'm a lumberjack!' I said, 'Really, you're a lumberjack?' and he said, 'Yes, in a mushroom factory!'

They all had a great sense of humor about their size. Kenny Baker, and his buddy, who unfortunately got accidentally killed in a car accident; the two of them worked together. They had been doing a show in town where they would play instruments and crack gags about themselves, so they were quite amusing in what they did and said and played music. They had done quite well at it and both had houses next door to each other not far from Elstree Studios. And they both had Mercedes cars, with the gears and seats brought right up and when they were sitting in their cars, you didn't know they were dwarves and they drove beautifully. If it was the two of them together, they would take turns driving to their night-time show.

They were getting near home and it was in an area of expensive well-to-do area of houses and Kenny Baker wasn't driving this time and he said to his chum, 'Can you pull over; I've got to spend a penny!' so there was a bank with a big H on top, so he stopped And a lot of these dwarves look a little bit odd face-wise; sometimes they have a little bump on their foreheads and some skull shape is different that makes them all look a bit odd. Anyway, Kenny Baker got out and he went behind the hedge and there was a police car coming down the other way, and he saw this car with the other chap sitting in it, who had this funny look about him, and around them were these big houses so he thought, 'Why is he sitting there?'

It was like a getaway car sitting there at half past three in the morning, so he pulled up and came around and knocked on the window, where they guy said, 'Yes, officer?' He said, 'What are you doing here at this time of night?' He said, 'Oh, my friend was taken short!' He said, 'Where? And he said, 'Up there,' so he looked up and Kenny Baker was standing there, who was about that high and he said, 'Taken short? He sure was!' and went off. Of course his wife was a midget too, and they had two children; one was a midget but one was normal-sized.

Did I tell you the other story about Larry Olivier? When they were trying to film him for the show and of course he had been a lord for some time. They were nothing to do with the film business this camera crew, but they had this special company that specialized in making these miniature talking heads, so they found a way of making them move by projecting a person's face on this rigid surface. So they were all referring to him as 'Sir Laurence,' and he hated that. I still called him Larry like I'd done for the past 25 years, but he said to them, 'Please don't call me that, call me Larry!' and they would say, 'Oh, yes, Sir Laurence, I mean, Larry!'

And then there's the story about Sir Thomas Beecham. The Beechams were well know for Beecham's Pills but he was also known for his conducting so everybody thought he was knighted for his music but in fact he wasn't; he was knighted for the pills. A lot of people don't know that. Anyway, Sir Thomas got the knighthood, he threw a party for his friends and relations and a local newspaper sent one of their young reporters to get a story out of it, and they all thought it was for his music. Anyway, this young boy explained who he was and they said, 'You'd better come in,' so he was sitting at this big table and trying to make contact to speak to him so he said, 'I'm a reporter and I'm here to report on him getting his knighthood for his music,' and he was told, 'No, it's not for his music, it's for the Beecham's Pills.'

Anyway, they eventually said, 'Sir Thomas will see you now, and he said, 'Yes, my boy, what can I do for you?' He said, 'I'm from such and such newspaper and I'm writing this story about how this happened; it is for your music, isn't it, because they told me it was possibly for Beecham's Pills.' He said, 'Oh no, it *is* for Beecham's Pills, but I'd like to think that my music is as moving as the pills!' I've got a book of Beecham stories, but I haven't had a chance to read it yet.

Sheelagh: Here's a photo of Albert Finney in *Murder on the Orient Express*?

I had to change his nose. He had a very boyish nose, so I had to give him a more grown-up nose so I put a nose on him.

And here's Christopher Reeve from *Superman*. Why did you cast his entire body if you were just building a miniature version?

I had to cast a lot of bodies on *Superman* for throwing them over buildings and things, using dummies in all different sizes depending on how they fit the set. If we were shooting on the real 42nd Street, they were the normal size, with the helicopter up there and Lois Lane falling down and Superman coming up and catching them, but when they were flying over Paris, they did a one-third size version, because you couldn't build a full-size Paris. So I had to make miniature bodies for some of the different sets. I did three-quarter size, half-size and one-third size so they could shoot accordingly. I did all the baddies as well, so it kept me busy for a while, I can tell you.

Here's a photo of Tony Randall for whom I had to make a bald cap. Of course to make it match, you have to look at the size of the pores on the artist and make them the same, so I would stipple it with different-sized sponges that were calculated to give it the same size pores and stipple it on over the edge of the cap and the graduate it until it goes smooth, so you have pores here but it's smooth further up, but sometimes the pores are quite heavy higher up, sometimes it's quite smooth, so you have to be able to do it according to how their skin is and match their pore sizes. Here's a picture of him again, for *The ABC Murders*.

Oh, and here's a picture of me; I did this when I was about 18. Guy Pearce the makeup artist said you take the pictures and then do the enlarging and during the enlargement you can change the bad things in the makeup. I said, 'Yes, but I didn't do anything to then,' and he said, 'Yeah, but I don't know that, do I? Go into my makeup room and do that makeup with all the aging and every-thing; I want to see you do it!' so I had to do it and they filmed it walking in front of the camera.

That's a great headline: 'Hopes of a Film Studio Career.' You couldn't ask for better publicity.

No, I couldn't, could I? And that's what did it. I did this as part of the Cine-Society as they called it in those days, where everybody had their own 16mm cameras.

And here's a photo from *Max and Helen*, one of your last films.

That's the very last major film I ever did. I've done commercials since then. I was 75 then. It was a very interesting true story. When I saw it, I was flabbergasted; they had cut it so much that you didn't know what the hell was going on. When they were in the prison camps together and they were sweethearts as it were, but he was shoved a long way off somewhere else so they were separated, but when he finally came back and asking where she was, none of the locals knew where she was, but by now she had a son by the German guy who was running the camp, the camp commander, and he was a real horror, and I had to make the son up to look just like his father so that it was obvious, which I did, and then when he goes to this flat, the son opens the door and he doesn't know this has happened and sees the son and thinks-

It's the young commander.

He knew she had this son by somebody against her will, so she wasn't married to anybody but she had become pregnant because somebody had abused her, so when this boy opened the door, he recognized him but didn't know he was a goodie, and that he was on the other side with his mother and he turned out to be a very nice boy, so that's how the story finished up as he learns the true story.

Here's a photo with Cliff Richard and the Shadows for one of his films. That must have been a long time ago, Maureen O'Sullivan, I used to make her up. The extraordinary thing was, in those days, it was a three-strip film, not one strip. You had very wide cameras and they took three films at once going through them. One was an emulsion that specialized in red, one yellow and the other blue and all the other colors in-between, so you had a three-strip film which was the only way they could get the entire range of colors, because they couldn't get one emulsion to have separate colors in it in those days, but there was always some disorder in it, because the red was far too sensitive, so it would make the reds very strong.

Up to then, for black and white, we had dark brownish-red lipstick, which you had to use for registering black and white to get a normal face and density of color to represent normal red lips, and it worked, but with color, we suddenly had to change to a very pale pink lips and with rouge, there was hardly anything there at all, and the girls hated it. As soon as they left us, they would go and put their own lipstick back on again.

And there were certain dancing girls we had with long hair and we made them up with this special makeup, but we also had to put a gray makeup on first over everything, because the emulsions penetrated the skin- the eyes don't, but the emulsion does and it goes underneath and picks up the red under the skin, so we had to blank that out anyway, in addition to doing any surface red, so you had those two problems.

What we had to do was put gray on all over first, and of course the girls weren't used to wearing anything like that, so they would go straight to their rooms and wipe it off and put the makeup back on again. Oh, so I was saying, we had all these girls who had long hair and we made them all up but of course we didn't do their ears because the hair was over them, so I would get a frantic call from the set that somebody decided that they would have their hair up and they actually shot it and when they saw it, there were all these red ears sticking out and said, 'My God, what went wrong there?' It had nothing to do with us, they were all covered and I had made a point of finding out if they were covered, but somebody decided on the set to expose their ears, so you got red ears.

Looking at these now, it's interesting because we were having to do the latest methods of eye shading and lining and highlighting. The thing was, you had to make the eyes look bigger. On the screen, the eyes diminish and the mouth diminishes, so you've got to enlarge things, not only taking it a little bit further but you've also got to put a slight shadow on the lower lip, so you've got to use a little brown pencil on top of the rouge and all these things, so you've got to check the overall shading, so that's how it had to be, and it's interesting looking at all those little details today.

Merle Oberon used to call me Bill Stuart, because my name is Stuart William you see, and at home, I was always called Billy. Nobody called me Stuart. I was always Bill or Billy at home, and some people in the studio still called me Bill while others called me Stuart or Stu, so she heard both names and thought my name was Bill Stuart and didn't know there was another name behind it.

Charles Laughton- I did many films with him. He was in nearly every other film at Denham Studios including the very first film I ever worked on. We did the eye bags with cotton wool and collodion and that's it. That's the only thing we knew in those days. This was very early day prosthetics. We didn't have any other materials to do it with. I used to use acetone to dissolve the collodion. Denham had the most fantastic back lot; it had everything. They've knocked it all down now, but it was fantastic, and I remember it well.

Part IV: 7/22/97

Anyone who's seen the 1989 Cameron Crowe film Say Anything will doubtless remember the scene in which Lloyd (John Cusack) opens a massive dictionary owned by Ione Skye's Diane, in which she has marked every word she's ever looked up, only to discover that virtually every page of the book is covered in Xs. That's pretty much the experience I had at when paging through Stuart Freeborn's copy of the British Film Encyclopedia, where he had checked off every film he had worked on, all the way back to his uncredited work in the 1930's. I agreed to take the book home and compile a formal list, which ultimately ran nine full pages, single-spaced, and I'm sure I missed a few.

On this particular summer visit, Stuart decided it would be nice to sit outside, surrounded by his stunningly beautiful gardens. Unfortunately, I'm pretty sure his house was also on the Heathrow flight path, which meant a lot of intermittent background noise; not a problem in a face to face conversation, but a huge difficulty when trying to transcribe that conversation months later...

Sheelagh: One of the things I was interested in, did you have any formal training, or did you learn on the job from the people around you?

I certainly didn't learn from the others around me. I was amazed at how the quality of what they did wasn't good. I recognized that, and thought I had done much better with my Beckenham Cine-Society, where I thought we had done much better work there than they do in here.

And that was amateur stuff.

That's right. I used to write the scripts and all the stories about aging people and all of that, not only the women but the men as well, with them young and then older, and turning an Englishman into a Chinese or whatever, bald heads; anything that called for interesting makeup. Do you remember Guy Pearce?

The man who originally hired you.

Yes, he was originally from Hollywood. In those days, he was probably one of the top Hollywood boys, and when Alexander Korda came to England (strangely enough, he came from Budapest, Hungary), he decided he would put the English film industry on its feet, because it was pretty poor. The Americans owned most of the cinema chains, and Hollywood was really booming, with some very good films, which were the main features.

If you were lucky, you might see a 'quickie-quota' after the first film, which was made in England. It was always the second film, so the quality never did reach anything at all, because nobody was interested. That's how I discovered it was, but I couldn't get into the studios. As I told you, I physically tried all sorts of ways to get into the British film industry, but they didn't want to know me. It's not because I wasn't good enough; it was the other way around. They were terrified, and they told me that later when I was doing my own films and started using some of those people and they laughed and said, 'We've got to tell you, all those letters you used to write, we saw all the pictures you sent, but we didn't dare answer them because you would have pinched all of our jobs!'

Little did I know that was what was happening, but that was the situation: they were never interested in doing anything because it was just a quickie-quota that didn't call for anything as far as special work. But that situation changed after Denham Studios, which changed everything. The other studios started developing a lot more, so it all sort of happened.

Sheelagh: So there was no real training.

Guy Pearce was a good makeup artist, but mostly straight make-up. He was good at that, and simple beard work, but he didn't get into anything too complicated. So I got the latest Hollywood way from him up to that point, but then we did a film with Anna Neagle, called *Queen Victoria*, where we had to go from young to old. He had a hell of a lot of people working for him to cover all these films, so I don't know why it was, maybe it was all those photographs I had showed him, but he picked me to work with him on it, doing things like where you stretched the skin to apply things, and then he would get me to start applying them, and none of the others had ever done that, so I got the best of all of that, because I was always working with him.

And then his wife was a little jealous, so if there was a very attractive new young actress coming in, she would create a fuss, so I got her, and I was making up all these actresses, who were big names in those days. I was only a young kid in the business but I was making up all sorts of people that were around in those days, and I knew why, because he used to get it in the neck if he made them up. So that was an extraordinary thing that happened.

And after we were applying the aging makeups and what we used in those days was cotton wool and collodion stuck on with spirit gum, and it was my job to take it all off again, so I would help him put it on the way he did it and I thought, 'There's a lot of room for improvement. I don't like this!' because the poor girls were all sore, so it was all right for the first day but they're getting more sore by the second day, so you had sore skin to put it on to start with.

I never put it on the same place, so I would cheat and put it in one place on the first day and put it up a little higher the next day and a fraction lower the next and then come back to the middle again but I would never put it in the same place two days running and nobody ever noticed it. I purposely cheated, because if you wanted a deep scar, which you often did, it could really become sore.

Anyway, we started having to do a lot of bald caps on certain films, and Guy Pearce was not a lab man at all. He did not go into making anything at all. I think it was George Bau or one of those guys a bit earlier than that; they used to send over bald caps, and it was early days over there too, so they weren't that advanced either, and there were problems with the bald caps, especially being sent over from the States by then, so things happened to them and they would get dried out or something else would go wrong, so you would put it on and sometimes it would crack into bits, so there were all sorts of reasons why they really didn't work. It might have been okay if you had just made it and put it on within the hour, but these bald caps didn't work.

I just thought, 'This is not very good; I could make them better than this!' At least they would be fresh, so I decided to experiment and Guy said, 'That's a good idea, come with me!' so he took me around to the other side of the studio where there were some empty rooms where the art department had just moved out, and he said, 'I'm going to take these rooms over, and I want you to make this your lab to develop and make all these things, like eye bags and bald caps and noses and double chins and that sort of thing.' I thought that was fantastic, but what were the others going to say?' He said, 'Don't mention it; don't let them know!' so that was a bit tricky, when they wondered where the hell I had got to at the time.

I got started making bald caps, and eventually they found out, because other people had seen me and said this Stuart Freeborn guy is working down there, so they found out, so it was okay, but it was very strange at first how all of that happened. Plus I was taught the Hollywood way by Guy Pearce, who was very good, so I got all of that, plus I was able to develop the other things from there, because things weren't quite right and he knew it, so I was working with entirely different chemicals and materials and all of that.

I would contact chemical companies like Dow Corning and I used to go up and talk to them and get them interested, or invite them to the studio to meet some of the actors and actresses they admired in the flesh and they loved that, so that was one of the little things I did, and it worked and they loved it. I would sometimes become very friendly with some of the actors and actresses, so I would say, 'Do you mind if we had lunch with you today?' They would say, 'No, not at all bring them in!' so they used to have lunch with some big names and they loved that.

I got a lot of free stuff that way, and they used to send a Rolls-Royce to pick me up, whereas I used to travel by train or taxi to get there, because I used to have a secondhand Ford 8, which was not very good and I didn't think I could drive it all the way out there, so they used to send a car to take me out to lunch. I was supposed to be picking their brains, but they were picking mine instead, because I did a lot of development work with their plastics.

You were making up actors, and researching new products in your spare time?

All the time. I was researching right to the end. I said to them all, 'Look, the main thing is I want is an artificial flesh,' which is not an easy thing at all. I explained the reasons why, which were the consistency and nothing must be toxic about it, because it was going to be applied to the skin, and neither could the adhesives or the solvents for the adhesives, so you had to keep all of those things in mind; there could be nothing toxic at all, and the quality of that flesh had to be able to stretch a certain way and have certain qualities that flesh has.

Flesh is unique in ways that plastic isn't, but there are ways you can make it that way by mixing it the right way, like PVC where you can get any kind of transparency you want. The way I used it, I could use solvents and things that weren't toxic, because it can be very toxic- obviously the fumes when you're cooking it, but normally it isn't when you are using it, so I would make all sorts of things out of it but then they didn't know how to foam it at all, so I developed different ways by using three different kinds of plasticizer, because if you used a certain quantity of one, it would screw up the foaming agent.

And then I found if I reduced that, another one would make big bubbles inside and lots of little ones on the outside, or vice versa, so I would change the color of it and I thought, well, none of these are working, but I worked it out that if I have a proportion of this one and a proportion of that one, it could give me (because they all gave me something quite different), something that I wanted and it worked. And then the boys from ICI came down and said, 'You found it!' They hadn't even got around to foaming PVC, so I had to go over there and explain how I did it. It was extraordinary really; you would think they knew about it.

Sheelagh: No wonder they sent a Rolls Royce for you!

Exactly. They said, 'You've saved us months of detailed work, which we could ill afford, because we were doing other things, and you've given us a leap forward on that and the reasons why with the proportions of different plasticizers and foaming agents,' so I figured out the combination and it worked, eventually.

Sheelagh: Did you have a good ventilation system in your little lab?

I certainly did!

Otherwise, wouldn't be sitting here now, would he?

Exactly. In a month's time, I shall be 84 and I still feel like I'm in my thirties! Anyway, what were we saying?

Sheelagh: About the ventilation system.

On *2001*, apart from the foam PVC, I needed a lot of polyure-thane, because there's rigid urethane in different densities- very hard, medium hard- and then you can also get flexible urethane in different densities so you could get the whole range because you needed them when you were doing these jobs. I got four of the boys out of the plaster shop and I went up to the top of the studio- I knew about the poisonous fumes from polyurethane when you're processing it; when you're mixing it and it's rising, that's when it's very dangerous, but I also knew that those fumes were a bit heavier than air, so they never went up; they always went down. I had worked that out too, so I talked to the powers that be in the studio and said, 'I want you to build me a big shed on top of the roof of the studio.' Out back, it was just open fields, so I said, 'At the back of this wall, I'm going to put a bench here, and I want you to put extractor fans all around the bottom under the bench.'

They said, 'Why not up there?' and I said, 'No, it's got to be down there!' I've seen those boys quite recently- I went up to Leavesden a few weeks ago- and they're still working and as healthy as can be, so it worked! More recently, I've been into their plaster shops where they're using polyurethane and they said, 'It's okay, we've got an extractor up there!' but it was pulling the poison right over their faces and I thought, 'It's wrong, you shouldn't do that!' Surely it's elementary to build them underneath the tables. They had no conception of these fundamental things.

Sheelagh: There must have been people who got badly damaged when you were starting out.

Stuart: There must have been. I was very concerned when we had to put a beard on an actor day after day for many weeks and you think, 'My God, we're taking it off with acetone; there must be something else!' I'm sure it's very efficient, but that's human skin, and it's not just once, it's every day for weeks or months, so all of that stuff worried me intensely. And with the wigs, it's been a sweaty hot day and they're in that room with the sun belting down and you've got buckets of Carbon Tech and they're washing these wigs and breathing in masses of fumes; I just thought it was dreadful. I remarked about it all the time and eventually it got sorted out. I've met artists years later and they're still all right. Maybe certain people have more resistance than others, so I got lucky.

During those early days, did you sometimes need a bit of ingenuity for problems that came along?

Absolutely. Right from the beginning, ingenuity was needed most of the time!

[Kath come in, offers to make coffee]

You volunteer your wife to make cappuccino?

We spent three and a half years in Italy over a span of ten years. I've worked in Italy before and since, but we worked in Italy for a certain part of every year for a span of ten years, which all added up to three and a half years. There were five different major studios and over the years we worked in all of them.

So your standard for coffee has got much higher.

I used to live on cappuccino for all those years.

Going back to the ingenuity, you had to think quickly in those early days.

That's absolutely true, there were lots of things. I can't recall them all now, but I know there were. I used to have this agreement with all the plastic and chemical companies that anything new that came out let me know about it immediately and they did. They would send me samples and I would work on them, so I was always up to date with the latest things that came out. But that also meant different solvents and adhesives, different this and that, and there were so many of them.

Sometimes I would get a call for a job that was six to nine months abroad somewhere, which called for a lot of that sort of work, so I would say, 'What do I take? If only I could get it all down to one thing, and the simplest solvent,' so alcohol, you can drink alcohol, fine, so it must be one of the safest materials, so I then put everything away and when I carried my box around, the solvent for everything was alcohol. Everything I had was alcohol-based, and I would take it off with alcohol too, as well as acetone.

Have I told you about Charlie Chaplin? I had been doing his makeup for quite a few days and one day, he said, 'That isn't alcohol, is it?' I said yes, and he said, 'Don't touch me with it!' I thought, 'Oh God, I've got nothing else; what do I do?

But it was only being applied.

It wasn't being drunk, I know, but maybe it would make him want to drink again, you see, because he was an alcoholic at one time, so he must have been concerned about that and thought it might do something, so coming in contact with alcohol was absolutely taboo. You do get these strange requests.

The other thing you've probably come across is you get calls from actresses who were very attractive when they were growing up, but years have gone by and they still get offers for the part of a younger girl, like they knew her to be, because they had seen other films in which she was younger, but some years have gone by since she made those films and her face is beginning to change a little, so there were several years when nearly everybody, 90% of the artists were having their noses done, some men as well, but mostly ladies, but the thing is, whether it's a nose job or an eye job, sometimes they take things away and for a week or so, it looks over the top and has to settle down. They really shouldn't work at all for a week or two depending on what it was, but they're offered a part and think, 'I'd love to do that part; I'll get the makeup man to see if he can fix me up and cover it all up!' So I knew all about this and the tricks of making it look normal, and I had so many noses; I had so many nose jobs.

There was one poor girl, a French actress who came over and her nose was scarlet and covered in grease, this special ointment she had to use, so they sat her in my chair and said, 'She's got to look beautiful! Sorry about this, but I guess you can fix it!' [Laughing] She had a scarlet nose, with grease all over it and you're not supposed to touch it. But I somehow managed it; leaving all the grease on, I did a quick cast of her nose using surgical plaster bandage and then made a proper cast out of it and made a really thin-skin nose .I didn't have to model it, because I already had the right shape and I put it on over the grease and then took it beyond where the grease was and keeping as thin an edge as possible.

The problem is, it had to be as subtle and soft as the real skin; otherwise you get resistance from the movement, which looks unnatural, so you've got to make sure that whatever skin you do it with has the same resistance or non-resistance accordingly. You don't want to get wrinkles in all the wrong places, so you had to think about these things when you're making a 'skin' nose.

I had another girl who came in and it looked like she had a false nose on, which looked horrible. I said, 'What happened to you? and she said, 'Oh, I had a nose job done-' she was a swimmer and a diver- who also did some film work. She was Spanish and what happened was, she said, 'I have to wear this,' and she took it off, and it was a horrible mess. She said, 'They told me I mustn't dive for so many weeks, but after six weeks, I dived, and it ripped it all off, all the stuff that was healing.' They said, 'We can't do anything now; it won't work, because it all ripped off, and there's nothing we can do, so you've got to wear a false nose for the rest of your life!' so she went somewhere and somebody made her a hard shell which pressed over it and looked horrible, but there she was, sitting in my chair and I had to get her on set in half an hour with a perfect nose. Once again, I did a quick casting job and made her a little shell nose and pressed it on and it worked. And up until a few years ago, she used to get in touch with me and say, 'Can you send me some more noses?' so I used to send noses to people for years.

Sheelagh: When did you start working from your own lab here?

I think it might have been on *2001*, because you couldn't get into the studio until a certain date, but there was work that might take you four or five months that you had to have ready, because they might want to use it on the first day of shooting, so that's why I set this up. I think I told you, that bit of ground wasn't mine but it was being sold, so I bought it, because it had that big workshop there, which was being used as a big greenhouse. The big one was there and I put all the others in. They specialized in trees and all sorts of flowers so it was a very large place.

I would say that must have been about 20 years ago, because I've been here for 25 years, so after I bought that ground, I hadn't used it that much, but I finally began developing it so I could start working on some of the early creatures and modeling them there and then I would take them down to the studio for George Lucas to okay, and he would say, 'Perhaps it should be a little bit this way or that way,' and I would say okay and I would change it a bit. So I got a lot of things ready here, before we eventually moved in to the studio. I spent a lot of time working on the apes for *2001*, because there was a lot to do, and I wasn't making creatures, so there's a difference between prosthetics and masks that have mechanisms in them, but fortunately I had a background in engineering, so that's how I was able to do it. I still had all my engineering tools and I could use my engineering experience, so I was very lucky to have that background.

Did you find you had to make more and more creatures as each film got bigger and better? By the time you got to the third Star Wars film, there were more than the first two combined.

It almost became a commercial for selling toys, because they made more money from the toys. That's the way it works.

Kath: I didn't like seeing too many creatures, because it gets overpowering and you begin to lose the thread of the story.

There must be a lot more pressure.

Yes, because with the first one, we didn't think it would be seen or even remembered.

What were we doing before *Star Wars* when George Lucas came to visit?

Kath: It was *The Omen*, because you were in the workroom doing the dogs when he walked in.

I know it was around that time. It wasn't *Superman* yet, because I didn't start *Superman* until after that. He looked so young at the time. He didn't come up to me first; he just came into the room and started looking around. I was working on these dogs, and I had to make a cast of a tooth because I had to make some phony dogs as well, because they couldn't take the risk of having the artists around real ones. They've got the trainer there, but you can't trust a dog that far.

Kath: I had to make up the dogs, because Stuart didn't do that. I went into this room that full of blood and dirt and started working on them, and he said, 'Oh, by the way, be careful of this dog Fluffy, because he can be a bit temperamental!'

I guess it was easier working with monkeys in comparison.

We were on that for two years!

Kath: Two years and six months.

I got a call from Stanley Kubrick, because I had done this other film with him, *Dr. Strangelove*, where I was making up Peter Sellers as these different characters. There were supposed to be five, but in the end, it was four, but he said, 'Stuart, I have a very interesting film for you. It's called *2001: A Space Odyssey.*' I said, oh yeah? And he said, 'It will take five, maybe six months,' and it ended up being over two years. That was a strange but interesting experience.

Kath: You have no social life.

At least we were working on it together, which made it better in a way, because I began working abroad much more in Europe and a hell of a lot in Italy and of course in the States and even Fiji and Kath wasn't able to come with me because of our sons.

You weren't both makeup artists when you met?

No, she didn't come into the makeup department for quite a few years and we got married and we had three sons after that.

When you were getting started in the business, you were making up the leading ladies, which was quite unusual, wasn't it?

I was very much aware that if you had an American actress who had never worked outside of Hollywood, a lot of them liked to choose their own makeup artist. As part of their deal, they would choose their own makeup person, and then they would say to her one day, 'We're going to England to do the picture, or maybe half of the picture, but you can't take your makeup man, because it would cost too much,' so they would think, 'Oh my God, who the hell am I going to get in England? My makeup man and I have been working things out for years?' I was very much aware of this, and I knew on the plane from the United States to England, this woman was thinking about it and getting more and more worried.

So she would come in, and I'd say, 'I understand you have your own regular makeup artist and you've worked things out together.' We would talk these things over and you would try and do them the way she wanted, but after a while, maybe you said, 'Just an idea, perhaps if we did this and this… would you be interested in letting me try that?' I had everything written down on these massive charts, and by the end, she would say, 'Can I take a copy of that chart?' That's what you had to do, because they were very worried about everything would look on that screen

So you met Kath before she was a makeup artist?

Kathleen is her name, but in the film business, somehow or another, she got known as 'Kay,' but only in the film business. In the family, it's just plain Kath, but Kay in the studio even though her name is actually Kathleen.

Sheelagh: So which name would be the right one?

I think you would say Kathleen.

What was the first film you brought her on to?

The reason was, they knew the audience was going to get fed up and would want something different, and then the 'kitchen sink' films came out, and they didn't last very long, but they were different so people went to see them, but then they got a bit bored with them, so there were only so many kitchen skin-type dramas you could do. They were dramas in the home, domestic dramas.

Sheelagh: So when did you first work together?

Well, this is what happened. In their minds, they were fed up with kitchen sink dramas, but it's many years since we've made a musical so they thought, 'We'll bring back musicals and have almost naked pretty young ladies in them!' so they started to bring them back again. And that made the whole body had to be made up, which as you know is not that easy to do. Colors vary according to different pigments and where the skin is stretched and not stretched, so there's a variation in colors. If you do it all the same, it doesn't look right at all, and it also takes time to get it all correct and then you powder it all off. And then of course they have to wear something over it, so you have to seal it so you don't have big trouble with the wardrobe and whatever you've done doesn't come off too easily on to those little bits of costume.

Anyway, if you're doing a musical, the makeup has got to be full glamour, not just straight makeup, so it takes a little longer, perhaps with separate eyelashes and that sort of thing, so you've really got to go to town with everything, so you had all these bodies to make up and I was thinking, 'My God, I'm never going to have enough time!' so we had a union meeting as it were, and I said, 'Look we're obviously going to be doing this kind of thing for the next two or three years,' so I suggested that if we were going to do be doing all these bodies, maybe we could get our wives in just for that period until it died out again, which we knew it would, because we thought this would be for a short time.

The union people discussed it and said, 'Yeah, we understand what you're saying,' so maybe eight wives came in to handle the bodies. They didn't handle the face makeups, just the bodies, so we had to teach them how to do that, but okay, they would concentrate on the bodies, so that's how Kath came in, because that was the period when our boys were getting married off and we didn't have to worry about them, so she came in just to do bodies, so most of them stayed for that period of time, which was two to three years and they all disappeared, but in between, Kath had got interested so I showed her a few things and maybe give her an artist to do and she was quite good at it, even better than I thought she might be, and then people got to like her, but she wasn't in the union, because they weren't going to put these women in the union, and there was never really any intention of any of them applying for membership, but she did and she got her ticket. Since then of course, she's done lots of her own films as head of department, so she starting going off and doing her own films and running the whole thing and became quite well known in the business.

Sheelagh: So roughly when would that have been?

Probably some 40 years ago?

Was it helpful to keep it in the family, if somebody was tough to work with but would be happier working with her?

That happened to a certain extent. Maybe there might be reasons to let her work with a certain person. Maybe she got along well with that particular person, and then she became quite well-known and people would ask for her.

Some of the big musicals of that time were a bit hit or miss.

The musicals of the very early Hollywood days were fabulous but it's changed now.

Kath: I think we need some strong stories and some really good scripts. That seems to be the weakest link at the moment.

I was just thinking about something else I was going to say, when we were talking about making drawings of things. With all these different people coming in and making suggestions, it meant you had to draw it, but it was much better if I just modeled it in clay and if they said they wanted something different, you would get a bit of clay and change it, so they can look at it all the way around, which you can't do with a drawing. So I did everything by modeling it, and I might change something on the spot so that became a good way of handling things and it's worth remembering.

A lot of artists can accomplish that with a computer design nowadays.

Sometimes it doesn't work, like the latest *Star Wars* film when they redid Jabba the Hut, which looked nothing like the original.

Kath: It wasn't even in proportion, was it?

It was very much smaller, so it could never have grown to that size in that period of time.

That must be disappointing to see.

It took four tons of clay to model it. I built a wooden structure and put chicken wire over it and then embedded the clay in it but I needed four tons of clay to model the whole thing.

Sheelagh wasn't with me when you and I talked about the problems you had with the guys inside Jabba.

Oh yes, the people I had inside. I had two guys up in the shoulders, and that gave me the right proportions, because this thing had to be 20 feet high, so if I got two guys sitting next to each other, the width of their shoulders and their arms are half the size of the proportion of a human, because you've got two guys there shoulder to shoulder, so they're twice the width and for the arms which came around, we made big hands with the fingers wide open. They both had four-inch monitors inside so they could see exactly what's going on, because the camera was fed to the monitors so they could see what they were supposed to be doing, and we spent weeks rehearsing all of this so we had two brains; one hand for one guy and one hand for the other so it looked like one brain inside operating it.

And we had another guy in the belly, because Jabba had this funny laugh, so he had to move the belly, so I had to make it all soft and nothing rigid there but firm enough to keep the shape blue flexible enough to go in and out, but there was a strong framework above it so it wouldn't collapse, so when he laughed, you could see his belly going in and out.

And going further down, you've got the tail and then I had one of my little dwarves in the tail, I think it was Deep Roy, who very coordinated because I wanted the tail to come up. Sometimes in the script, he would knock people over with it, but that tail was quite heavy, so I thought, if I put a weight inside it to counterbalance it so it would be easier for him to bring up the tail, but when you're doing that part of it, you need eight cables instead of four. If you just raise the tail, you've got that weight to bring it up, and the same to bring it down, or you could say, just leave it to gravity, but you really want to have control both ways, so I had what looked like a dustbin lid with four cables on it, but when it does an 'S' bend, the top becomes the bottom and the bottom becomes the top, so you've got to have another set of cables for that.

So I had all of these cables together, going through a flexible to down the center so he had both hands on them to make all those movements. I also wanted little movements in the flesh as it were, because I thought we needed rippling movements in the skin, especially in the tail, so I thought, instead of using the weight, if I have an electric motor, I could adapt that motor to make these rippling movements in the skin, which is what I did, and since he was a bright little chap, if both hands were on the cables, he could have one foot to switch on the motor and the other to vary the speed of it so he could make any kind of ripple that was necessary, and he's got a monitor too so he could see how to work the tail, fast or slow accordingly, so he was doing that with both of his feet and both of his hands on the cables, so even though he was a tiny fellow, he was very strong. He had a black belt I think, and he was a stuntman as well, so he did all this for me.

Wasn't Nick Dudman working as one of your assistants at that point?

I don't think he was with me on *Star Wars*. He wasn't in the film business, but he kept ringing me, and I thought I would give a chance and Daniel Parker too, who is doing all right now. They came in pretty much at the same time, although I can't recall which way around it was now. Daniel's father Charlie Parker was a buddy of mine for years. I taught Charlie Parker; when I started at Denham, I had been in the business for about a year and then Charlie Parker came in. Guy Pearce had also come in, and he was a Mountie. There was a Hollywood film that went to Canada and used to the local boys so they used him because he was a tall, handsome guy and he used to teach people to ride horses and was very good at it, he got me to ride on weekends. But they took him back to Hollywood and finished the film, but then he decided to stay, and because he was a good artist, he got a job in the makeup department, and he specialized in beauty makeup. He didn't really go into the other areas. That's when I came in and he used me to develop that side and help him on that side. He really didn't have time to go into it, because he was running this huge department with all these people working for him.

So when somebody needed a character makeup, you ended up doing it.

Yes, I did, so I was involved with all of the films, even though I didn't get credit for it. He didn't get credit for most of them either. People didn't get credit back them.

It was the same in the US studios, where the department head got the credit.

The four Westmore brothers came from Tumbridge Wells. There were hairdressers in Tumbridge Wells and moved to Hollywood where they made it. I met all the sons who working at different studios, and they used to say, 'There are more Westmores than there are pan sticks!'

Sheelagh: In those days, did the head of the studio go along to all the production meetings? Would he then take that information to all the makeup artists?

It was very much left up to us. When I first went up there, he was sent this newspaper cutting so he looked at it and invited me up. He asked if I had done the original photographs and printed them up and I said yes. He said, 'Have you got any of them with you?' I had all rolls of ten by eights so I showed them to them and he said, 'Did you enlarge these?' and I said yes. He said, 'Well, you can have a bit of cotton wool on a stick, can't you, and you can fiddle with things, so if you've got a line on a bald cap or nose or something like that, you can soften it up, can't you?' I said, 'You could, but I didn't,' and he said, 'I don't know that, do I? I've got a lot of makeup in my room; do you see this picture of an old man with a bald head and a beard? I want you to go in there and do it so I can see for myself!'

So that he knew you weren't retouching the photos.

So I went in and made myself up and of course it took longer, because at home I had all my mirrors and lights fixed up so I could see it, and he had little side mirrors in the main room so it took me longer, and he was in his office outside, and suddenly I heard him say, 'Are you done?' so I thought he was getting anxious or worried because I was taking too long, so I could have gone on for a much longer time, and it wasn't as good as I could have done it, but I said yes and he came in and said, 'Is that it?' And I thought, 'Oh no, he doesn't like it?' but he said, 'Right, were going to go down to the set and film it,' and I had never been on a film set in my life, so we walked down the corridor and I saw all sorts of well-known actors and actresses in the flesh for the first time in my life; people like Orson Welles.

Anyway, he sat me down and they filmed it, and he went over and chatted with the director and came back and said, 'We've only got this one chance and then they've got to go to another stage, so when they finish shooting this scene, I'll put you in front of the camera and do what has to be done. I've got to go back to my room, but there is the telephone; ring me when they're ready.'

So I waited there nearly an hour, and I thought, 'Oh my god, the makeup must be falling to bits by now!' but the director suddenly said, 'We're on the wrong stage!' and all the lights went out and everybody went off and forgot about me completely, so there I was, sitting there in pitch dark. I remembered the phone number but it was dark and it was a dial phone so I had to work it out on the dial, putting my finger in the holes, so that will be this number and that number.

So I called and Guy Pearce answered and I thought, well, at least I've got that right. So I told him what happened and he said, 'Stay there, I'll be right down!' so he came down and said, 'Which door did they go out?' I said, 'That one over there,' so he went out that door and disappeared for a while and came back and said, 'They've got one more shot to do on the other stage and then they will be coming back in.' In the meantime, I thought the makeup was looking awful.

The electricians came back in and put all the lights back on and they wheeled the camera back in and the director came in and said, 'Okay, look straight into the camera, turn left, turn right and then walk around and come back into camera again,' so I did all of that and Guy Pearce said, 'Right, come up to my room and take off the makeup,' so I went up there and he said, 'I can't say anything yet, we have to wait for the powers that be.' In those days, it was two or three days before you saw the rushes. Anyway, he said, 'The powers that be will make up their minds what they want to do about you,' and then I got a letter saying, 'The powers that be are very interested; will you please come up for another interview?'

Before that, I spent all my time going up to the studios and trying to crash in, so I got fired from my regular job for not turning up. Anyway, my father was going through his mail and said, 'Here, looks like another letter for you,' so he threw it over. The first time I got a letter from them, I didn't have any money at the time, so I talked to a friend of mine, who said, 'Well, I'm not working either, so I can't give you any money; I'm sorry!'

I said, 'What a pity, I've got this offer to go in and see these people, and I've been trying for years to get in and here it is, and I can't get there!' And then my friend's mother came in and said, 'I heard what you were saying; I'll lend you the money!' This is a woman I had scared the daylights out of, making myself up as Hyde or Frankenstein, standing under the lamps on the street, so everybody knew me because I was scaring the daylights out of them. I said, 'I'll pay you if I get the job,' and she said, 'Somehow, I think you will!' She gave me the money and I went out there.

The second time, it said, 'The powers that be were very interested in the test you did, so will you please come up again?' So this time I asked my father, and he said, 'Oh… all right. I had already sold my bike for ten bob because they didn't have any money and wanted to buy things like spirit gum, so I had to sell my bike, so I couldn't even cycle there! Anyway, I went up there and there was Guy Pearce at his desk outside the makeup room and he said, 'The powers that be have decided to take you on?' I said, 'What, in three or four months?' and he said, 'What do you mean, three or four months? Now!'

I said, 'But I haven't got anything-' and he said, 'Don't worry, come with me!' and he took me down this long corridor and opened the door and there was a big room, full of makeup artists, all working with artists behind them and he went over and pushed a couple of them apart a bit and another guy came in with some makeup stuff which he put on the table. I said, 'With all these films being made, how do I know what to do and what period it is?'

He said, 'All you've got to do is ask the artist. With all these pictures you had, I can see you know about periods, because you brought in pictures of beards and things, so you know about some of these periods, because these are the beards they wore in 1905 or

1860 or whatever it was, so I'm sure you know it all. If you just do what you've done in these pictures, that's what we want.'

And before I knew where I was, some guy sat in the chair and I said, 'What picture are you on? What period is it?' So I did a quick makeup and put the beard on according to what I remembered, and he went out and another guy sat in the chair, and that happened all day. It was an extraordinary way to start. In those days, we laid them on, because they didn't make beards, so it was all loose hair work, which is great, because I learned all about loose hair work.

There were actors like Alec Guinness who refused to wear a lace beard, because it stretched their face out, and if they moved, it could pull away the lace, so it was all loose hair. You started with their own sideboards, so you put on a fine edge across the ear, lift up the gap and then you bring the hair up and go in this gap with your blending hair, which blends in with the color so when you comb it out, it's all the same color hair and you've got a graduation in the sideboards, which makes all the difference in the world. If you put those little ridges in their own hair, you can mix it with their own hair. [Stuart shows us how he had an area set aside for teaching] I was originally going to do ordinary makeups, but for those who wanted to go on to special effects makeup, I had the labs there to show them modeling, casting, foam rubber and all the other techniques; making teeth or eyeballs, but it all started with ordinary makeup.

So you've got an entire school ready to go.

It's all ready to go, but I get busier and busier. There's nobody to teach all of this now.

[We all move inside the main shop building]

This is the creature from Spectre?

That's right. Peter Mayhew was in it. Gene Roddenberry and everybody else came over and they said, 'We want you to do this particular creature because we haven't got anybody tall enough,' but they had seen Peter Mayhew play this very tall character, so we used him… I nearly got thrown into jail for this. It's faded a lot now, which is the trouble with this material: it all goes whitish, but it used to be very transparent and realistic-looking.

[Looking at another head cast] I had to go over to Europe and it was a true wartime story and they were trying to make this guy talk and he wouldn't talk so they knew he lived over there and his mother was there, so they chopped her head off so it would be shocking for him when he recognized her in front of him. It was very realistic, and very fresh with the bones and the blood, so I had to go to this special place and there was supposed to be someone there to meet me when I was going through customs, because I had that in a couple of cases, and they didn't speak much English so I said, 'There should be somebody here from the film!' but there wasn't, and I thought, 'What's going to happen to me? I tried to explain it to them, 'Look, it's not real; feel it!' but fortunately for me, somebody did turn up from the film we were making, but thank goodness, because it was an uncomfortable few moment.

Which actor is this over here? Is it Jack O'Halloran?

That's right, *Superman II* with Terrance Stamp. There's Terrance Stamp's body, because I had all of those bodies to make. There's Sarah Douglas, who was playing the other baddie.

[Stuart starts showing all of his life casts]

Here's Herbert Lom. He was in the Pink Panther movies, but this is from something else. Here's Greg Peck; he had a similar build and bone structure so it would fit him. If somebody had a bigger nose, that throws it off completely, but you can almost disguise somebody by giving them a bigger nose, so it's amazing what a difference it makes.

[Showing us work stations ready for students] It's all ready to go. But everything is so complicated nowadays.

How complicated can your life be now?

Well, it is somehow. I don't know what it is, but I don't have to think, 'What am I going to do today?' because there are so many things, I just don't have to think about it. It's all there and I can never catch up with what I would like to do, and I don't have time to do something else until I finish that!

Part V: 8/11/97

This was the only pilgrimage that Sheelagh made to Esher on her own. I can't remember why I wasn't available, but I assume I was doing something else work-wise, and I kitted her out with lots of extra audio tape and batteries for the visit.

The big surprise during that night's dinner-time debrief was that Sheelagh and Stuart spent a big chunk of time together in his attic, one wall of which was stacked floor to ceiling with out-of-date makeup products. In fact, Sheelagh proudly showed me some vintage black and white makeup Stuart had given her, which had long since expired, but was hugely valuable as a teaching aid. She also brought back a couple of hackles (a lethal-looking barbed device using for blending together pieces of hair) and a couple of wig blocks called 'red-heads,' so I know she was in seventh heaven following that visit…

[The conversation starts with Stuart talking about keeping a bottle of gin in his makeup room, during production of *A King in New York*] I knew Chaplain, but he could be a so-and-so, especially because he was directing as well as acting. He got annoyed with one of his actors, who wasn't doing it the way he wanted them to do, and that was poor Dawn Addams, so he laid into her and said, 'Look, I'll show you what I mean!' so *he* did it, and damnnit, he did it better than Dawn Addams, and you could see what he had in mind.

Chaplain had a different mind from everybody else. He had a super-sense of doing things and acting in certain ways and expressions and whatnot that none of them had. They were pretty damn good in their own way, but he had this sense, and he was trying to get it into them. There were times when she was suddenly going to tears, and of course I had mascara on her, so I had everything ready for cleaning her up, because this would happen several times a day, and I would also give her another tot of gin, which she seemed to like, so I always had it ready and that calmed her down and I got the makeup down again and she would go on with the picture.

Did Chaplain ever explain what he wanted, or did he always have to show it?

He had to show it. He would finish up by showing it, and they realized that he was doing it that much better, so I could see it or they could probably see it too and think, 'I know what he wants, but I can't give him what he wants!' Sometimes they would crack up, but Dawn would start to cry, so I had to take her off, calm her down, give her a tot add of the old bottle and talk to her and get her by getting her mind right again, and then taking her by the hand and taking her down again, and then she would have another go at it, we got through the film even though there were times we weren't going to make it.

What happened to her in the end?

I don't know what happened to her after that, but she played in quite a few films. I worked with her again once or twice, but I don't know what happened to her.

So these are some of the tools you used for making your own teeth?

That's right. I made the teeth myself, so I would really look and study and see the kind of teeth they needed. Teeth are interesting, as far as how many different complications there are with teeth and the reasons why people have different teeth, and the way they fit into the skull, there's a lot more to it than you would just think about teeth. There's much more to it and I do like to get it right, but boy did I open up a can of beans there!

Anyway that's what we had to do, with all these different tools here, including this drill here. And then I would reshape everything and I could make any kind of teeth I wanted, including animal teeth, which I did for Chewbacca. I would polish them up and put the color in them. I was using different colored acrylics, so when I poured them in the mold, I would put the slightly transparent part in first, the thinnest bit, and on top of that would go the denser whitish color in that area and up above that you would start to put in a little bit of brown on top, so you've got a natural looking tooth but the color is all embedded in it as you go.

Why do you have a hackle sitting there?

Well, it just happens to be there at the moment. It's not usually there, but sometimes I don't have a place to put everything, I've got so many hackles.

I see a box over there that says 'Peter Sellers Noses.'

Yes, and there's another one that has Peter Sellers' teeth. I made dozens of them. The boys in Hollywood would keep phoning me up and say, 'He's off filming somewhere in Europe, and we've got to start shooting on him right away as soon as he gets back here, but we need a set of teeth. You've got the teeth; would you make the teeth for us so we've got them ready when he gets here?' I knew a lot of those boys already from when they came over here to work and I had done a lot of Hollywood films so I got to know them all and we became buddies.

So are you still helping people out that way?

Not as much lately, I must say. [Stuart is going through bits and pieces on a huge table] Anyway, let's see what we got in here. More KY, surgical adhesive. I've got quite a few eyebrow pencils. Here's a box of hairpins. There's all sorts of stuff in here. I've got to get this drawer reorganized; I had them in proper drawers all together.

That's a nice little pair of scissors

Yes, I use that for mustaches. I did so much hair work and you've got to have all the right bits for it.

You've got some interesting photos here, including what appears to be some characters made up to look like paintings.

I did a number of interesting commercials, and this one was for a very well-known drink- so well known, I forgot what it was! Anyway, you see them walking around this art gallery filled with pictures of famous people from the past, and they're looking around and there are different drinks placed every now and again, and finally, they pick up the one they're advertising and they're drinking away, when suddenly there are all these pictures of famous people there, so you track back a little bit and you see the people in the pictures reaching out for this particular drink and then you see them knocking it back in the picture. I had to make up all these people looking quite different and they chose them so they looked entirely different-looking and I had to make them up to look like the people in the picture and then put them in the pictures, so that was great fun. I did all the preparation here, making up all the teeth and toupees and got the whole lot organized and then figured out the makeup and whether or not it was going to be prosthetic pieces to change them, and it all worked very well.

[Looking through the drawer] Are you sure you've got enough tongs in here?

I have done a fair bit of makeup in my time! [Pulls out an old pair of crimpers]

I've never seen an old pair like that! A modern electric pair yes, but never an old one like this.

And some old brushes. You can't get any that soft anymore. I'm hanging on to those. Here are some metallic pencils- if you're doing a musical or maybe a stage makeup that has to shine, you've got all the metallic pencils for that.

'An invisible adhesive by George Bau;' what is that?

He was the guy in Hollywood before anybody else made foam rubber for prosthetics, so he started it all. He was a top makeup artist at Warner Bros, George Bau and his brother. I met both of them, and we used to talk for hours about things, because I was interested in foam rubber, so who better? They made all these different things. For some reason, he committed suicide years ago; I don't know why. But that's a bit of history. It really takes me back, thinking about those people.

You've got some of the old Leichner sticks!

Yes, there's history if ever there was.

You can't get those anymore.

No, I'm sure you can't. These are in the original box as well. When I first started, there were no books on anything like film makeup, because in England, nobody really knew that much about it, so they used what they had learned on the stage It's what we called 'slap and tickle' in those days! The only books I could get were on stage makeup, but I knew it wasn't good enough for film, but it gave me the basics. I also used to go down to Wardour Street and got to know everybody there and chatted them up, so I used to get a load of stuff and that's really how I started. When I was doing my own makeups in the studio years before, it was Leichner and me, and I learned all the theatrical ways from the books.

Which stage makeup book did you have? Was it the Corson book?

I can't remember, it was so long ago.

I believe Leichner used to do their own makeup book too. French's did one.

That's right, I remember that!

I can't believe all these boxes; Peter Sellers noses, another that says *2001-*

Those are the mechanics for the working of the mouth and snarling and the apes showing their fangs. The Peter Sellers box is not just noses, but teeth as well. I remember when he was in a show and had to leave early but they wanted to shoot on, so I had to put that face on a double, so what I used to do was, I made a special set of teeth for the double, exactly the same shape but ground them right down so they were just shells so they would go over the double's teeth but I had an acrylic material that set in a few minutes, so I would mix it up, put it in and press it on to the double, so I now had his shape inside them. He used to use them quite often, because he was Peter Seller's double. He was always wanting to go off for one reason or another. I used all these teeth on Peter; I made him Japanese at one point with these teeth. I also turned him into the March Hare, one of the creatures in *Alice in Wonderland*. I think some of these extended teeth are actually from *2001*. It was a thin mask, and they changed the shape of his mouth.

When did you do *Alice in Wonderland*?

It's strange, I used to do film after film in those days, so you would go on for year after year, doing 30 or 40 or 50 films in a row. I've tried to remember them all, but I can only remember maybe 80% of the films I worked on. I tried to keep track of them and I've got up to 350-odd marked down. I've taped over 300 of them, but I know there are still more that I've done.

Here are some ape-man ears; some large ears that I did for the apes in *2001*.Here are some PVC noses; unfortunately with PVC, the fumes can be very poisonous when you're cooking it, but the great thing was, you could do them in a quarter of an hour. I told you about some of the actresses that had nose jobs done, so I could make a nose for them in a quarter of an hour, which was very useful to be able to do, and pressed it on. They're perfectly harmless once they're made; it's just the making of it that was dangerous. Here are some feathers- I had to make the owl in *Alice in Wonderland*, but it disappeared. I would have loved to have kept that owl. Here are some more ears- I made a *lot* of ears. For Peter Sellers, I had to make behind-ears from acrylic. I cast his ear and made it in foam rubber and then bent it forward and put acrylic on it and smoothed it off to get the exact shape I wanted. I found the Japanese ear would come forward a little bit, so there was just that little bit of difference. And when I did the nostrils, the nostrils were lower and the middle a little bit wider. You've got to do both the ears and the nostrils.

You've got a box that says 3M Hair. Is that the hair that shines 100% in light?

I think it probably is.

It's just like the paint- I didn't know you could get hair like that!

I'll have to look in my files to see what it was for, because *I'm* interested now. I've probably got it written down somewhere; I tried to write everything down. Did I ever tell you about the time I needed negative glue? Sometimes they needed shots of people who glowed in the dark as it were, so I had to find something that glowed for the face and hair.

So that would be 3M.

I found they also wanted them to be different colors, so that was another thing I thought was impossible, but I thought I would have a go at it. We used to have 3M beads; I used them for front projection. There was the old-fashioned back projection where you've got a screen projected behind them, but front projection has millions of little beads and each glass bead is half-mirrored, and each bead has got to be the right way around, so how the hell do you make sure those beads are facing the right way on the screen, so I had to figure that out myself, because I could buy the 3M beads and I could use them for a lot of different makeup effects, and then I thought, 'If I could only get them on the hair!' but it's got to be one-one way only, and if it's got to be a glue on each hair, how are you going to get it to not all stick together?

That was my big problem. I knew I could get beads on the hair, because I first got involved with that on *Superman* when they sus-pended the real artists so they got cord thick enough and strong enough to hold them, and then they had a 3M screen at the back and they were filming against it in the picture that was projected on to the screen to come in to the picture with the artists in it; it also showed up on the cords, so you could see the cords because they didn't have those 3M beads on it, so we had this problem and I suggested- silly me, of course, we were in the rushes and they said, 'It's no good, you could see the ruddy cords!'

I said, 'May I make a suggestion? Why don't we just glue these beads on to that bit of cord?' They asked how we could do that, that I said, 'I don't know, but I'll think about it,' so I found out how they get them all the right way up using a magnet, so you just run a magnet across them, and then I glued them on the cord and got them all the right way around and hung it up, so when they presented the picture on it, you had these 3M beads on the cord.

So I later thought, how can I do that on a fine hair? So I took it one step further, and I thought what I needed was a negative glue so that it pushes away if that's possible and I found one! It was a negative glue, so I could then put the beads on the hair, but very fine beads, because they did different sizes of beads, so I got the finest ones they make, very tiny ones on the hair so you could project a color on them and that would reflect back and you could make it any color you like. You can see somebody come in with white hair and it can be all the colors of the rainbow! I also used that system on a film I did for TNT. I think we used Peter Mayhew (who played Chewbacca) as the character because I was working with them at the time, so it could have been that one, so I think we used them in the hair.

So what was this negative glue?

I hope I've made a note of it somewhere, because I don't remember it now. I was so busy at the time.

This box says 'Mateus Rosé-' is that the wine?

That was for the commercial I was telling you about before, where I had to put those actors in the picture frames so they were all alive. This was the hair I used on all the different characters. Goodness knows why I would use a color like that, but I obviously did. It was the way it was painted, because it had to be exactly like Van Gough. Mateus wine; that was it.

What you were doing here? It appears to be a frozen bust of Christopher Reeve.

You do a lot of work on film, but when it comes to the editing, they find that they're half an hour over, so they cut things that don't change the story. If it happens to be one of those special-effects things, they'll think, 'Oh, we can lose one of them!' so that happens to your work many times with a lot of things I did.

This was something we did for *Superman,* but they ran over and found they got too much, so it was unfortunately cut, but it was interesting because I learned a lot. Lex Luther was trying to bump him off, so he was trying to kill him in every way, so I had an interesting makeup challenge for every one of them. You see him walking through flames for example, so that was interesting, because he's got to be able to see and he can't close his eyes and his hair must not catch on fire, so you see him actually walk through the flames, so that was one of them.

And then if that didn't work, Luthor would go the other route and try freezing him and see if that killed him, because you've got to be able to kill a person from Krypton somehow but he didn't know how. He tried everything he knew, but shooting was no good because it would have just bounced off him. Burning him was no good, so he thought about freezing him, so you saw Superman trapped in this little room and you see him beginning to freeze, so I had these different sized crystals to put on his eyebrows and eyelashes and hair, building up slowly.

I was building up the early stages of it so you see the ice forming and you finally see him in a big block, where you could see him inside but it's solid, which I think I told you about before. I did a lot of painting and drawing in my early days at school, so I thought, you've got two bottle; one half full of water and one full and when you're painting that bottle, what do you do to make it so you recognize immediately that one is full, one is half-empty and one is empty? The same problem occurred here, so I did it by making the inner shape with quarter-inch plastic that I had so I grounded it down and polished it and made it all smooth and it worked.

[Looking at another box] 'Fiber-Optic Beaded hair and Negative Glue- it's here!

Stuart: That's the fiber-optic stuff we were just talking about. I had them in all different sizes and thicknesses. Did I explain the reason for that? This was another thing they cut from *Superman*. We did a lot of work on it and this is another one of the things they cut, which was a pity because it worked well.

Lex Luther has bought Nevada on this side near the coast of Los Angeles all the way down and that is the most expensive land on earth, that district, going all the way down to San Diego going all the way up to Canada, and the fault goes between Los Angeles and Nevada all the way right down, the San Andreas Fault. If an atomic bomb was to explode over the top of it, the whole of Los Angeles would slip into the sea and then this part of Nevada, which is not worth very much at all now, would become the most valuable land in the world!

So they're moving these two bombs, one from there to there on such and such a date, which they put in the newspaper strangely enough, so all they want to do is pinch this bomb because they know where it's going so they are going to steal this bomb, take it over the top of Los Angeles and drop it down so it explodes over Los Angeles, but there is a snag: not too far away, Superman is going to find out one way or another; he always does, so he'll get there and grab the bomb and push it out into space, but there's another bomb being transported and he can't do that to both of them at the same time, so they have to pinch them both.

So get the two bombs, down they come and one goes off and Superman comes along and is pushing it out into space and he knows about the other one so they are about to explode that one and they think he won't get there in time, so the camera is there and it does explode and it's coming out and you see Superman coming underneath it, coming up through the center of the explosion and he's got this power of absorption so as you see the explosion going out, he absorbs it and it all starts going into him and he gets redder and redder and redder until he's red-hot, so of course they have the makeup department doing it, don't they?

Naturally, but I could never make out why they came to me, but I did the whole bloody thing, I did the explosion and everything. I told the camera boys that I could do it with fiber-optics and I would get a whole range of fiber-term optics in different sizes and as they come out, they are spinning at different speeds, so you could go as slow or as fast as you want so you could make them go in or out in conjunction with the way you push them out or pull them in, those two movements.

I also had a red light that comes in slowly as you wanted it to, so it comes out the end of each one of these fiber-optics, so it can be white or it can go red, so I've got the miniature of Superman himself, the whole body with his arms up and that is on a motor and I've got control of that motor- I'm doing all of this, you see, so I'm spinning the motor, and of course it's nothing to do with makeup air or putting eyelashes on or anything like that, but I've got these two levers and I'm turning him and it's all tied up with the same electric wiring, so it's all spinning on this control and meanwhile I've got a special mirror to reflect into the camera. You can't use an ordinary glass mirror, but I knew that fortunately, so I had to get one specially made.

And then you got Chris Reeves spinning and I've made this tube the exact same shape as Chris so when you look at the end, these two sides come out a bit like his arms so that's the same shape, and I had been on quite a few films where they used front projection and what they always do is on one half, that's got a big black screen so you don't get anything reflected there into this two-way mirror, so the camera goes into that and you've got the picture of the actors and you've also got screen at the back of the picture that is projected on the back, so it all comes into the camera through that two-way mirror, but you got to see through that two-way mirror to see what's on the screen at the back, so you get two images in one now into the camera, and you've got the projector projecting on to the beads, and that is the explosion that we've done.

Now, my effects have got to come into it. I remember thinking at some point, one day where they've got that black velvet, I'm going to use this for some special effect. I remember saying it to myself, and it could be something to do with makeup, and lo and behold, it did happen, so all of these tubes I had made here, including the one I made with the shape on the end, pushing them out and controlling the different speeds plus the control of the red light that would come and go as you wanted and that was all one unit that was set up, so I was able to control it and it's also spinning at the same time with Chris seen through the mirror so he was coming into the camera as well, and I said to the camera boy, 'Look, I don't know if at any point the light power will be sufficient to register in combination with what else you are doing.'

He said we could do a test on it, and I said, 'I wish you would!' so we did a test and there was no problem at all, so I knew it was all going to work, so I went ahead and did it all. We filmed it, and as you see him spinning, you see it all going up, with all the different shapes becoming more and more red and in different sizes, which looked more natural as part of the explosion, and then I slowed it all down and you see it going the other way into him, and it all looked fantastic and Chris looked red-hot as he absorbed it all.

That's what I needed all these different sized fiber-optics for, because all the little particles had to be different sizes; you couldn't have just one size. I figured they had to be different sizes, so I talked to the company, who was fascinated by the whole thing, so they helped me tremendously because it was good advertising for them.

I also had a bunch of miniature dummies for flying scenes with the miniature sets, so I had to make them in different sizes, modeling and casting them and making them in various sizes. There was Christopher and Lois Lane and Terence Stamp and Jack O'Halloran. I had to do them all. [Opening another box] These are Chinese fingernails. I would cut them up because they are all this long, so I would make the mold and press them out and cut them down to different sizes. I used them quite often, because you can't buy things like that. Here, I got blood of all kinds- I used to make my own blood as well. Here are some special mouth blood capsules, which you can swallow if you like and it doesn't hurt you. Here are some Fu Manchu nails, which were some of the original Chinese nails I showed you. Here are some rat teeth. And aromatic tears. Clown noses, a whole case of them. Some pieces from *Alice in Wonderland*, including a black velvet beauty spot. Here's some of the snow that you normally spray on Christmas trees, which I used on one of the Superman films.

What is in this box?

Nipple molds and nipple cover molds. During the era of musicals, sometimes they would be wearing a really thin dress and you would have to smooth them down because they didn't like their nipples showing through the fine silk dress, so I had nipple covers made to cover them. They were just made of foam rubber. You would stick them on with a touch of surgical adhesive.

Here are some bald caps.

Those are PVC caps. First of all, I would stipple with another plastic that dried quickly and according to the coarseness of the sponge and the speed at which it dried, you could make pores in the 'skin,' which would graduate. You would start them *here* and go up, so when you put the bald cap on, you had the hard line and then the area where it was smooth, so I would stipple in the pores to look the same as the skin and I would let that set and on top of that, I'll paint the PVC skin that dries matte because I've got a matting agent in it, but the quality of that is it would take the makeup the same as human flesh does and it doesn't change color, so you've got the graduation of pores and then the material to take the makeup so you can't see it anymore. I would just make the bald cap and put it on the artist.

So you would stipple and then put on the sealer.

I would put the sealer while it's on. You also got the actor perspiring, so you get beads of perspiration. Do you know how to get rid of that?

Short of sticking a pin in it?

Do you make bald caps? You get a plaster cast, and you paint the bald cap material on, and with a very fine tool, you make tiny holes all over it. And then you paint the stuff on and little bubble will come up and it will leave a tiny little hole in that skin. You do six or seven layers but you wait for the little bubbles to come through on each one and you end up with a natural little pinpoint which you cannot do by putting a needle in it, because it will close up again so you can't make a round hole, but you don't have to; you just make the holes in the plaster- I could show you some of my molds, that I would use for making bald caps with those very fine holes and it doesn't take long, because it very quickly comes through, and then you do another layer and let that bubble come through again for each one, and then you've got little holes all the way through, which you cannot make after the cap is made. So it's very easy. And all day long, it's got these holes that you can't see but the air is coming through to keep them cool, and if any moisture comes through, it comes off naturally, not bursting out.

According to this box, it's got Peter Sellers in it!

It's one of the seven characters he played in one film [*Undercovers Hero*], Kyoto the Japanese character; upper and lower teeth, ear sticks and chin sticks, which took away his double chin and made him look 25 years younger. Oh, here's another trick for bald caps. Maybe you got a character that you put a bald cap on, but he's not bald, so you have then got to put on a sparse toupee so you can still see his bald head through it, so that's got to be made of fine lace, hasn't it? If you paint spirit gun on top of the bald cap to stick it on, you're going to see shiny stuff coming through, so the trick that I found before I started using that matting agent, going back a few years, instead of putting the glue, whatever glue it is, you don't put it on the cap itself, because it only needs to be on the lace, so what you do is put it on the lace.

So you haven't got it in the holes, just the fine piece.

Exactly, so you put the lace on and using a brush with a little bit of isopropyl acetone, you just run it down in between where the glue has already dried into the lace and that's enough to stick it down, and it goes exactly where you want it to. It's very simple but it works.

Here's a box that says 'two-way optics.'

Those are for putting behind the eyeballs, so they can see out but you couldn't see their own eyeballs behind it, so I had to get them made in varying degrees because you needed different densities, so I had to do lots of tests to figure out what I needed.

LONDON FILM PRODUCTIONS present a

VICTOR SAVILLE PRODUCTION

"DARK JOURNEY"   1937

Directed by VICTOR SAVILLE

VICTOR SAVILLE handles a big crowd scene on the
set at Denham. The set represented the Grand
Hotel in Stockholm, a favourite meeting place
for international spies. CONRAD VEIDT, VIVIEN
LEIGH and ANTHONY BUSHELL are all playing spy
roles, and this exciting film is packed with
thrilling incidents, both on land and at sea.
Other well-known players who are in the cast
include JOAN GARDNER, URSULA JEANS, AUSTIN
TREVOR, ELIOT MAKEHAM, SAM LIVESEY and MARGERY
PICKARD. The photography is by GEORGES PERINAL
who has handled the camera on many London Film
Productions.

(Stencil no. V.S.1/14.)

LONDON FILM PRODUCTIONS present a

VICTOR SAVILLE PRODUCTION

"DARK JOURNEY"

Directed by VICTOR SAVILLE

Karl von Marwitz (CONRAD VEIDT), in command of
a German submarine, stops the boat on which
Madeleine (VIVIEN LEIGH) is travelling in order
to arrest her for espionage. A British Q-boat
intervenes, however, and sends out a 'panic-
party' to cover up their real identity.

(Stencil no: V.S.1/20.)

LONDON FILMS present a

VICTOR SAVILLE PRODUCTION

"DARK JOURNEY"

Directed by VICTOR SAVILLE

A scene in the Grand Hotel, Stockholm, in the
year 1918. Karl Marwitz (CONRAD VEIDT) is
dining with Madeleine Godard (VIVIEN LEIGH),
with whom he is in love, although he knows
that she is working for the French Secret Ser-
vice.

(Stencil no: V.S.L/10.)

LONDON FILMS present a

VICTOR SAVILLE PRODUCTION

"DARK JOURNEY"

Directed by VICTOR SAVILLE

A scene in the Grand Hotel, Stockholm, in the
year 1918. Karl Marwitz (CONRAD VEIDT) is
dining with Madeleine Godard (VIVIEN LEIGH),
with whom he is in love, although he knows
that she is working for the French Secret Ser-
vice.

(Stencil no: V.S.L/10.)

LONDON FILM PRODUCTIONS present

"KNIGHT WITHOUT ARMOUR".

Directed by JACQUES FEYDER.

MARLENE DIETRICH as Countess Alexandra.

Caught by the Red Revolution, Alexandra is im-
prisoned and bought before A.J., (ROBERT DONAT),
an Englishman posing as a Russian Commissar.
They fall in love and attempt to escape from
Russia, suffering at the hands of the Reds, but
eventually reaching the White Army headquarters
at Saratursk, where Alexandra is treated with
respect and kindness. A bath is welcome after
her long and tedious journey across country.

(Stencil No. L.F.P.22/19.)

Clockwise from top:
Marlene Dietrich,
Knight without
Armor, *Robert Donat,*
Dietrich, Donat.

LONDON FILM PRODUCTIONS present

"ELEPHANT BOY"

Directed by ROBERT FLAHERTY and ZOLTAN KORDA

SABU as Little Toomai

Toomai's father has been killed by a man-eating
tiger, and the great elephant Kala Nag mourns
his master's death. Toomai entreats the natives
not to shoot the elephant, which has gone tem-
porarily insane.

(Stencil no: L.F.P.8/4.)

Above, right: film unknown, dated 1938.

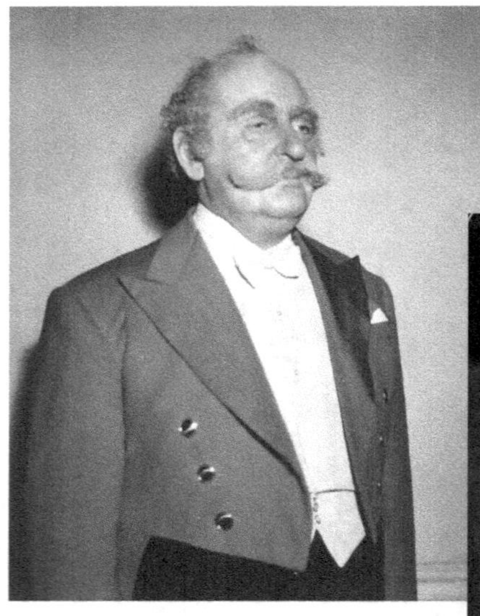

As a makeup designer, Freeborn would often a character's makeup and facial hair.

Above: Knight Without Armor.

Above: Knight Without Armor.

Above: Dietrich and Donat, Knight Without Armor.

Knight Without Armor.

Patricia Ellis as Jeanette Dupont, Paradise For Two.

*Above, right:
Charles
Laughton,
1930's*

Vivien Leigh as Cynthia, Fire Over England *(1937)*.

Miriam Hopkins, Paradise For Two *(1937).*

Jack Hulbert, Paradise For Two.

"THE RETURN OF THE SCARLET PIMPERNEL".

Produced by ARNOLD PRESSBURGER.

Directed by HANS SCHWARTZ.

A unique 'still' showing the three disguises
that the centre figure wears in the film.
He is BARRY K. BARNES who plays the part
of Sir Percy Blakeney, and is one of the
most recent additions to London Films Star
Ranks. These disguises are the work of
Guy Pearce, London Films well known
make up expert.
(B.C.1 - 22.)

LONDON FILM PRODUCTIONS present "I, CLAUDIUS"

Directed by JOSEF VON STERNBERG. Produced by

ALEXANDER KORDA

FLORA ROBSON as Livia. She is the widow of the great Emperor Augustus who is proclaimed a god after his death. Although she admits to murdering her husband and other relatives 'for the good of Rome', she begs Claudius to make her a goddess after her death, her reason being that the immortals can do no wrong.

(Stencil no. L.F.P.20/5.)

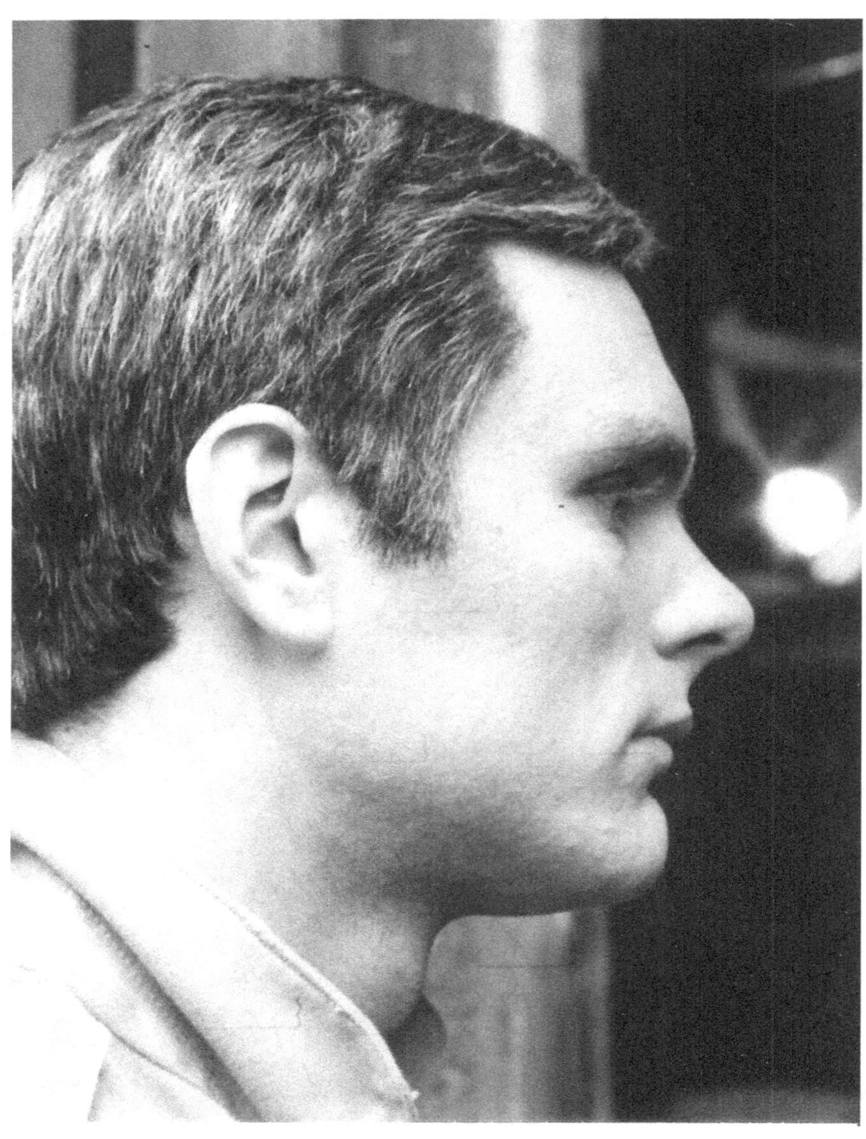

Keir Dullea, 2001.

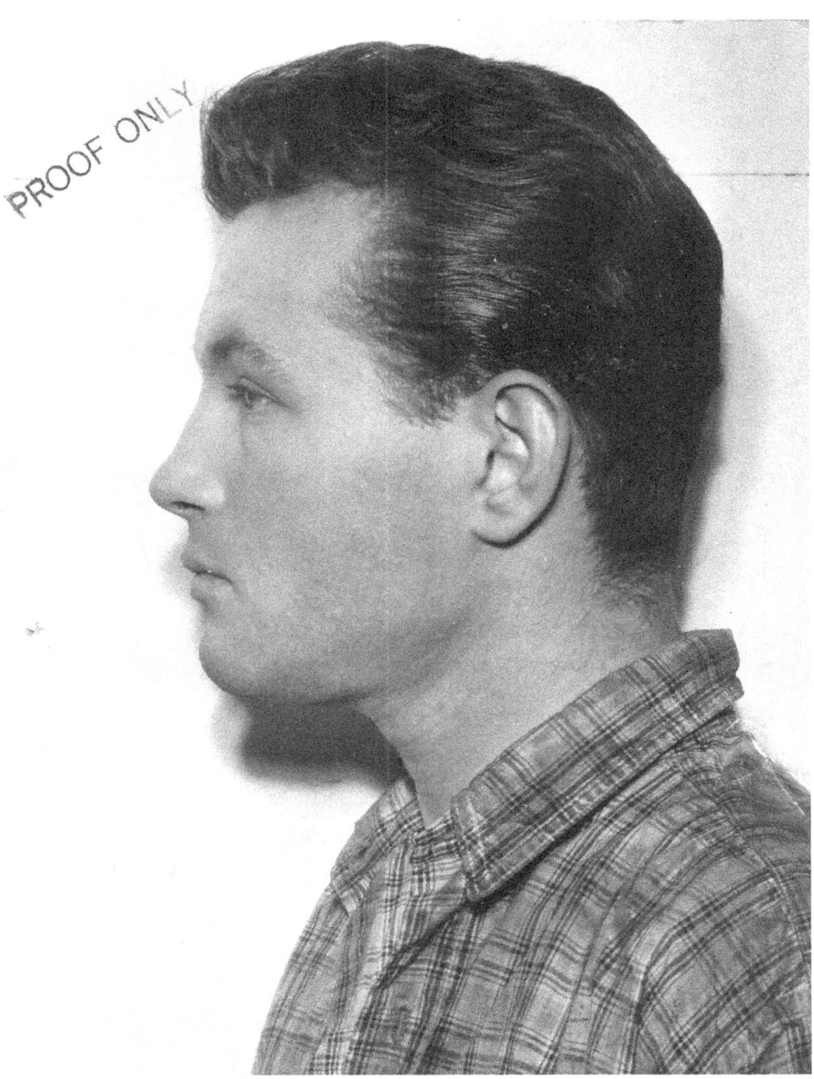

French-resistance-fighter-turned actor, Jacques Sernez

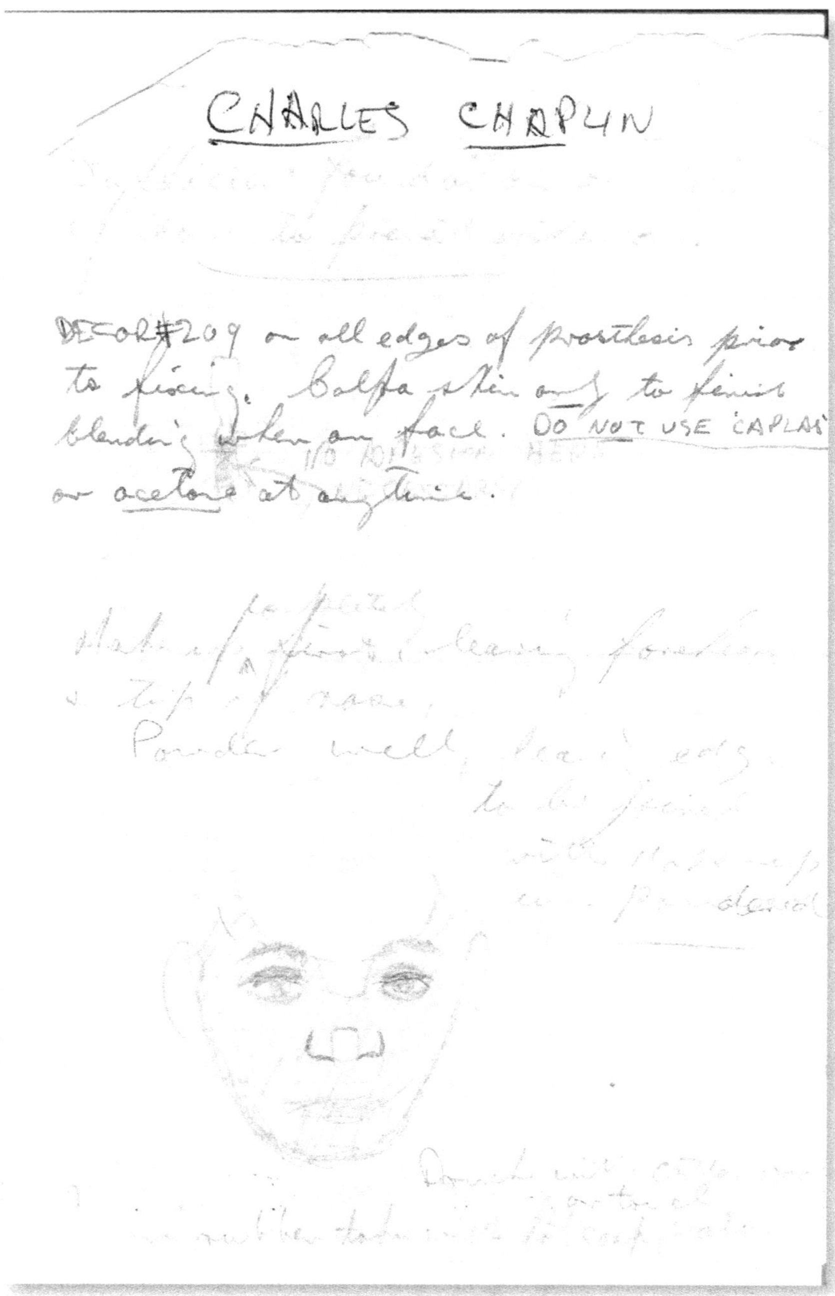

Makeup notes for a project involving Charlie Chaplin.

Press on tape at tip & draw up
adhere to forehead, press in at
bridge of nose, press on sideways
strip. Press on plastic nose piece
(already glued) press on forehead
piece, finish off edges with
"Bolpa", stiple all over pieces
with N9 + 665H, then N8, N5, & T.4 LPs
on nose. going off to face, powder well.

LONDON FILM PRODUCTIONS' DENHAM STUDIOS

Set amidst the beautiful Buckinghamshire countryside, these Studios are the largest and most
efficient in Europe. The seven huge sound stages
cover over 120,000 square feet, and the entire
buildings cover 28 acres of the total 165 acres
which comprises the estate. Surrounded by
lovely woodland and gorgeous scenery, with the
River Colne flowing for over 1½ miles through
the grounds, this is an ideal spot for film-
making, affording great opportunities for ex-
terior scenes of every conceivable type. Denham
will undoubtedly become the centre of Britain's
great film industry, and the modern equipment
installed in the Studios will ensure that every
picture turned out will be of the very best
quality.

(Stencil no: G.F./13.)

JOINED APRIL 1936 TO THE LAST DAY 1954

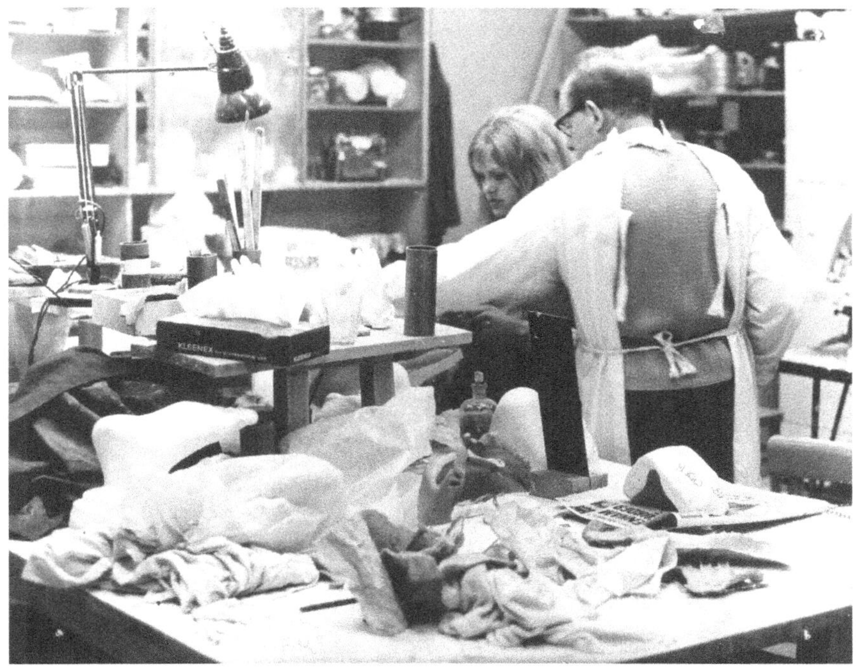

Freeborn in makeup lab, and with one of his monstrous creations.

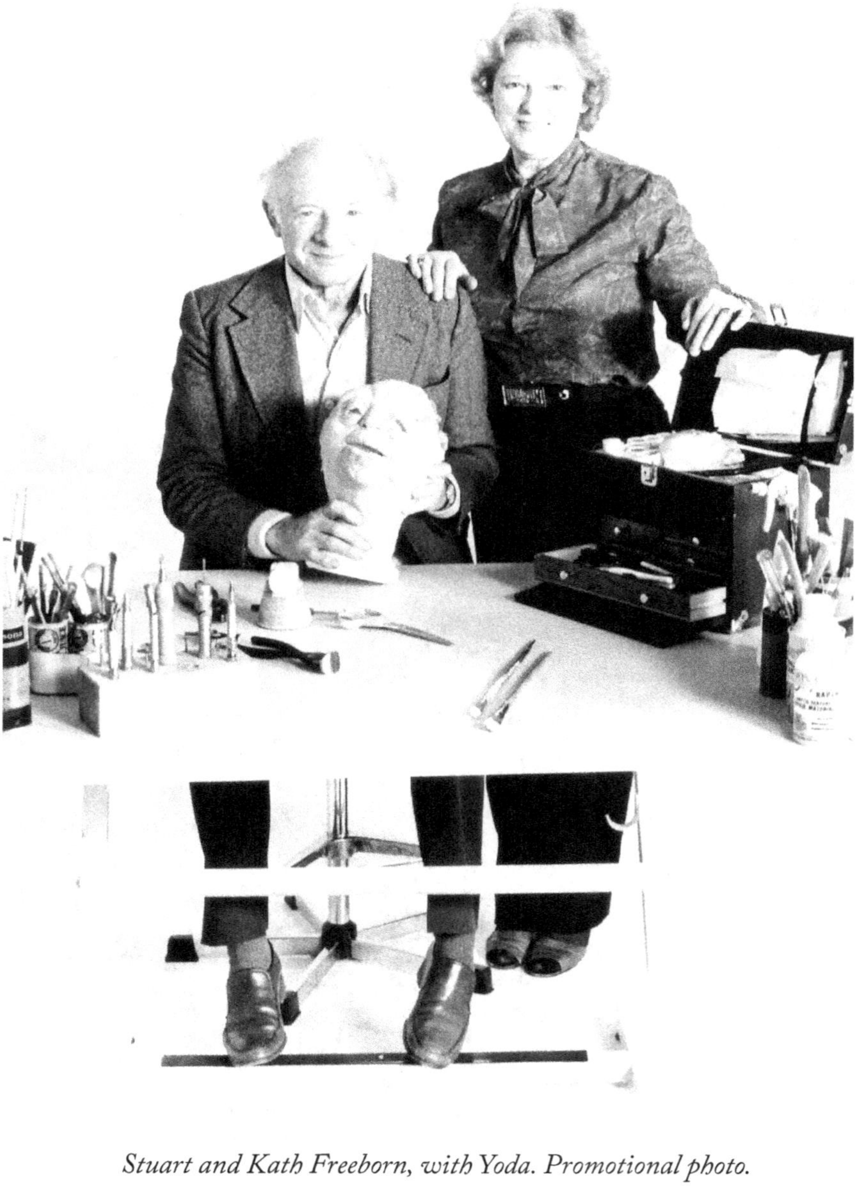

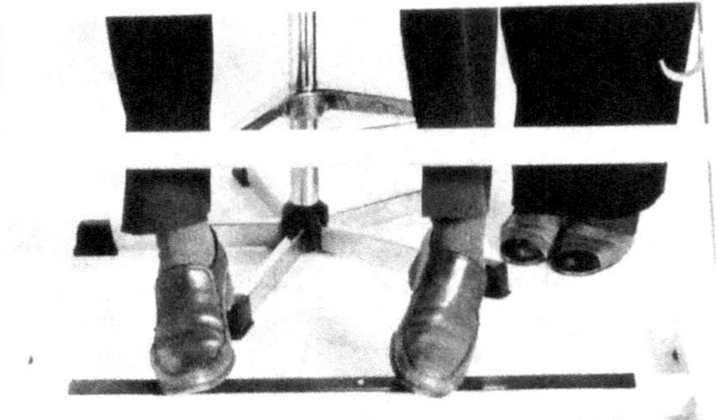

Stuart and Kath Freeborn, with Yoda. Promotional photo.

Above: Tefal ad prosthetic makeup, below: mask pieces from 2001.

Above: Selection of pieces from 2001. Below: the author with Stuart and Cath Freeborn.

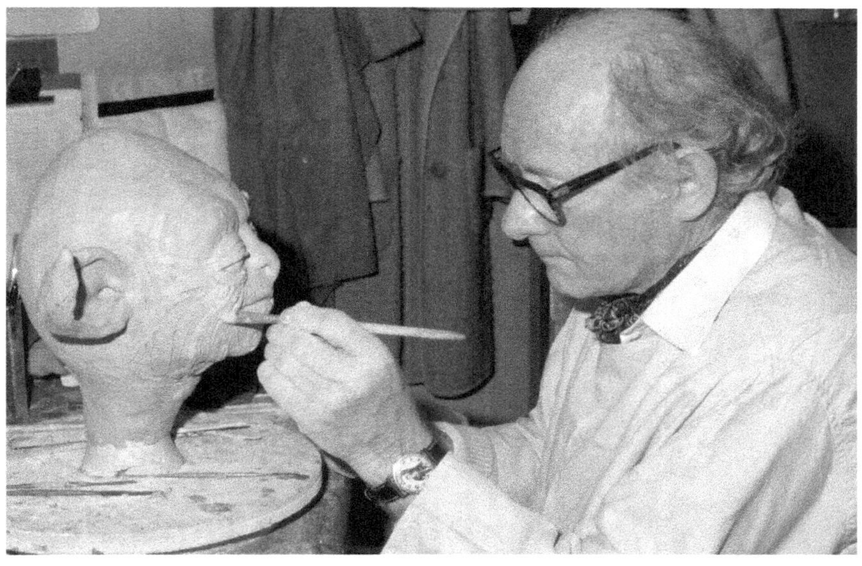

Above: Freeborn sculpting Yoda. Below: Yoda cast, sans teeth and eyes.

Above: Prosthetic makeup from Tefal commercial.
Below: Early makeup room, Denham Studios

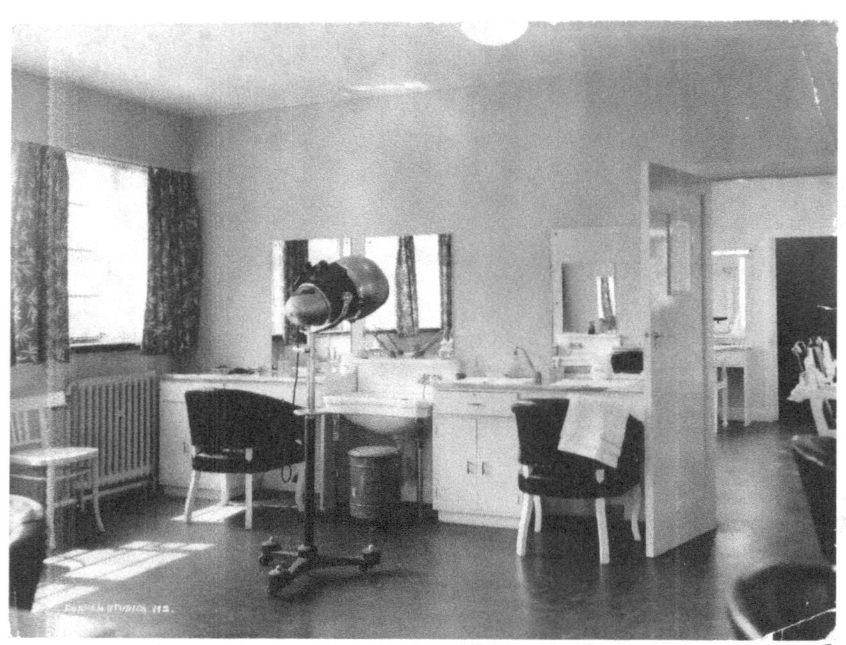

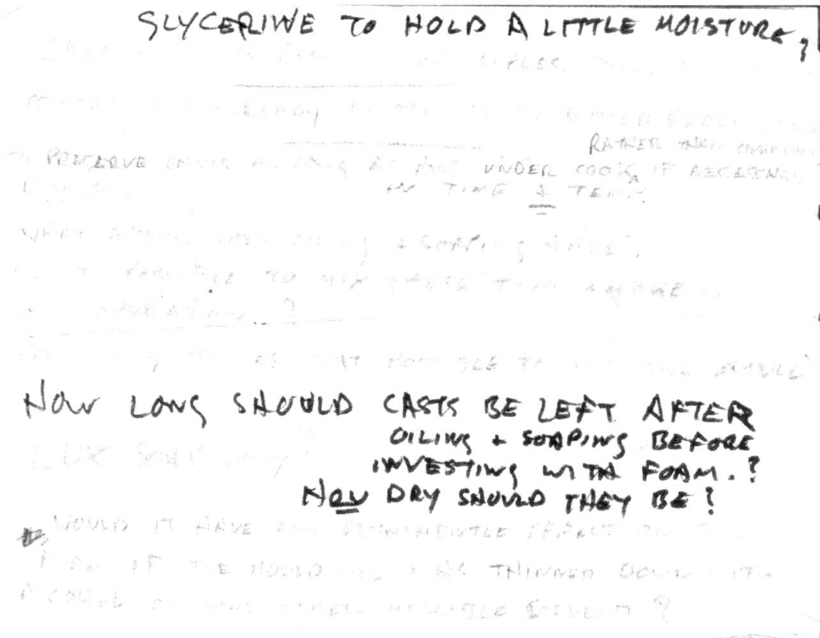

Above: Partial call sheet from 2001 (1966).
Below: makeup notes, film unknown.

2nd UNIT	CHAPTER II PRODUCTIONS LTD.			Call Sheet No: 94A (Studio)	
PRODUCTION: "THE EMPIRE STRIKES BACK"		DATE: Thursday, 26th July, 1979.			
DIRECTOR: HARLEY COKLISS		UNIT CALL: 08.30 hrs.			
SETS: EXT. LUKE'S X-WING (Blue Backing)		STAGE 8: Scs: 232. 265. 269pt. 375. 2─			

ARTISTE:	CHARACTER:	D/R:	M/UP:	READY:
KENNY BAKER	ARTOO	133	10.00	AS REQD.

ART DEPT./PROPS:	Cockpit dressing. Rocking fx.
SFX:	Cockpit practicals. Artoo Practicals. S/BY readouts.
CAMERA:	Vistavision fx.
BLUE SCREEN:	Via Stan Sayer.
EDITORIAL:	Moviola on set. Footage as req.
CATERING:	AM & PM breaks for 50 persons on Stage 8 please.

DOMINIC FULFORD
Assistant Director

Above: Call sheet from The Empire Strikes Back, *Below: Freeborn's prosthetic notes scrawled on the back of an old call sheet.*

RUBBER RESEARCH
NELTS.

ZINC OXIDE
BENTONITE.

POTTASSIUM   THE SAME? →   RM SULPHOR   HAVE
SULPHATE.   DISPERSOL L/R

ASERITE ~~WHITE~~ WHITE
S.S.F.?

VULCAPOR   RENEW ?
Z.DC.?

HIGH SPEED WETTING AGENT.
VULCASTAB BX   "   ZMBT.
+ AS FORMING AGENT.

VULCASTAB LW — STABILIZER FOR FOAM ?

NONOX CI?   ANTI-OXIDENT ? SPECIALLY PREPARED

OLEIC   RR. FORMING ?   LA
2 CANS LATEX 60%

DUNLOP 6811   AB+C.   POSSIBLE TO
6 WKS ON SNIP.   WHIDBY.   SELF CENTRIFUSE

ART FINISH - SPECIAL NOTES.

TRANSFERANCE OF FUR. (ANIMAL SKINS.) REAL.
TO ADHERE TO A SYNTHETIC ELASTIC SKIN OR ELASTIC
MATERIAL i.e. BUTTONED ELASTIC, ALWAYS STRETCH
~~ELS~~ MAN MADE FIBRES, KNITTING.

TRANSFERENCE OF HAIR. (ANIMAL OR HUMAN)
INTO.
WAX. FOAM RUBBER, POLYURETHANE (RIGID-SEMI RIGID-VERY FLEXIBLE)
ACRYLIC. P.V.C. (IN ALL FORMS)

SPECIAL FOR ART FINISH ON ARTIFICIAL LIMBS.
TO MATCH EXISTING HAIR ON PATIENTS OTHER LEGS-FEET.
ARMS-HANDS. ETC.,

SPECIAL NOTES ON FLEXIBILITY OF MATERIAL USED TO COVER
ARTIFICIAL LIMB. SO AS NOT TO PUT TOO MUCH RESTRICTION
ON LIMB MECHS, & PERHAPS TO ASSIST IN RETURN TO (NORMAL) REPOSE
POSITION

Freeborn's makeup notes, film unknown.

HAUNTED HONEYMOON PRODUCTIONS LTD.,

"HAUNTED HONEYMOON"		CALL SHEET NO: 51
DIRECTOR: GENE WILDER		DATE: TUESDAY 19 NOVEMBER 1985
STAGE: 4		STUDIO CALL: 8.30 a.m. on set
SET:		SC. NOS:
1) INT. RADIO STUDIO		1) 10 N
2) INT. RADIO STUDIO	S/By	2) 12 N

ARTISTE	CHARACTER	D/R	PICK UP	MAKE UP	READY
GENE WILDER	LARRY	M'home	8.30 on set then make up		
GILDA RADNER	VICKIE	73	11.15	11.45	1 p.m.
HOWARD SWINSON	EDDY	76	–	7.45	8.30
CHRIS MUNCKE	ANNOUNCER	76	–	7.45	8.30
DAVID HEALY	P.R. MAN	78	–	8.00	8.30
ANDREA BROWNE	PROD. ASSISTANT	88	–	7.30	8.30
BILL BAILEY	HOST	80	–	7.45	8.30
MATT ZIMMERMAN	RADIO ACTOR	90	–	7.45	8.30

ORCHESTRA

Sax – Trumpet – Trombone		141		7.30	8.30
Bass – Organ – Violins 1 & 2					
Cello		131		7.30	8.30
Conductor: Andy Ross		133		7.30	8.30

STAND-INS:	FOR:			
Jack Dearlove	Mr. Wilder + (Double Producer)		8.00	8.30
Mercedes Burleigh	Ms. Radner		"	"
Alan Harris	Utility		"	"
Alan Meacham	Double Sponsor + Utility		"	"
Norton Clark	Utility + Double Engineer		"	"
Chris Spooner	Ms. Browne		"	"

<u>R E Q U I R E M E N T S</u>

PROPS:	Scripts, mics, tea, coffee, cigarettes, etc., Sound fx, table
WARDROBE:	As per script –coats, hats etc., for Vickie and Larry
MAKE UP NOTE:	As per Stuart Freeborn + (Poss. moustache for Alan Meacham double/ Sponsor)
CAMERA DEPT:	As per Fred Schuler

November, 1985 call sheet for Haunted Honeymoon.

SOUND DEPT: As per Simon Kaye + playback required("Always in all ways")
                + 2 strings

LIGHTING: "On Air" sign required practical etc.,

SFX: As per John Stears practical consul lights etc.,

ART: 1. Studio dressing

RUSHES: TBA

PROD. NOTES: 1. Motorhome to be practical from 7.30 a.m.
                2. Fireman to standby from 8.30 a.m.

CATERING: a.m. and p.m. trolleys for 70 people please

TRANSPORT:

CAR (ROY)   Pick up Mr. Wilder at   TBA   to Studio by 8.30
CAR (PETER)   Pick up Ms. Radner at   11.15   to Studio by 1.00 p.m.
CAR (LEN)   Work to Prod. Office instructions
CAR (BRIAN)   Work to Prod. Office instructions

SPECIAL NOTE: THERE IS A CABLE ATTACHED TO THE ENTIRE PERIMETER
                OF THE SET. THIS IS FOR SOUND DEPARTMENT PURPOSES —
                IF AT ANY TIME THE CABLE NEEDS TO BE MOVED PLEASE CONTACT
                SIMON KAYE IMMEDIATELY.

                        DAVID TOMBLIN
                        ASSISTANT DIRECTOR.

HAWK FILMS LTD.

CALL SHEET   No. 66

PRODUCTION "2001: A SPACE ODYSSEY"	DATE	TUESDAY 22nd March, 1966

UNIT CALL 8.30 A.M.	WHERE WORKING STAGE 4	DISCOVERY — CENTRIFUGE

ARTISTE	CHARACTER	DRESSING ROOM	MAKE-UP	READY ON SET
KEIR DULLEA	BOWMAN	C201 T.	7.30	8.30
GARY LOCKWOOD	POOLE	C204 T.	7.45	8.30
NIGEL DAVENPORT	HAL'S VOICE (GUIDE TRACK)	C103 T.	–	Standby for call.
STANDINS. ERNEST FENNEMORE	for Mr. Dullea	Crowd	8.00	8.30
JOHN KELLY	for Mr. Lockwood	D.R.	8.00	8.30
CAMERA DEPT.	35mm Camera required.			

Above: Partial call sheet from 2001.
Below: makeup notes for Revenge of the Jedi.

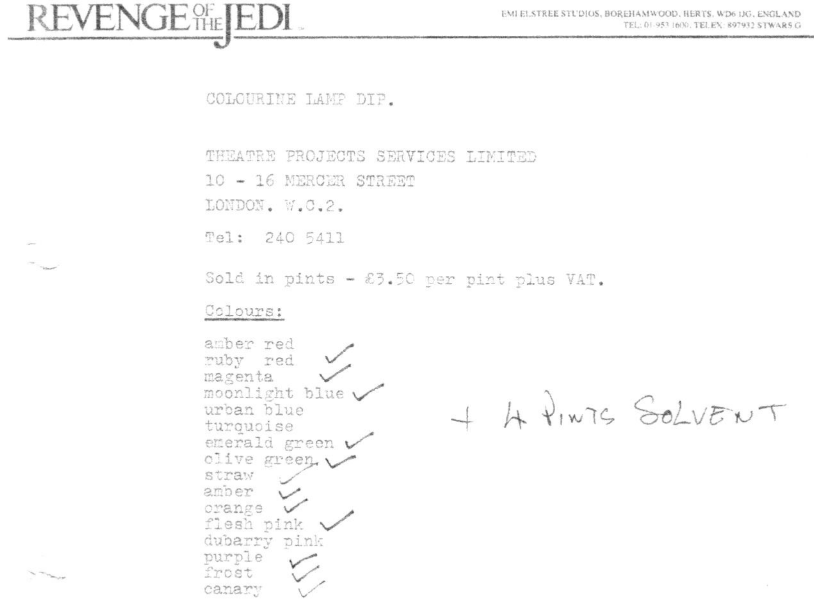

STAR WARS

REVENGE OF THE JEDI

EMI ELSTREE STUDIOS, BOREHAMWOOD, HERTS. WD6 1JG, ENGLAND
TEL: 01-953 1600, TELEX. 897932 STWARS G

COLOURINE LAMP DIP.

THEATRE PROJECTS SERVICES LIMITED
10 - 16 MERCER STREET
LONDON. W.C.2.

Tel: 240 5411

Sold in pints - £3.50 per pint plus VAT.

Colours:

amber red
ruby red
magenta
moonlight blue
urban blue
turquoise
emerald green
olive green
straw
amber
orange
flesh pink
dubarry pink
purple
frost
canary

Life Casting List

Rubber Cape

Comb

Life Cap

Spirit Gum + Brush

Acetone + Brush

Gaffer Tape

Water Tray for Plaster Bandage

Gypsona Plaster Bandage

Bowl for Casting plaster

Spatulas

Scrim

Vaseline

Wooden Modelling Tool

Alginate   - GLYCERINE (2DROPS PER CUP)

Cups

Mixing Bowls

Alginate Brushes

Bandages

Modelling tool for nose

Long Bandages for Mould edges

Cotton Wool

Tissues

Facial Cleaner

Clay + Clay Wash + Brush

Strong String

Surform

Scissors (Plaster)

Scissors (Cap)

Scissors (String)

Vibrator

Mould Stand

Jugs for Plaster or Water

Salt

Pen + Paper

Bucket

CALL SHEET   NO: 27

PRODUCTION: "OH! WHAT A LOVELY WAR"   DATE: SATURDAY, 27th APRIL, 1968.

UNIT CALL: 8.30 a.m. ON LOCATION

SET: INT. TINSEL PALACE ROOM.

ADDRESS: West Pier, Brighton.   PRODUCTION OFFICE:
TEL. NO: Brighton 24091 Ext. 12.   Brighton 26584.
CONTACT: Mr. Jack Taylor, Pier Master.

DIRECTOR: RICHARD ATTENBOROUGH.

ARTISTE	CHARACTER	LEAVE HOTEL	HAIR	M/U	ON SET
INT. TINSEL PALACE. Sc. Nos. Pick-up shots of Pre-War Sequence, 295, 296, 297 (1918) DAY.					
RALPH RICHARDSON	SIR EDWARD GREY	9.20 am		9.30	10.30
IAN HOLM	POINCARE	8.20 am		8.30	11.15
KENNETH MORE	KAISER	8.05 am		8.15	9.00
JOE MELIA	POPPYMAN	9.15 am	W/B 9.25		10.00
PAUL SHELLEY	JACK SMITH	8.20 am	W/B 8.30	9.00	10.30
JOHN GABRIEL	LENIN	9.20 am	W/B 9.30	10.00	11.00
FRANK FORSYTH	WOODROW WILSON	9.50 am	W/B10.00	10.30	11.00

STAND-INS: FOR:
HAROLD SANDERSON   SIR RALPH RICHARDSON)
FRED CLARKE   IAN HOLM   )
ALEX NORTH   KENNETH MORE   )   8.00 a.m. at Drill Hall for W/robe.
ALEN BENNETT   JOE MELIA   )
MAX HAMLEY   PAUL SHELLEY   )   Ready on Set 8.30 a.m.
JIMMY SCOTT   JOHN GABRIEL   )
MAURICE CONNOR   FRANK FORSYTH   )

CROWD: AS:
JAMES KHONJIE   POPPYMAN'S ASSISTANT   8.00 am Norfolk for W/B. On set 8.30.
1 MAN   AUSTRIAN SOLDIER   )
2 MEN   GERMAN SOLDIERS   )   8.00 am Drill Hall for W/B. On set 8.30.

MAKE-UP, HAIRDRESSING **TEST**:
JOHN MILLS – HAIG – to be made up and hairdressed at Norfolk Hotel, time to be advised.

R E Q U I R E M E N T S

PROPS: As per script and breakdown to include: all continuity props for
           pre-war sequence. Cricket scoreboard and panels. Official documents
           pens, ink, red tape, water in jugs, glasses, conference table, papers
           on table, spectacles for Woodrow Wilson.

EFFECTS: White Smoke.   FIREMAN: Required at Tinsel Palace.

NOTE: THE ART DEPARTMENT HAS ADVISED THAT ONE HOUR WILL BE REQUIRED TO REDRESS
           THE SET FOR 1918 SEQUENCE.

CATERING: All meals and breaks for 100 people.

NOTE: 1.   IT HAS BEEN NOTED THAT CERTAIN MEMBERS OF THE UNIT REFUSE TO CO-OPERATE
           WHEN ASKED NOT TO MOVE AROUND OR TALK WHILE THE RED (SHOOTING) LIGHT IS
           ON.   A VERY SERIOUS VIEW IS TAKEN OF THIS ATTITUDE AS IT IS DIFFICULT
           TO SHOOT UNDER THESE CIRCUMSTANCES.

Note 2:   Please note that the telephones installed on the West Pier are intended
           to be used for urgent local calls or emergency calls to London.

           Any person wishing to make other calls should make them from their
           respective offices or public telephone, rather than blocking the
           switchboard at Queen Square.

P.T.O.

Call sheet for Oh, what A Lovely War *(April, 1968).*

PAGE 2.

TRANSPORT:

Unit Car: (Ron):   To pick up Sir Ralph Richardson from the Metropole Hotel at
                   9.20 a.m. and take to Norfolk.

Unit Car: (Bob):   Pick up Kenneth More from the Bedford at 8.05 a.m., Ian Holm
                   Bedford at 8.20 a.m.   Joe Melia from the Metropole at 9.15. a.m.
                   and take the above Artistes to the Norfolk Hotel.

Minibus (Bill):   To work to Allan James' instructions.

- - - - - - -

RUSHES: To be shown on completion of the day's shooting at the
                   Norfolk Hotel.

                              CLAUDE WATSON
                              ASSISTANT DIRECTOR.

"The Great Muppet Caper!" - Call Sheet No: 60 (cont'd)   2.

3) <u>INT. BALLROOM</u>   Sc: Nos: 72pt. 70pt. 73pt (DAY)

  i) OPTICAL - KERMIT SINGING
 ii) PIGGY PEEKING THROUGH CURTAINS - <u>INSERT</u>
iii) PIGGY BRINGING JEWELS OUT OF RAINCOAT - <u>INSERT</u>

JIM HENSON	KERMIT	from above
FRANK OZ	MISS PIGGY	" "

<u>STAND-INS</u>:   from above

<u>PROPS</u>:   Jewel necklace for MISS PIGGY's Coat.

<u>SOUND</u>:   Playback required "MISS PIGGY".

<u>WORKSHOP</u>:   KERMIT in Tuxedo.   PIGGY in backstage outfit and
hairstyle, then wet raincoat and wig.

<u>CATERING</u>:   a.m. and p.m. breaks for 65 persons, please.

<u>RUSHES</u>:   Admin Theatre at 5.30pm.

<u>TRANSPORT</u>:   <u>Car 1</u> (IVAN) Pick up Ossie Morris at 7.45am and
transport to Studio.

<u>Car 2</u> (FRANCOIS) Pick up Anita Mann at 8.30am and take
to University of London Swimming Baths by 9.00am,
Malet Street.

<u>Car 3</u> (KINGS) Pick up Louise Gold at 7.30am, Kathy Mullen
at 7.50am, Steve Whitmire at 8.00am and transport to Studio.

<u>Car 4</u> (KINGS) Pick up Bob Payne at 7.50am, Brian Meuhl
and Ed Christie at 8.00am and transport to Studio.

<u>Car 5</u> (TOM) Pick up Tim Rose at 7.30am and Leslee Asch
at 7.35am and transport to Studio.

<u>Car 6</u> (KINGS) Pick up Bob McCormack at 7.30am and
transport to Studio.

<u>Assistant Director</u>:   DUSTY SYMONDS

<u>SCHEDULE
NOTE</u>:   Please note that the USA Street first shooting date
will now come forward one day to Thursday, 11th December,
on Stage 3.

A call sheet for The Great Muppet Caper *(1981).*

Life Casting List

- Rubber Cape
- Comb
- Life Cap
- Spirit Gum + Brush
- Acetone + Brush
- Gaffer Tape
- Water Tray for Plaster Bandage
- Gypsona Plaster Bandage
- Bowl for Casting plaster
- Spatulas
- Scrim
- Vaseline
- Wooden Modelling Tool
- Alginate
- Cups
- Mixing Bowls
- Alginate Brushes
- Bandages
- Modelling tool for nose
- Long Bandages for Mould edges
- Cotton Wool
- Tissues
- Facial Cleaner
- Clay + Clay Wash + Brush
- Strong String
- Surform
- Scissors (Plaster)
- Scissors (Cap)
- Scissors (String)
- Vibrator
- Mould Stand
- Jugs for Plaster or Water
- Salt
- Pen + Paper
- Bucket

Freeborn's notes for a Tefal ad prosthetic head.

HEAD		
C I R C		
T / T F		*Mike Cotterel*
E / E O		
E / E B	8"	
E / E F		
NECK	15"	
– BODY		
SHOULDER TO SHOULDER	17"	
FINGER TIP TO FINGER TIP	46"	
SHOULDER TO FINGER TIP	16"	
SHOULDER TO ELBOW	8"	
ELBOW TO WRIST	8"	
WRIST TO FINGER TIP	$5\frac{1}{2}$"	
NECK TO CROTCH	26"	
WAIST	32"	
COLLAR BACK TO WAIST	15"	
COLLAR BACK TO FLOOR	38"	
HIP TO FLOOR	20"	
KNEE TO FLOOR	11"	
HEIGHT	4'–1"	
CHEST	$34\frac{1}{2}$"	
HIPS	37"	
CENTRE BACK TO MIDDLE CROTCH	11"	
CENTRE FRONT TO MIDDLE CROTCH	11"	
INSIDE LEG	16"	
THIGH	10"	
FOOT	12" or $8\frac{1}{2}$9"	
SHOE SIZE (ENG)	4.	

Measurements for actor Mike Cottrell, as an Ewok in Return of the Jedi.

Top, Freeborn's home lab even made artificial eyes and teeth, above Freeborn and his horse team from Top Secret.

Freeborn's makeup notes for Peter Sellers, most likely Dr. Strangelove.

Sellers

Sellers

Sellers

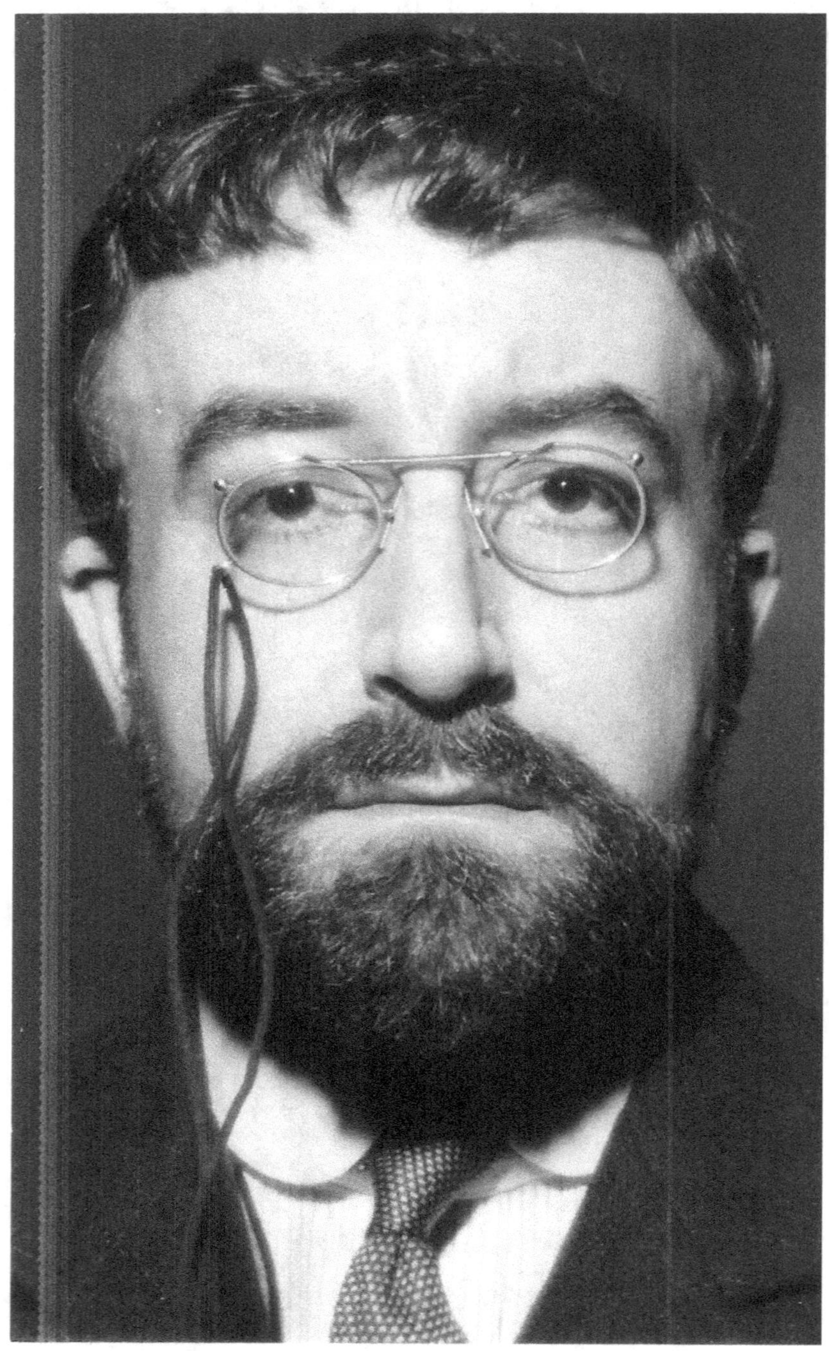

Sellers

Film Prosthetics

60 The Grove,
Isleworth, Middlesex,
TW7 4JA
01-560 3565

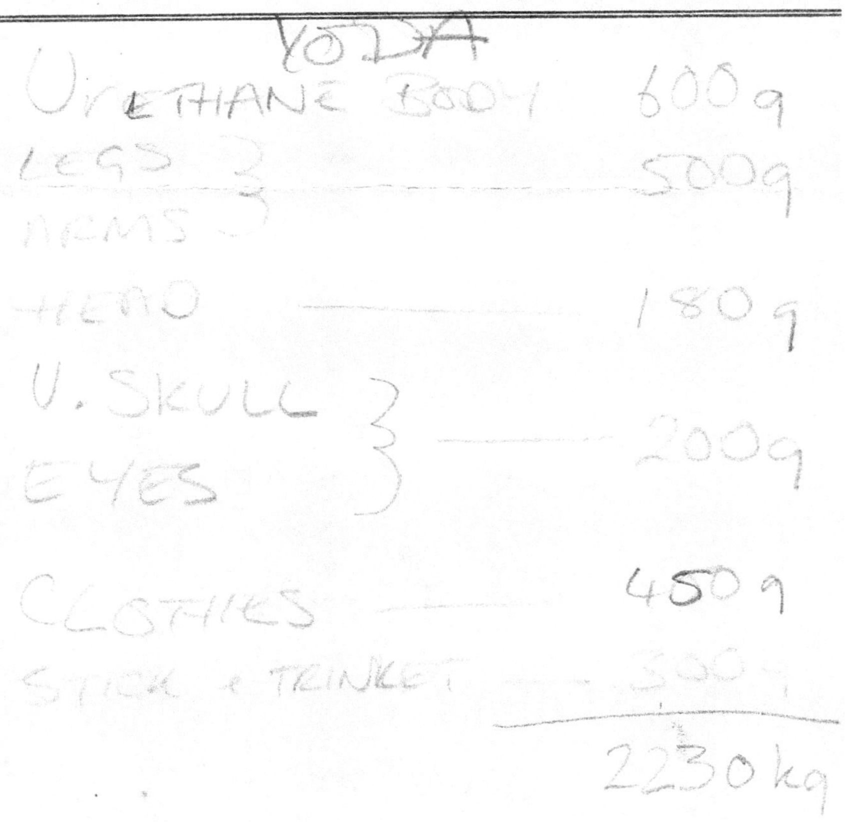

Freeborn's notes from 'Empire, calculating Yoda's total weight.

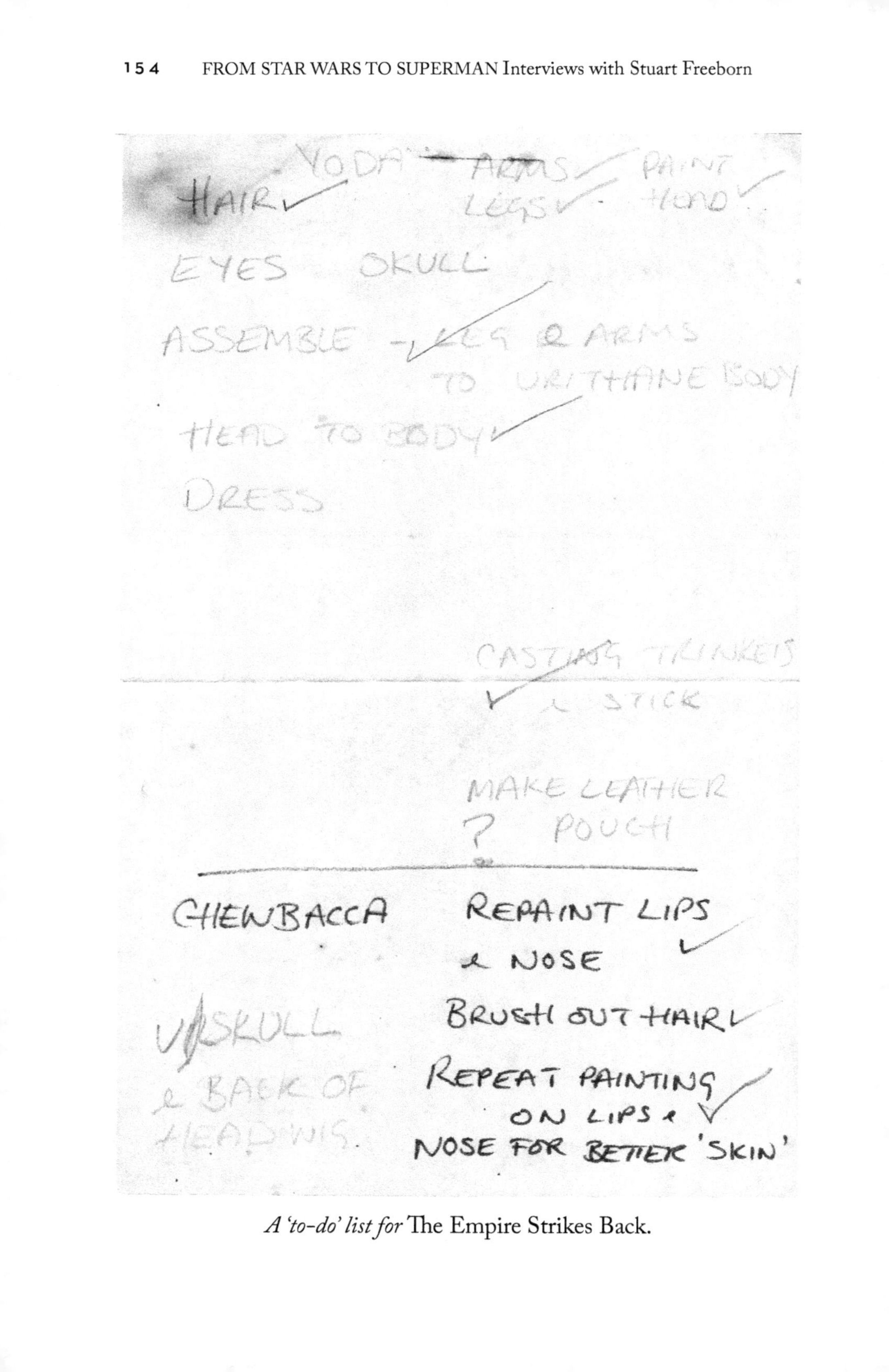

A 'to-do' list for The Empire Strikes Back.

Stuart Freeborn

4344

DOVEMEAD LIMITED   ISSUED 26/9/77

'SUPERMAN'

MAIN AND 2ND UNIT

SCHEDULE NO 5

DATE	SET OR LOCATION	STAGE	SC NOS	CHARACTER & SPECIAL REQS	
MONDAY 26/9/77	MAIN UNIT EXT FROZEN NORTH	007	344/346 DAY	LUTHOR EVE	
	2ND UNIT INT LUTHOR'S LAIR	D	127A PT DAY 239C PT DUSK 238 PT DUSK 183 PT DAY	SUPERMAN LUTHOR EVE OTIS	DOUBLE EVE
TUESDAY 27/9/77	MAIN UNIT EXT FROZEN NORTH	007	344/346 DAY	LUTHOR EVE	
	2ND UNIT INT LUTHOR'S LAIR	D	259 A/B NIGHT 232-238 DUSK PTS	SUPERMAN EVE OTIS LUTHOR	DOUBLE EVE
WEDNESDAY 28/9/77	MAIN UNIT EXT FROZEN NORTH/FORTRESS	007	375 501/506 DAY	SUPERMAN LEX LUTHOR LOIS EVE ZOD URSA NON GUARDS	
	2ND UNIT INT LUTHOR'S LAIR	D	259A/B PTS NIGHT 232-238 PTS DUSK	SUPERMAN EVE OTIS LUTHOR	DOUBLE EVE
THURSDAY 29/9/77	MAIN UNIT EXT FROZEN NORTH/FORTRESS	007	501/516 DAY	SUPERMAN LEX LUTHOR LOIS ZOD URSA NON GUARDS	
	2ND UNIT INT MISSILE	L	230L/M DAY	OTIS	
	INT OVAL OFFICE	L	463 PT	LUTHOR	

A September, 1977 main unit/second unit filming schedule for Superman.

Early storyboards for the key flying sequence in
Superman.

2
Clark climbs up onto wall
S163B
"Clark, don't don't!" etc.
S163B-1
Lois pulls herself up onto wall with Clark
S163B-2
Talk, talk...
S163B-3

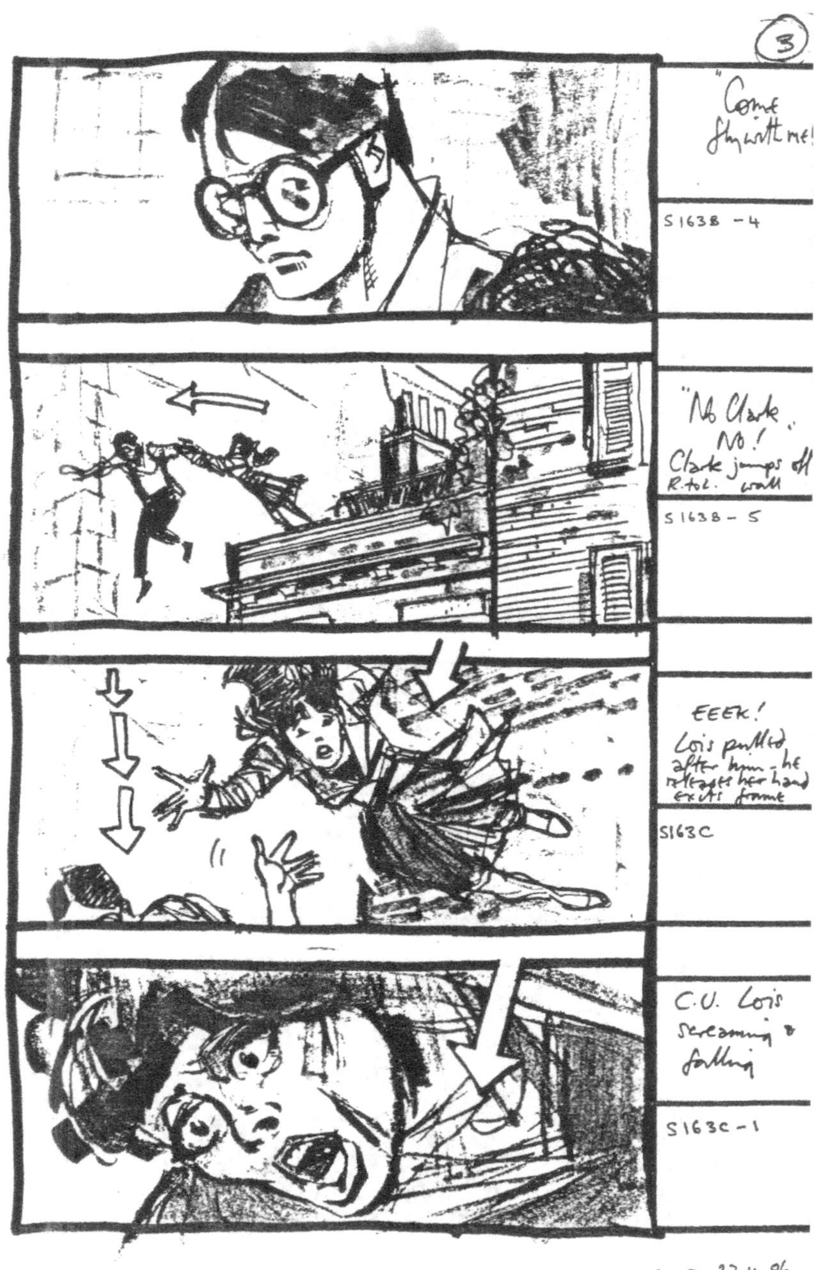
3
"Come fly with me!"
S 163B - 4
"No Clark. No!"
Clark jumps off
R. to L. wall
S 163B - 5
EEEK!
Lois pulled
after him - he
releases her hand
exits frame
S163C
C.U. Lois
screaming &
falling
S163C - 1

④
Superman,
wearing Clarke's
glasses catches
Lois, flying up
R. to L.
S 163D

Lois removes
spectacles..
S 163 E

..tucks them
in the belt of
her dress.
S 163 E — 1

Together, they
fly up thro'
Metropolis.
S 163 E — 2

ISSUED 27.11.86

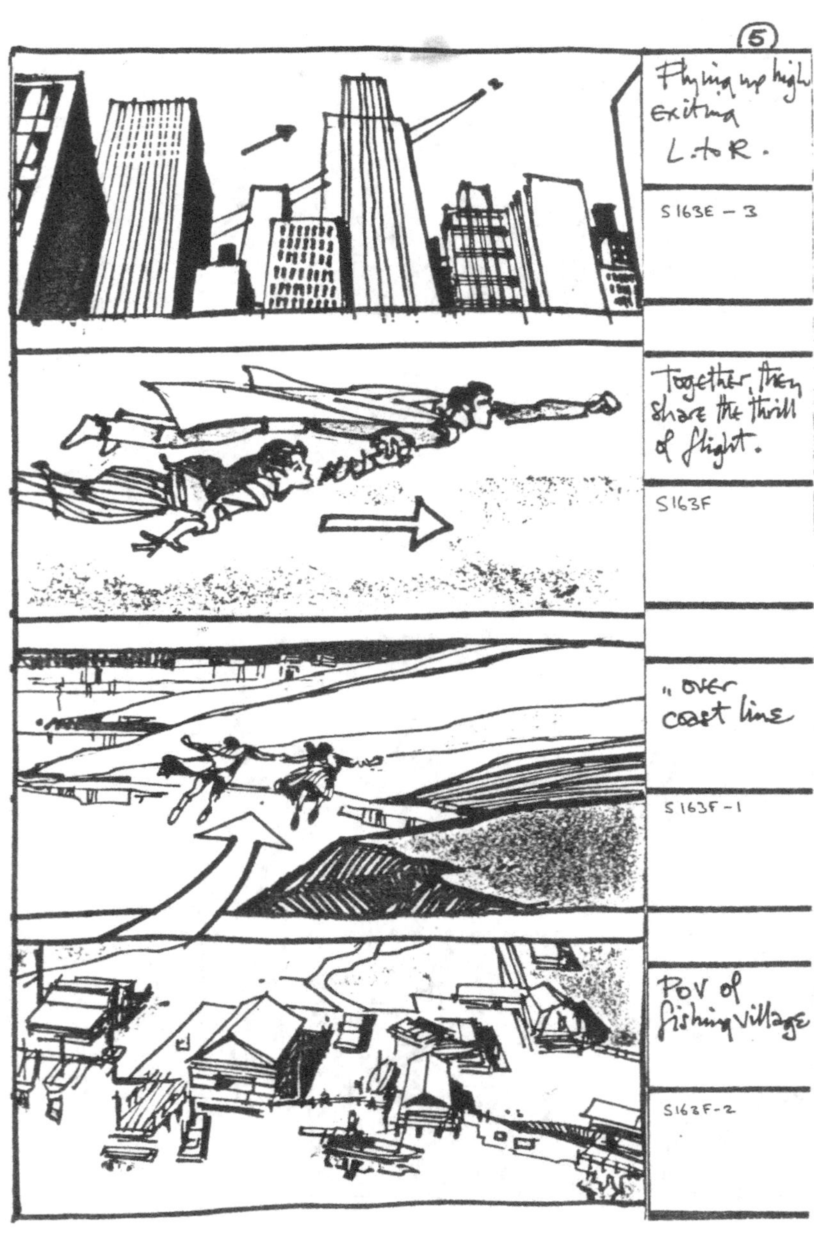
5
Flying up high
Exiting
L. to R.
S163E – 3

Together, then
share the thrill
of flight.
S163F

" over
coast line
S163F – 1

POV of
fishing village
S163F – 2

Issued 27·11·86

6
C.U. Fishermen working on nets, +/or lobster pots - Contrail in the sky L. to R.
S163F-3
Superman & Lois sweep over the Countryside L. to R.
S163F-4
"They look down
S163F-5
POV.
S163F-6

(7)
They smile at each other sharing the pleasure ..
S163F-7
P.O.V. up & over snow covered pine hills
S163 G
P.O.V. .. into more dense land .
S163G-1
They fly on L. to R.
S163G-2

8
.. Cut as they Enter frame from L. turn and fly straight at CAMERA ..
S163G - 3
.. Entering frame from above & straight at CAMERA — over a lake?
S163G - 4
Lois really enjoying it.
S163G - 5
POV. Snowscape — farm
S163G - 6
ISSUED 27.11.86

(9)
They swoop -
diving down
then climbing
up again..
SI63G - 7
.. high up over
the country side
SI63G - 8
on & on,,
SI63G - 9
PLAINS
flashing
over
winter wheat?
SI63G - 10

10
PLAINS
low and very fast L to R.
S163G-11
Superman indicates — "go on your own"
S163G-12
.. slowly withdrawing his hand..
S163G-13
Her face says: "Can I — Is it possible?"
S163G-14
ISSUED 29-11-76

11
C.U. His hand
letting go of
hers!
S163G —15

" immediately
she veers off!
S 163G — 16
B.G. non-
descript
countryside.

"zig-zagging?
Suddenly she
gets the hang
of it.
B.G. low hills
S 163G —17

"it sails off
to the R. and
he breaks away
B.G. Hills/
Rocks.
S 163G — 17

ISSUED 27.11.8

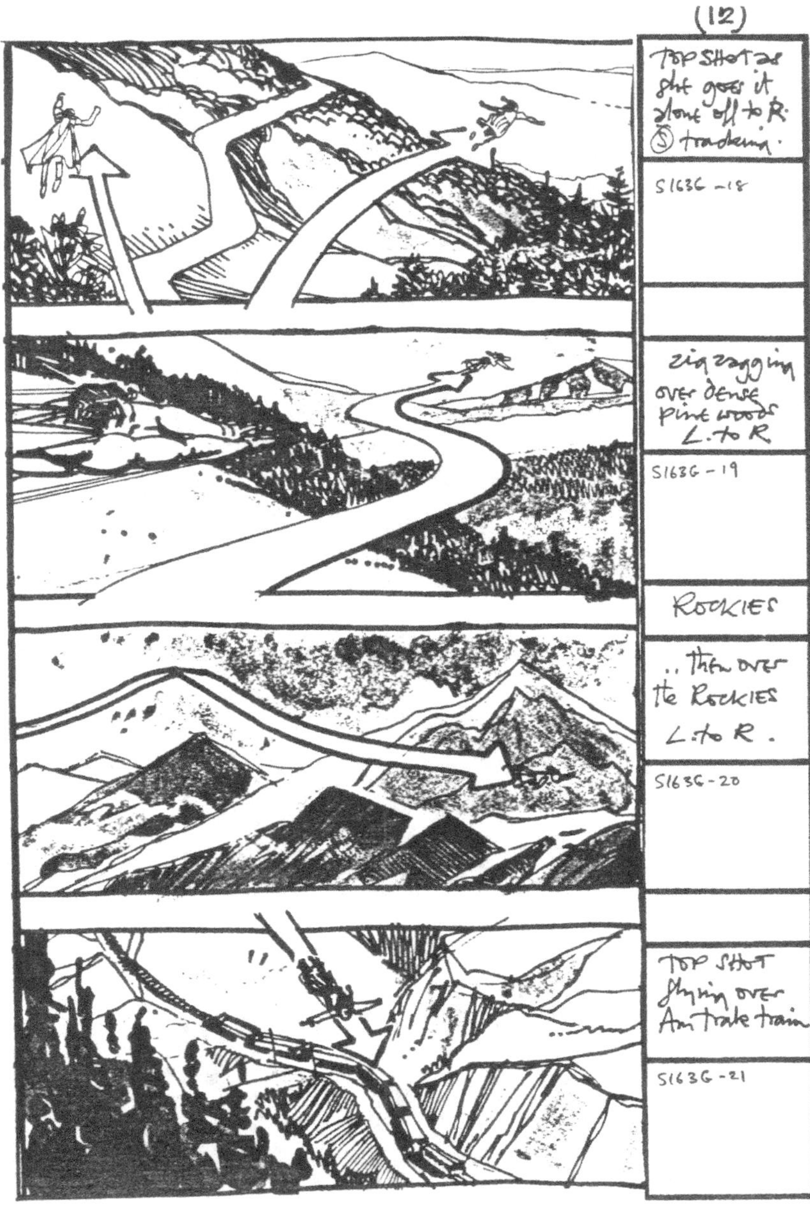
(12)
TOP SHOT as
she goes it
slows off to R.
(5) tracking.
S1636 -18
zig zagging
over dense
pine woods
L. to R
S1636 - 19
ROCKIES
.. then over
the ROCKIES
L. to R .
S1636 - 20
TOP SHOT
flying over
Amtrak train
S1636 - 21
ISSUED 27.12.86

(13)
Lois
delighted
S163G-22
Her POV of
the train.
S163G-23
closer -
the same
S163G-24
The train passes
L. to R. as she
flies close "
S163G-25

Part VI: 10/8/97

This was probably the only visit we ever made where we quite literally ran out of time. Stuart's solution was quite simple: 'Come back tomorrow, and we'll pick up where we left off!' This time, there was plenty of ground to cover. I had borrowed a lot of reference material from Stuart, including several books from which I had copied key passages and marked as important. I had no idea for example, that Stuart had been in a near-fatal jeep accident while shooting The Bridge on the River Kwai, until I read about it in David Lean's biography, and there was no way I wasn't going to ask about it this time (although we didn't get around to it until the following day).

More importantly, I finally got to visit the attic, which was a surreal experience. The ceiling was low, which didn't affect Sheelagh or Stuart at all, as they were both little more than five feet tall, but I immediately hit my head in an overhead beam and nearly knocked myself out (I still have a tiny scar on my forehead to prove it).

The attic workshop was quite similar to the rooms downstairs, filled with mislabeled drawers and all manner of film artifacts. As noted in Sheelagh's visit, a bust of Christopher Reeve as Superman dominated the center of one table, covered in what looked like ice crystals; it had been used to test an effect for one of the films. Every cranny and crevice was filled with something interesting; one could spend a week up there and not see everything, so it's not all that surprising we had to come back the following day to finish up this part of our conversation…

Let's start by talking about your work with Alec Guinness, which we touched on in our last conversation. The first time you worked together was *Oliver Twist*?

That was his second film with David Lean. They had worked together on a film I missed, because I was already working on something else. I knew him quite well, and had worked with him before, but I was off when he did the other one, which was another Dickens film. Alec Guinness was the same age as me; I think we were 34 when we did *Oliver Twist*, but this was like two years before when he did that other film, so he was 32 or even younger.

And then Lean said, 'We're going to make *Oliver Twist*, and I want you to let me know about the actors.' I had books on all of the actors, whether they were the old ones, medium ones and young ones, as well as what they specialized in doing, and he wanted me to suggest half a dozen different actors who I thought would be easiest to turn into a good Fagin, so I chose several actors, and he said, 'Hmm, yeah, I'll think about that.'

A couple of days later, we were filming on set, and he said, 'This Saturday, if you can, I'd like you to come with me, we're going to have a meal up in Charing Cross Road in London and we'll will discuss it.' I thought, 'That's a bit odd; why don't we just do it the way we normally would, in his office or something?' But we went out, and were sitting there having this meal, and he was talking to the camera boys and one or two other heads of department, and then he looked at me and said, 'Have you had any more thoughts about Alec Guinness?' I said, 'Any one of those, I would like to have a go at.'

You hadn't picked Alec Guinness?

No, I hadn't, because I just came back from this other film and we were still working in the same studio, so I saw him as this young lad, or and he seemed very young, and suddenly, David Lean said, 'I've had a thought; what would you say if I suggested Alec Guinness? I think you've met him!' I said, 'Alec Guinness? He's just a young boy!' And Fagin is an elderly, nasty Jewish character!

He was the exact opposite of what you were supposed to be looking at.

Exactly! So I looked at him puzzled and he said, 'As you know, I had him on my last film, and I think he's a brilliant young actor, so I'd like to try him so if you could make him up to look like Fagin, I'd like to see how he gets on with it and see if he can play that part. I think he could!' and I thought, 'Oh my God, I don't know if I can make him up to look like Fagin!' because he had a clean, smooth face.

So this would be a big test for both of you.

Stuart: Exactly that. And Lean said, 'As a matter of fact, you're probably wondering why I've got you all up here. Across the road is the theater, and Alec Guinness is playing over there. They'll be finished any time now and he'll be coming over here, so I want you to get to know him and talk to him about it.' Five minutes later, in walks Alec Guinness!

Anyway, I liked him very much, he was a great guy, but I thought, 'This is a challenge if I ever had one but I'll go along with it,' because I could see that David Lean was very keen on him, and I liked Alec Guinness, so there it was. A few days later, we arranged to do a makeup test on him, so I was looking through the drawings and cartoons, because they were all characterizations; they weren't true life characters. They were larger-than-life characters, so I thought, 'What do I do here?'

I went back to Lean and said, 'I've got a little problem here: this is not for real, this is just a cartoon. Everybody knows the character only as this cartoon, so how far can I make a natural human being look like that? Do I do a really cleaned-up one, making him look normal and natural, but then the public wouldn't recognize him, or do I do it all the way like the cartoon, which wouldn't be a normal person?'

He said, 'Yeah, that's a point and I get your meaning. Tell you what we'll do: you may come up with the cartoon look first and the next day we'll do him with you cleaning him up a little bit.'

When you say 'cartoon,' are you talking about an illustration?

It was an illustration, yes. I got some books from the library with cartoons in them, so that's what we did. When I did the original 'cartoon' version with the full works and an extra big nose and everything as he had in the cartoon, I thought, 'My God, we can't mark Jews because they've got big noses, but this is an extra big nose and people are not going to like this at all! I had some funny feelings about it, but it's Jewish anyway and people don't mind that, looking like they happened to have big noses, fine, but this is different.

So we did that and when he saw it, David Lean said, 'You know, I like that one, but let's see the other one, when he's cleaned up.' I still made him look like this particular character, Fagin, but all cleaned up, with a smaller nose and less wrinkles and things, so he was cleaner all around, and you know, he looked just like Jesus Christ, which was *not* the character we wanted! So it was obviously no good- Jesus Christ wouldn't play a part like that!

If you did it one way, you offended the Jews, and the other way offended the Christians.

So David Lean said, 'Forget it, we'll go for the first one regardless. People know he's Jewish and they know he's a cartoon character; it's just somebody's imagination!' so that's what happened, and in the end, that's what we did. I did exactly what I did in the first test and David liked it just as it was whatever I did.

I was in at five every morning, taking half an hour to set up my bench for the different makeups, noses, eye bags, bald caps and hair and the different colors and whatnot. Alex Guinness would come in about 5:30 and sit in my chair and he was wonderful. He didn't speak at all, he just said, 'Look, I know you've got a problem and it's very early, so I'll keep awake, I won't allow myself to go to sleep, but I'll leave you to do your job. I won't interfere in any way and I will only move when you tell me to.' And he was fantastic. He had all of this in his mind and he was so with me on it; and that made my job so much easier. With some people, it would have been so much more difficult, but he was like that every morning.

I did that makeup for 52 days, and the problem was in those days back in 1948, was that we were still using the old stage technique of false noses.

This was before foam latex?

Exactly that and this is the one that changed me. After that film, I went into plastics and foam immediately after that, because the problem I had was that for 52 days, I had to model that nose to look the same, which took about three and half hours every morning. But we didn't shoot it day after day after day; there were big gaps, so there might be a couple of months when Alec wasn't working and we were shooting all of the other stuff and then he would come back and I would have to remember in detail the shape of the nose I did.

I developed a system that I've used for other things as well as noses, up to the day we went to foam noses, but I still use it for other systems; I thought, there must be some way… when I model, I do a life cast of the artist first so I've got his nose there already, and I model the nose on and I know exactly the one that's been passed in the test, so I do a cast of that nose too and I thought, there must be some way of putting the wax in those two plaster casts, squashing them together and taking them apart and taking out the wax: I'll put it in a fishbowl, so as it's floating around, not one but you do dozens of them floating around in water. So I put it in, pulled it apart, so that one and that one are all squashed in and to squeeze it out, it forces the surface of it into the plaster and it pulls it apart. I tried other things like painting a skin on it and all sorts of things but they never worked. I tried all the little tricks I could think of but it didn't work, I couldn't get it out. Anyway, I thought, there has to be an answer to this-

This was the nose inside the plaster?

Inside the plaster, the negative and the positive, and I couldn't separate them. But with all the different tricks like powdering it or painting plastic skins on it, I finally figured out what it was: it was in the pores and it was a hell of a job getting it off the plaster once you pressed it into it. But I thought, wouldn't it be marvelous if you could just pop them out, pick them up put them on, smooth the edges off and paint my plastic skin over the top to make it up?

The sticking point was separating the wax from the plaster?

It was a total disaster. Nothing would work, and then one day I went to the canteen and I thought I would have a cup of tea, and it was tea in a mug without a handle, so I got this mug which was still hot, so I put it on the table, because it was too hot to drink, so I thought I would cool it down, but as it happened, I still had the mug in my hand and I had some cold milk, so I poured the milk into the cup of hot tea, and I had to put it down quickly, because it got hotter, because the cold milk going into the middle of it pushed the heat outwards, so it got hot. I looked at that and thought, 'That's it, that's the answer!'

I rushed to my lab while my brain was still analyzing it in detail and I could see what I could do. If I reversed it, if you put something cold in the middle and it goes out, if I put something cold on the outside and it goes in, it's going to melt the wax inside and therefore, it's not going to have all that pressure. It releases all that pressure, pushing it into the surface and it might work. It's more likely to stick, but there's far less pressure on it now, because it's mostly liquid on the inside and not necessarily the outside, because I fill the wash basin up with cold water or put some ice in it so it's really cold, and if I keep it all wet, that will keep it from sticking while I'm pressing in, because there's water there already, and then I found to get the temperature right for the wax, I put it in a cup of hot water and by several tests I did, if I would just bear having my finger in it, it's just at the right temperature that I would take it out, plunk it in the plaster cast, take the wet cast that I've just taken out of the cold water, so that will keep it cooled off on the outside and drive the heat in, which will now melt it inside in the center, but it's still hard on the outside, which is the reverse of the milk in the cup, so I could see all of this happening. If I went hotter, it would melt the wax, but this was where it was just under the melting point.

So if it was any hotter, you would destroy the wax?

If you melt it completely, exactly. So I found if I could just bear it on my finger, that was the point where it set and I could do it when it got it to that temperature. I would take the molds out, plunk it in and squash it, and then I put it in the water and opened it up and floated out beautifully in the water with thin edges and not destroyed. It was beautiful, so from there on, I got my fishbowl and made dozens of them, plonked them in and it worked.

This is a system that I trained all my boys to do. If you're modeling anything and you want duplicates of it so you've got lots of molds, I do the same trick, so instead of modeling it up each time and trying to imitate the first one and get them all the same, I do the same trick and turn them out by the dozen. I've got all the molds, so I put one in each mold and re-cast them. I could put a dozen in foam rubber or whatever in the oven and cook them using the same idea and it worked all the way through.

And it all started from this wax nose.

From the wax nose. That gave me the idea, and I've used it ever since. It's been marvelous, saving a lot of time and messing around and they all come out the same.

So you could build up a backlog of noses that were exactly the same.

That was a major step. After that of course, I worked with foam rubber.

How long did you do this makeup on Guinness before coming up with the idea?

Unfortunately, it was three-quarters of the way through. I had been trying everything and it hadn't worked. I knew what I wanted to do and I could see it, but it wouldn't work. I hadn't got this idea of mine, of the heat transferring from one place to another and catching it at the right moment, with molds as cold and wet as you could get them and doing it underwater.

So it was too late to do you any good on this film.

I was still getting in at five in the morning and making him up. I had other artists to make up too, so I had to get him finished and then work on quite a few others who had bald heads and beards and god knows what else, as well as Alec. So that's what happened, and Alec was thrilled. He loved it, and he was doing a damn good job and David was right; he was brilliant.

How many times have you worked with Guinness over the years?

Not that many, strangely enough. On *Star Wars*, my son actually worked on him and had to put a beard on him, and I worked with him since on one or two films, but not that many, strangely enough. I was under contract for three years at Denham Studios so you knew that's where you're going to be. After the war, that was all gone, so you didn't have contracts with the studio. You just picked up a film, and when it was finished, you were fired and hoped you had another one as soon as possible.

Didn't Alec Guinness win an Oscar for that role?

He could well have done; I'm not sure about that. I don't know that there were that many Oscars going around in those days.

If you look back at the number of performances helped by the makeup, this is definitely one of them.

And it isn't often an actor will give credit to the makeup artist. Albert Finney did that on *Orient Express*, and Chris Reeve did too, and also Wendy Hiller on *Orient Express*. You know that story?

I know you had to age her, but she had very sensitive skin?

Her skin had been damaged by somebody else putting makeup on. That had done a lot of harm to her, so she had this problem. She did a lot of theater work too and made herself up for the theater, but this was something she did for television, where they wanted some aging and whatever it was. Somebody had put on a material and I'm not sure what they used but normally you use latex and stipple on two or three layers until you get it to the right thickness according to the depths of the wrinkles. It's something you learn from experience, and then you stretch it in different ways, so you've got it all planned out in the shape of the wrinkles. Sometimes they're pretty straight and sometimes they're tight curves, but you've got to plan where to stretch to get those curves just right around the face, around the eyes and everywhere else.

Unfortunately, it's not an easy thing to do, and I think it was probably the first time she had to do it and it wasn't done right, so Wendy Hiller's pores had been damaged, and she found difficulty in doing her own makeup. She had been to the doctors and got some special cream that she put on for theater makeup, so it wasn't too bad.

The thing was, they tried to pull it off, and you can't do that. There are special techniques for that, and then she was going to do this film and I was called up to do this film in Elstree, but it was too late, because I had already said I was going to Oslo on a Sean Connery film. I had been up there first and talked to them, but it was delayed, so Sean Connery came to me and said, 'Would you do this film with me?'

I thought, well, the other one is delayed, I don't know when it's going to happen, so yes, I'll do it. But then they got the money to do this other film and they got another makeup artist to do it, who was very well-known; I actually trained him in the early days at Denham Studios- after I had been there for a year, my boss, Guy Pearce told me to reach these other young lads and this guy Charlie Parker was one of them, but he was a very good straight makeup artist for girls and things like that, but he didn't go into the lab. He hated it and didn't want to know about chemistry and things like that, so he never developed on that side.

Anyway, they got Charlie Parker to do *Orient Express*, and Wendy Hiller had to age quite a lot. On top of that, she had to look like she tried to make herself up but badly, so the mascara was all over the place and her lipstick was uneven, which was not an easy job for a makeup artist, when you're normally trying to do it as perfect as you can and you've now got to do the reverse.

So I was in Oslo and Charlie Parker used to call and say, 'Stu, can you help me, I've got a little job here; what would you recommend? What can I use?' He had heard about this latex problem that had given her this trouble, but foolishly, he had no idea about chemistry or anything, and he decided to use bald cap material that was dissolved in acetone of all things, but he didn't know anything about it, and he foolishly tried to do it with this bald cap material all over her face, which of course it made it a thousand times worse, so she was in a terrible state, all fiery.

They rushed her off to a Harley Street doctor, who said there was no way he could see any way that people could put makeup on her without doing damage, so it was all very bad, but she badly wanted to do this film and wanted to play this part, but she was very uneasy about it. I had worked with her on several films before, so I knew her quite well, so when she asked, 'Is there anyone else who could do it?' they said, 'But look, here's the letter from this Harley Street doctor who said nobody could do anything about this; this was a situation where she mustn't have anything on her face until it's better, so that meant she wouldn't be able to play the part. But somebody had suggested me for some reason, so they sent me a letter from the doctor saying this was the problem, but she would dearly love to play the part. They said, 'Somebody suggested you and she said she knew you and would be happy if I would give it a try.'

So I met with her and looked at her face and they explained that not only her skin had to breathe, and at the end when you take it off, it's got to come off easily without tearing the skin, so I had to keep those two factors in mind. So I thought, I'd love to do it for her, because she's a lovely lady, so I thought about it and got an idea. I thought, if I used latex on its own, I knew I would have a problem and it does seal up the skin and with her skin condition, it wasn't possible to do that, so I had to do something else.

I thought, if there was some way to take it off; for instance, if I could mix gelatin with the latex, the gelatin would make it much easier. If I pressed on some warmed skin freshener that would melt and dissolve the gelatin and it would crumble it all the way. I could try it out and test it first to remove it, so I thought, her skin has got to breathe, so I thought, supposing instead of putting it all over, I would do it in streaks leaving the skin absolutely bare in-between. I don't know, it might not work at all, but it might so it's worth a try.

Of course I had Kath working with me on all of these things; on the old age makeups and the pulling bit and stretching the skin, you need somebody else to do that, and she knew exactly where to put her fingers and how much to stretch while I stippled that bit on there and there are so many thicknesses on there and less on there, so we were doing all of that, but at the same time only doing it in streaks and then doing the stretching, so her skin was exposed to the air at the same time. I did a test with her to see if it was comfortable or it was smarting or hurting her too much and I said, 'Let me know if you feel it's doing you any damage.' She said, 'I would like you to try it, and I will let you know if I feel uncomfortable, but I will keep my fingers crossed, because I would still love to play this part!'

So Kath and I worked on her and did a test, all in little streaks and it worked much better than I thought, because I thought, maybe it's going to be more difficult to get the wrinkles, but we got all the wrinkles we wanted with just the streaks. The trouble was, mixing the gelatin and the latex, the gelatin, if I got it too hot, the latex would congeal. If the gelatin wasn't hot enough, it wouldn't melt, but I found with tests, I had four degrees only that if I could keep within those four degrees, I could melt the gelatin and it would not cause the latex to congeal.

And then when I got this temperature just right with trial and error, so it was mistake, mistake, mistake and finally I got it to a point where I had a thermometer so I knew the temperature and I knew the gelatin and the latex would stay all right at that temperature, so they just overlapped a little bit, and it was in-between that bit that I got the temperature just right, so I could mix the two and they blended together. I kept it in the bottle at that lukewarm temperature and wrapped it all up and rushed it into the studio and we put it on and it worked.

Doesn't gelatin break down under studio lights if it gets too hot?

Mixed with the latex, it stayed on perfectly all day without any problems. At night she had some special witch hazel skin freshener, so we warmed the witch hazel, put it on a sponge and laid it on and it melted and it all came off beautifully. She also gave me some of the special cream she put on and knowing it was a greasy sort of material, I blended that in with it too, so it was in the mixture, so that helped, so that was three things together. The witch hazel was just to take the latex off at night; the warmed witch hazel took it off gently without peeling the skin. Being warm and a solvent, it dissolved the gelatin and the latex came away beautifully without any pulling. And we got all the way through the film with it and there was no problem at all. She still had a certain sensitivity of course, because it wasn't cured, but it didn't make it any worse.

She then went to France and did a film and she wrote a letter to me from France and said, 'I've just heard I got an Oscar for the part I played when you made me up. Quite frankly, I shouldn't have got the Oscar. You should have done, but I never would have played the part if it hadn't been for you.' so that was nice of her. She also said, 'I wanted to tell you, my skin is in perfect condition and there are no problems!'

Didn't you have Albert Finny in that film too? You had already done Tony Randall as Poirot, so this was a different approach.

Completely different, because it was a different character and the director had his own ideas too, so they weren't purely mine, if they said, 'It fits him better this way or that way,' so we came up with a slightly different look but it's still Poirot.

You said he had mentioned some makeup he had seen on television?

I think it was probably the Wendy makeup that he mentioned. Unfortunately, poor old Charlie Parker never got into that kind of work. He should never have taken the film on, really, because it wasn't his kind of work. He was brilliant at normal makeups and characterizations with highlights and shadows, but applying prosthetics, he wasn't into that, and Albert Finney had to have a false nose, a bald cap and thinning on the top and various other things to make him look like the character of Poirot, but he couldn't get that nose right, so they would go into rushes every day and people would say, 'What's happened to the nose?' because it stood out from a mile.

That's when Charlie Parker himself and said, 'Stu, I want you to come in to the rushes with me today,' so I could see it, and he said, 'I've got problems, as you can see; would you mind taking over the principal characters with these heavy makeups?' which included Albert Finney and Wendy Hiller, so I finished up doing all the principals in the end and that got him out of trouble. I said, 'Just one thing, allow me to promise; I don't want any credits; it's your film, so leave it that way and we'll say no more,' so he said thank you very much and that was it.

So if this was '65 or '66, you had the technology to use foam by then.

Stuart: Oh yes, I had done a lot of it by then. *2001* really put me into that.

Wouldn't this be *after* that?

Kath: We did *2001* first and then we did…
Orient Express was after 2001, wasn't it?

By the way, I ran into a girl with her mother, who was supposed to be on the new Kubrick film for just a couple of days, and she's now been here for five months.

[Laughing] Five months! Five months, he said, I still have the letter upstairs: five months, maybe six, and we were on it for over two years! So that's the same story.

Kath: That's what they did with the two astronauts, isn't it; they kept them hanging around. Gary Lockwood and Keir Dullea.

Gary Lockwood and Keir Dullea never got on very well together. They were always arguing; I think it was because of your war in Vietnam that was going on at the time, and they had completely opposite views about it, and they were always arguing about it. They were completely on opposite sides and all they could talk about was that, so they didn't get on at all.

How many films did you do with Kubrick?

Just two. I did *Doctor Strangelove* and *2001*. He asked me to do others since, but I was too tied up, thank goodness. Quite frankly, I wasn't too keen to go back with him.

You must have had a reasonably good experience on *Doctor Strangelove*; otherwise you wouldn't have gone back for *2001*.

Well, he was all right on *Doctor Strangelove*. He wasn't too bad at all on that, and I rather liked him. We had a lot in common. His sense of humor was the same as mine, so we always had little jokes, and also he was good at sleight of hand magic tricks, and I did a lot of that in my young days too. I used to entertain, trying to get into that entertainment world. It's a bit different now, but I used to do it with magic of all kinds, with coins and cigarettes and string and sleight of hands with the fingers. I haven't tried it for many years now, so I don't know if I could still do it, but he would come up and I would say, 'What about this one?' and he would say, 'Oh, I can do that one!' so we used to do that every morning and exchanged a few sleight of hand tricks, so he was great,

But on *2001*, he was altogether different. He came up and explained, because he realized I was puzzled about his different attitude which was not as friendly as it was, so he said, 'Stuart, I would like to show you this letter,' and it was from the boys on the coast, if you know what that expression means: the money boys on the Coast, and it basically said, 'When the hell are you going to show us something?' I don't know if it was deliberate, and I have a feeling it was, but he hadn't let them know what he was going to do. He said once he got them committed and got over here and shot something, they were committed and he could go on further. He knew it wasn't going to take five or six months- I know he must have done- but in his mind, he knew it was going to take a lot longer, so I don't think he had told them, because he hadn't shown them enough that would make a film to be finished in that space of time.

They were saying, 'What the hell is going on over there? Why don't you show us something?' so he said, 'I'm showing you this,' and I realized that mentally he was under enormous pressure. They knew he wanted to do it and it might even be a big one but they wouldn't have let him do it if they knew it was going to take that long or cost that much. And then I suddenly realized, so I went along with him. A lot of people didn't, because he got more and more difficult, so an entire department would leave and then another one, but I thought, 'I'm going to stick this out regardless, because I've got faith in him, and I know it's really going to be something, so however difficult it is, I'm not going to let it hit me at all, so I will carry on as though I never heard what he said and all the difficulty is was going to be,' so that's what happened in actual fact.

Kath: He did ask you to do *Clockwork Orange.*

Yes, but after two years of putting up with him, I thought, I've got to give him a rest. And I had other offers too that I wanted to do. And then *Star Wars* came up and there were three of them and four *Superman* films in-between, so I was full up. I had no gaps in-between, so I never got around to doing them.

And he didn't do that many films after that.

No, he didn't. *A Clockwork Orange* and *Full Metal Jacket* and that was about it until the one he's doing now. I suppose he still lives in Elstree- we used to pass his house and he would be coming in and out.

Because he was such a perfectionist, did that filter down to the makeup?

I was learning so much that I knew that it was far more important for me to put up with what he was being like, but it made it easier knowing that it wasn't really him and remembering how he was on *Doctor Strangelove*, so I stuck with it. I was also getting opportunities to develop my knowledge, like with different plastics. I had all the big chemical companies coming down and they were fascinated by my showing them around the studio and I made a point if possible to have lunch with some big star or whatnot. That kept their interest, so they loved coming down to the studio and keeping me up to date with all the latest plastics and new things that hadn't really hit the market yet. I was the first to know about anything new, especially artificial flesh or the nearest thing to it, which was not an easy thing to imitate with plastics or any other material, so I was into that all the way through the film. Over the span of two years, I learned so much, it was unbelievable, so I thought, 'I've got to stick with this, because I'll never get an opportunity like this again!'

It also ended up making things easier on *Star Wars*, having already done the R&D for *2001*.

With Chewbacca, I did the whole thing in a fortnight: modeling him, making him and putting in the mechanics. I knew exactly how I was going to make it work, so I didn't have to do any trial and error, because I had already done all the monkeys, and this was almost identical to what I did with the monkeys after it took me four months to develop them. With *Star Wars*, I was able to do it in two weeks, because I got all the little bits and pieces already made, like the little acrylic toggles and things like that. I've still got loads of them, so I didn't have to make them and I knew what to do. It's just the modeling; that's all it was.

It's interesting to look at your early monkey tests compared to the final creatures. What you were originally supposed to do was a lot simpler, the way it was presented to you.

Oh yes, just a few bumps on the forehead and things like that, and that's about it.

So things really snowballed.

Only because they couldn't photograph them. Fifty percent of a film is full length of the artists, but I said to Stanley, 'How can you have them stark naked full length?' He said, 'Oh, don't worry, I'll shoot them from the waist up and then in long shots or in close-ups,' so he tried that and it didn't work, because you've still got to get your full lengths, and the only way to do that was to go back another million years or so when there was sufficient hair all over the body.

I'm assuming those stages were amusing and frustrating at the same time.

That's right. So he said, 'Stuart, I want you to fix their crotches so you don't notice anything!' I had all the boys and girls lying on their backs and I was taking casts of all these crotches and making flat things and he said, 'Don't worry about it, a little bit of fur here and there and nobody is going to notice!' They shot for about a week and I said, 'Stanley, the whole thing about this is, they have to procreate for the future stuff, and you won't have anybody in *2001* if they're like that!'

He said, 'Yeah… maybe you're right; we'll have to go back another million years!' so that's what we did in the story. He asked me how far back we would have to go, and I said I had been all through the books and the nearest things to human beings would be these apes with hair covering them, so before you could shoot on them without noticing anything wrong, so that's what happened.

You had a scene of a monkey nursing, which must have been a challenge.

That was a last-minute idea. Every single artist had to be cast; I couldn't make just one suit to fit all of them, because they had to fit exactly, so we life-cast not only the heads, but the whole body, hands and feet and everything. Wardrobe was going to do the 'costumes,' and they were hiring ape skins, but of course they couldn't make them fit, and Kubrick went mad and said, 'These are no damn good! What the hell are you doing?' In the end, they got fed up with it, because they didn't know to make a costume that looked like a monkey and put it on, so they said, 'Look, this is not wardrobe; we do costumes, not animal skin. That's the makeup department!' so Kubrick phoned me and said, 'Stuart, I want you to come up to my office. The wardrobe department has made a statement that it's not wardrobe. It's makeup, and I've got an idea that they're right!'

So I went up there, thinking, 'I've already got enough to do!' I hadn't perfected the other things yet, so I was there seven days and nights a week and then they threw this at me on top of everything, so it was a question of, how the hell was I going to make these suits and the feet? If the camera is on the floor and when they walk towards the camera and their feet come up and they're all pink underneath and almost black on the top, so there were all these little details I had to do, like make them pink underneath. And then they wanted the females in milk, with their breasts a bit different because they're now feeding the baby monkeys, and I thought, 'My god, I can't get babies and life-cast them and put suits on them!' I phoned up Mary Chipperfield from the Chipperfield Circus, which was well known in England; she and her employees supplied animals for films, so I got to know her on many films she had come down for, so I said, 'Mary, I've got a problem.'

I explained to her about this scene with a female monkey, and said, 'From my books on apes I've got, there are none that I can see that show a female monkey in milk, when she's feeding the babies; do you breed them?' She said, 'Oh yes, we certainly breed them down here,' so I said that was interesting, because I wanted to see what the nipples are like and the color of the nipples and breasts, so she said, 'We don't do that; they all drink out of plastic cups!'

'I can't tell Stanley Kubrick that! He wants to see them suckling from the breast! The only other thing I could think of was, I need- ed two little baby chimps.' She said, 'Yes, fine, I'll send a trainer down with a couple of chimps,' and I said, 'I need them for about a week; we've got to get used to them and they have got to get used to us, and I've got to make them up, because it's only halfway- it's human and it's chimp, so it's half and half. The ears would be big- ger than a human ear but not as big as the full chimp, so I've got to do a big of makeup on them, because when they're babies, they're a very light color and then as they get older, they get black patches and older still, they're black all over.

I had to work all of this out according to photographs of different characters, so we had these two baby chimps, Joey and Jimmy and we played around with them and got used to them and they got used to us, and then Kath would make up one and I would make up the other and put things like earphones over the top with the ears on, and a bit of hair over the top of that, so we covered their ears and to match our ears, and made up all these white bits and toned it in more to match ours. They would sit there quite patiently while we did it, but as soon as we let them go, they would run towards each other and lick it all off, so we would have to smack their bums and say no, but they would do it again, so I would have to run out there two or three times.

On the third time, as they went to run together, we would do that [clapping his hands] and they would come back and we would fix it and they were all right, so they learned. So that's what we did, and we shot it and it was beautiful, and I got the breasts just right. It took another three days- I had to make the foam rubber smell like real chimp flesh, and look like and feel like chimp, because we had the real monkeys down there, so we filmed them and I studied them and the five little holes running through and the problem of, when they've suckled all the milk out, how do I fill up the bladders quickly instead of holding them up on set for thousands of pounds a minute for the hold-up? In the end, it was no good trying to put it up their jersey, which was too much of a hassle, so I got these cow injection gadgets, the big ones and filled them with milk and attached them to the nipples and squeezed it in, so that filled them up very quickly and worked a treat.

Anyway, it was all working fine, and then Kubrick said, 'I want to shoot on them next Monday!' so I spent all weekend preparing the milk and putting it in the frig so it would keep, but getting it to the right consistency so that when they suckled, it would come out right but not leak out if they didn't suckle. It had to have the right consistency and keep things at the right temperature, so we kept it at the right temperature in the frig so it wasn't too cold, but at the same time it didn't go off.

So we got it all timed to put it in on the Monday, but he didn't work on this particular Sunday, so on Saturday he had all these chimps down and they were all jumping about and fighting and all that sort of business, so he shot all of that (I thought) and then on the Monday morning, we got the two chimps all fixed up with the milk and everything and sent them down, and he hadn't finished what he had wanted them to do with them jumping around, so he had to use these two who had the milk, jumping around with all the others, and after a couple of minutes of jumping around, the milk started squirting around! I was busy doing something else, because I thought it was being shot already, so I thought it was all done, but he said, 'Oh, just send them all back to Stuart!'

So they all came back to me and I had to clean them up and make up a fresh lot of milk. I said, 'Stanley, look, you cannot do that, for God's sake, give me a chance! When you've got them, they're all set, so they can suckle from the breast and that sort of thing and it will work fine,' so he finally did it and they shot it and it was fine, but when they edited it together, they chopped it off at the end so you never see it. I saw it once, maybe on the screen, but it was cut on telly, where it was cut a lot, so after all of that, you generally don't see it but I did see it the first time it was on screen.

You showed it all to Kubrick with the facial mechanisms and he said, 'Great, now make it do *this*…' Directors don't understand you didn't build it to do that.

That's exactly what happened. There were two groups, which were enemies, but all they do is [snarl] and show their fangs. Sometimes they get into a fight, but most of the time, one group scared the other off. Since the artists were inside these masks, I had this protected mouth that came out much further, because Kubrick said, 'I want them to look much more like apes than humans, and I shall be shooting them in profile, so I want the mouth out in front of their own. They can't use their own mouths!' There was going to be a full mouth in front, with a false tongue that licked the lips and everything else, and the mechanics to make the head work. When they opened their mouths, it opened the false jaw automatically and I had a two-inch gap between the teeth. The top lip came up three-quarters; the bottom went down half an inch.

Enough to expose the teeth.

Enough to expose the fangs, top and bottom. So I took them down to Stanley and said, 'I think I've got what you want now.' He looked at them and said, 'Hmm… hmm,' and I knew that meant he liked it. Otherwise he would really blast you, so no news was good news; it's as good as saying, 'That's fine!' He asked me how I did it, and I explained the cables and things to make it all work- I always did that- and I could see him thinking. You can tell when somebody is thinking, so he now knew I could do that, so he was going to push it further; he's going to push me as far as he can.

Lo and behold, the phone rang half an hour later, and he said [imitating Kubrick] 'Stuart, I've been thinking about this, and I want them to snarl with their teeth closed!' and I thought, 'Oh, you rotten sod!' I knew he was going to come up with something, because he knew exactly by opening it, what made everything work, so now I had to do it without opening the mouth, so I had to work out how the hell I was going to do that, because it was the opening of the mouth that was the motivating force for all the other movements! I knew he had done it to me before with things like that and I knew him by now, so I didn't care what he asked for, I was going to make it work somehow or another. I never fail, so if he wants it to do that, I'll do it.

I got to thinking about it and I worked out a way of doing it. All I had to do was make it so there was a little bit of a gap [dialogue momentarily inaudible] so the jaw of the mask wouldn't open at all at this point, because I've got a little freedom now before it connects to the false jaw, so they can now put their own tongue through the front teeth, and I added two little toggles to the acrylic toggles I had already made, that came from the fishing line that operated from the hinges of the false mouth, that pulled the top lip up and the bottom lip down.

So I've now got two toggles on the top one that did the same thing, because I brought them down in front of the artist's own lips, which was the back of the throat part of the mask, so all they had to do was open his mouth a little bit, put his tongue out to that toggle and it would raise the left top lip a bit, and to the right, it would raise the right side, and if he rolled his tongue between the two, he could snarl, and it worked beautifully. So I said, 'Stanley, I think I've got what you want; do you want to have a look?' so he came in–

How long did this take?

It must have taken me another week to work it all out, make the extra toggles, fit them and try them. He came up and the artist did what I told him to and snarled and once again, Stanley said, 'Hm… hmm…' Away he went and I thought, 'I wonder what he's thinking now to cook up!' but fortunately he couldn't think of anything else in time, so that's what happened and I think we got through the film without failing on anything that he asked us to do. He tried hard, which is good for me, because it made me do things I never thought I could or would have done, or even thought of trying and it's only because he set me up on this that I had to beat the situation and do it. I didn't have any choice.

A lot of people who talk about your work on *2001* seem to focus on the apes, but not on the old age makeup you did on Keir Dullea, which was quite complex.

It was. The veins were all pulsating, and I was standing behind the camera with a little bulb pulsating them. I know it would have stood a close-up, but for some reason, Kubrick was a little bit scared, so he didn't come in anywhere near as close [with the camera] as I wanted him to. I felt he could, but for some reason, he thought maybe something wouldn't be quite right, so he was a bit nervous about it.

The character wasn't so much old as ancient, was he?

Yes, he was very ancient. The script was a bit difficult to understand anyway, I have to say, but he was described as being somewhere around 120 years old, or so I was told.

And a very young actor to transform.

He was 24, so we had to gradually get up into that age, but I had so little time. I hadn't had a reason to take a cast of Keir Dullea. I had been casting all the apes, but Keir Dullea was a straight make-up as a young guy. That makeup was a bit complicated, because I had to make him look very subtly, without anyone really noticing any differences that the years were going by and he was getting more concerned and changing in his personality, so there were different things I did in the makeup. Right at the beginning he was young-ish and full of fun, but he was going on these very long trips and things were happening and they didn't know where or what was happening. If you go into a simulator, it's similar to that. The brain has to work it out, and going through space, which a human being had never done before, with all these different outside visions that he was getting, the brain has got to have an answer to it, so to simulate that, the brain has to give you an answer to it, and that caused him to think in a certain way and go along with it, which was something he had never experienced before mentally, so the answers were coming to him with this strange way that the brain does work.

When you dream, they are simulations of your experiences, so you might be mentally disturbed through things that have happened, or maybe there's some physical pain you're suffering while you're asleep and the brain gives you an answer, therefore you dream. Well, it's the same sort of thing with all this going out into space. It's almost like a dream, and your brain is letting you visualize all these things that are not really there, but this is what it looks like and that's what the audience didn't really understand. All of those fabulous visions are only in his mind and not for real. It's all a simulations, and it's the brain giving the answer. It's all a dream that he's going through, and at the end of it, he has to look completely mystified. After all, he's only a human being, but with all this long-distance traveling and whatnot.

What did you do as far as the makeup is concerned?

There were subtle differences in my highlights and shadows, hollowing out the eyes and things like that, and doing a slight aging to make him look that little bit different, according to the moods he would be experiencing and suffering through during that time. There were a lot of subtleties that I had to stop and think about.

Stanley had given me a rough idea but not going into those details, but I had to try and make it look real, because that's what would happen. And also, you would get the other crew for instance, that's put to sleep, so they are in their hibernation coffins and when it's time for them to wake up to take over, because the humans are not going to live that long anyway, and when we go out into space, they say it's almost certain that is going to happen, so we had the specialists with us all the way through the film, who had succeeded in doing this with rabbits and other creatures and it works.

Given certain chemicals and temperatures and all of that, they were semi-frozen, but they were able to slow the heart be down so they lived that much longer, so they say it's possible and it works with these creatures. They hadn't done it on a human being yet, whether they have done it now or not, I don't know, maybe they have, but they were very close to and they said it was very feasible. They had been working on it for quite a long time and said, 'We are going to go out into space so this is what we've got to do and it will happen,' so that was interesting. So we had all of these things, and one has to bear in mind when you're working on this kind of film that you have to go into these subtleties and show them.

So it was expanding your mind at the same time.

Exactly that.

How many days did you do the full aging makeup?

It took quite a few hours to do it. We were shooting it all day, so I said, 'I don't care what time I start, if it's three in the morning if necessary so you can have them on set by 8:30, but try and shoot it all in one day!' Because it was something they sprung on me quickly; it originally wasn't going to be in there, so it was something extra they had put in.

That he was going to be aged?

Yes, that wasn't in the original script. It came up quite a bit later, so I didn't have a lot of time to do anything about it because I was still doing all the other things that Stanley wanted. Making up the artists was just a small part of my job, but I was still perfecting all the other creatures and masks and things for the other scenes. I needed to do a life cast of him to do it, because I had to make all those pieces, and as I say, we only had one Sunday off in three so I was working 16 to 18 hours a day, seven days a week. I was pretty damn tired, but this meant I had to work on my one Sunday off to get Keir Dullea in to do a life cast of him, because I was full up with doing other things all day long, and now I had model all those pieces, seven different sections separately modeled to make foam rubber pieces and cook them all.

I put them in the oven and very early the next morning, and took them out very early the next morning when they were about cooked. I didn't even wash them, I had no time, but fortunately for me, they were perfect. This was still the early days of foam rubber, so nine times out of ten you had to do it again, but they came out right so I was so lucky. I put them straight on him and did the whole thing without any trial or error; I didn't have time to practice it, I just did it for the first time, once only, and it was an enormous strain doing it, so I said, 'All right, please try and shoot this and tell the folks that you are going to be shooting late so they expect to be working late,' so we did. Fortunately they knew the problems I was going through, so it was pretty late and I went on the set to see how it was all going and Stanley said, 'Stuart, I'm having a few problems here; I don't think I'm going to shoot it all in one day; what about carrying on tomorrow?' I said, 'Please, don't do that! I'm sure the rest of the crew will understand.'

And you didn't have another set of pieces ready.

I said, 'I can't make them in time; it's not possible!' There were one or two people who wanted to go home, but the majority of them said, 'We understand; we're staying!' so they stayed and finished it. Some of them went, but they managed to get other people in. Fortunately for me they were on my side and knew what I was going through so they stayed put and finished everything in the one day, so that was it. They couldn't come back and say, 'We want another little bit of this!' because I was still fully occupied with everything else and didn't have time to fit it in anymore.

Did you ever speak to Mike Westmore when he was doing *2010* and had to replicate your makeup?

No, I remember thinking about it, and expected to hear from him, but I never did, so I thought okay, fine, he's making do on his own, so he never did, no. I think he did quite well, considering it was a difficult thing to do. It wasn't quite the same, but it's a difficult job, being thrown in there like that. I know what it's like, and it's not easy doing something like that, when somebody else has done it and try to make it look the same, but I thought he just about got away with it.

Was *2001* worth the two years you put into it?

It was, yes. It was tough for me, but I was young enough to take it, so I thought, 'This is it, I'll never get another opportunity like this!' It was wonderful, because I learned so much and money was no object, so I could bring in specialists from chemical companies to advise me on different things that I never would have been able to talk about on another film, so I took advantage of that. I had to anyway, to succeed on that film and make things work. But I wouldn't want to do another one like that less than every five years or so! One experience like that is enough.

You worked with Kubrick on *Dr. Strangelove*, which featured Peter Sellers, who could also be quite demanding, so you had a tough actor *and* a tough director. Was that difficult to resolve?

Not really, because I still did what I wanted to do and the artists (fortunately) usually go along with me. Peter Sellers knew me well enough, because I had done something like 16 films with him, and it was usually some heavy characterization, so he trusted me enough to not question it at all and just get on with it.

On *Dr. Strangelove*, it was three different parts he was playing. He was also going to play the pilot who drops the atomic bomb instead of that lovely comedian fellow who played it in the end, but I had many meetings with Kubrick and Peter Sellers at Peter's apartment in Hampstead, so I used to go up there and the three of us would talk about it and Peter said, 'I don't think I want to play two American characters; I've got to have two entirely different characters; a southern drawl and an American president accent, so I'm a little bit scared of taking those two characters on!'

Kubrick said, 'Oh, don't worry, I want you to play all four parts,' so I did makeup tests for him as the southern pilot and we shot it for about a week, but instead of the southern drawl, he would suddenly come up with the American president accent, which didn't fit at all, and Stanley would say, 'Cut, no, this is the other character!' Peter would get fed up and go screaming mad, so in the end, he said, 'No, I can't do it, I'm not going to do it!' which upset Stanley but anyway he didn't do it and Stanley had to get Slim Pickens, who was a lovely little fellow and great fun, so Sellers just played the three parts in the end as the president and the other two characters.

Were they supposed to look completely different, or was the conceit that it was obviously Sellers playing all three characters?

I never knew why they wanted one actor to play so many parts. I often used to puzzle over that, and why they didn't get other actors for that. What was the idea of him playing all these different parts? But they seemed to want it that way, and the more parts they could make an actor play- I don't know if it was cheaper or what it was- but I can't imagine it would be, because they still had the artist working for whatever many days it was, so I could never really work that one out. And it wasn't just Peter Sellers; it was one or two other actors as well, who played several parts, but especially Peter of course. There was only one film out of the 16 I did with him where he just played one character, and it was serious acting, no comedy and he was brilliant. I didn't expect that; I thought he was used to playing comedic characters.

Did you work with him on *Being There*?

He was in the States at the time and I was working on another film at Pinewood or somewhere, and this American lady turned up one day and said, 'Peter Sellers has sent me over from the States; he's coming over to do this film, *Being There* and he would very much like you to do his makeup.' I said, 'I'm very sorry, but I won't be able to, because this one is going on for so long.'

She said, 'He'll pay you anything you ask!' and I said, 'That's really nice of him but I can't do it; I've got to keep my name in the profession, so I can't suddenly chuck a film however much it paid. It's entirely against my principles; I would just take my normal salary and that's it if I could do it, but I would never do that to anybody, so I'm very sorry, tell him thanks very much but I will not be able to do it.'

She kept coming back day after day, because he told her to try again and again, but in the end she went away and I never saw her again, so I don't know who did it. I understand it was a very good film and I would have loved to have done it, but it was just impossible.

Do you find a lot of comedic actors aren't that funny in person?

Peter was very moody. There were times when he would be great fun and chatting as one of the boys. He was great in the early days, and he was never moody, but unfortunately because of complications in his married life- I knew his wife and I used to go to his home, and then something happened- I think he had a bit of an affair with Sophia Lauren and that busted it all up, so they separated, and of course he would try to live with, or marry, the leading actress of nearly every film he worked on. I would see that going on and think, 'Oh my God!' But there were times when that all went wrong, and he would come in and be so moody.

There was one character that took me a long time, like a three-hour makeup with everything on him, so he sat there and I thought, 'Oh God, he's in one of his bad moods!' But this time he was quiet, so I did the whole thing and when I finished, he said, 'Call Burt for me,' Burt was his man, his driver and the guy who looked after him. He was always sitting in the hall outside, so I opened the door and said, 'Burt, the governor wants to see you!' and he said, 'Let's go home!' so he went home with that three-hour makeup I had just put on him and that was it. That's the way it was.

After that, he went to the States to make a film. I had worked with Britt Ekland, and I knew Britt and did one of the Pink Panther films with her, and he married her and went to the States. This was a few weeks after he married her, but she already had a film to do in England and then was going over to join him. I was making her up, and the phone on my makeup bench went off and it was Peter. He said, 'Stuart, have you got Britt with you?'

I said yes, 'and he said, 'I'd like a word with her!' I was just fixing the eyelashes on her, and she picked up the phone and said, 'Oh, hello, Pete… oh no, I can't, I can't… no, I've been shooting for three weeks already… no, no, I can't!' She finally put the phone down and said, 'He wants me to go over there and forget this film and just walk out!'

We carried on filming for the day, and the next morning, same thing, the phone went and it was Peter again. She said, 'No, Pete, I told you, there's no way I can do it… oh, well, all right!' and I thought, 'She can't mean it, something is going to happen!' Anyway, I had the makeup ready on my makeup table ready for her and I sat there waiting, and the assistant came out and said, 'Britt, will be in any moment!' so I sat there waiting for to turn up.

Half an hour went by, the assistant kept coming in and said, 'Where's Britt?' I said, 'She hasn't turned up yet; that's unusual, she's usually right on time.' An hour went by and the director came in and said, 'What's happened to Britt?'

I said, 'Well, I would say she's on an airplane at this moment, going to the States!' He said, 'Oh come on, don't be silly,' and I said, 'Well, we'll find out, won't we?' and she *was* on that plane that morning, so instead of coming in , she was flying over there and that was it, they had to scrub everything they had shot and start over again.

I don't know whether they sued him and made him pay for everything; they probably did, but I don't think he cared very much about it. [This was March, 1964 and she was working with Attenborough. Fox sued her and put her on suspension for two years]. Anyway, we got Mia Farrow in to take her place and we started all over again with Mia Farrow. I liked Peter very much, in many ways, but he had these bad bits, so unfortunately he was capable of that.

One thing people tend to forget is a makeup artist is also a psychologist, a marriage counselor and all sorts of other things.

Oh yes, you do get quite a lot of that, which you have to put up with.

Did you do any of the Pink Panther films with Peter?

Yes I did one with Sellers, the first one he did in Rome, *A Shot in the Dark*, the very first one. Actually, *Shot in the Dark* was the one I did, and that was the second one. The first one was called *The Pink Panther* and the second was *A Shot in the Dark* and that's the one I did. He went out to Rome and asked me to do it and I said, 'I'm sorry, but I won't be finished in time,' but then I finished and that's when Kubrick wanted me for a film; I don't remember if it was *2001* or *Dr. Strangelove*, so I said I had to be back in time for that.

He said, 'Look, I've got another film to do back in England, not another Pink Panther,' so he wanted me to do that one which I did, with some complicated makeups, and he said, 'I won't have time, I've got to know exactly when I finish *The Pink Panther* in Rome, I've got to come back and start it immediately,' but he had to have all the makeups sorted out and the director had to see them in order to know that they are going to work.

He So said, 'I want you to come to Rome with me, all expenses paid and we'll set you up in a nice hotel, and in the evenings and when I get any days off, I want you to make me up and we'll film all the different makeups and we can send them to the director.'

So I went to Rome and did it, because I had a few weeks in-between and was able to do that. I didn't make him up for the film, that first one; the Italian boys did that one. Anyway, I came back and we did this other film and from there on, I did the film with Kubrick, and after that I did another Pink Panther, the one we just mentioned.

[A gap in conversation, as we look at a long list of Stuart's films]

You worked on *A Matter of Life and Death*?

We did that at Denham Studios. This was just after the war, because I went back to Denham, which didn't close up until 1950-something, maybe 1952.

[*The Million Eyes of*] *Sumuru*, that was the one with Shirley Eaton, who was in the 007 film *Goldfinger*, where she had to be painted gold all over, naked, so all she wore was the gold paint. The problem was of course, you have to have at least four inches of skin exposed.

I Was Monty's Double. During the war, they wanted to make the journalist think that we were going to make a bigger test of North Africa and around that way. They couldn't use the real Monty, so they sent their spies out to find somebody who looked like him and there was a comedy actor who looked extraordinarily like him, who they saw on stage and brought him down and put a little bit of makeup on him to make him look more like Monty, not 100% but good enough from a distance. And they put the costume on, and he was acting like him. This guy was still alive by the time we finished the film; I knew he was ill because sometimes when I had him in my makeup chair, he would go funny and I would have to wake him up, but he did the film.

This was based on a real person?

It really happened. So I had to make him up three different ways. I had to make them up to look like he was the double made up to look like himself and then made up to look like Monty and then as the real Monty because we had to have shots that were supposedly of the real Monty, but they couldn't get the real Monty, so I had to make the actor [M.E. Clifton James] up three different ways. So he was playing himself, made up and the real Monty, they were subtle makeups.

Because you didn't want the audience to lose track of who they were looking at.

Exactly, it had to be just enough to show it's not this one or that one, or this time it's that one, so people were convinced it was the one it was. There were subtle little bits of makeup, with enough difference to make all the difference, but they still all had to look more or less the same. The thing was, we flew out from Heathrow to Gibraltar, which was where this actor had actually flown to start all of this, and I was sitting next to him on the plane as we were going out there to film it. We had already done quite a bit of shooting in the studio, but we were now going to the actual locations where it all happened. So we were just going past Barcelona and over the sea down to Gibraltar and this actor suddenly grabbed me. I said, 'What's the matter? Are you feeling okay?' and he said, 'It's bringing back memories. This was exactly the spot where when I was in the plane and it really happened during the war when the pilot said, 'I've got a problem…' It was him and a few other people on the plane, and the pilot said, 'I might have to ditch and we might have to drown, because something is done wrong and I have a shortage of petrol, and we mustn't be found alive, because millions of lives depend on this!'

Wait, the actor who played Monty's double *was* Monty's double?

It was the same guy. So he was now in a plane, the same way he had been in real life, and I happened to be sitting next to him when he said, 'My God, this is where it was almost certain that we were going to have to die!' So the tension was terrible, but we finally made it, We came into that little bit that was half in the sea in Gibraltar where you've got to hit it right with the first few inches; otherwise you could fall off the other end back into the sea and the rocks, so it was all very tricky. They said it seemed like they were going to have to ditch, knowing what it meant that they mustn't let the enemy know that they were doubling in any way, so that was the true situation that really happened.

Anyway, we went on and finished it and went to all the places in North Africa and along the southern coast of Spain where he exhibited himself, because they were hoping that some of the spies around would say they had seen him and he was there. So that all happened in real life and we were doing it all again, with the same guy, so that was amazing.

Dam Busters was another interesting one. It was a true war-time story, where we sent the bomb to blow up the dams in Germany.

I don't suppose you've heard the real story? In actual fact, a guy painted this particular bomb, a big bomb that was underneath the plane, and by spinning it backwards, they would drop it at a certain height-it had to be at exactly the right height-and the only way they could do it was to put a light there and when the light got to a certain point, they knew they had got exactly to the right height, and they would drop it at a certain distance from the dam, it would then spin backwards and then run down. They didn't want to hit it; it had to explode at the bottom near the water without exploding, so by trial and error and spinning it backwards, it would slow up enough and the little spinning would still run it right to the bottom, so they got it weighted just right for it to do that and then blow up. So it bounced a few times and then went down. They tested it in a place that was originally built for propellers on boats and trying out different shaped propellers so that's where he did all his tests on the bomb, so we went and shot it all there same place he did during the war. So the dam busters blew up several of the dams, which then flooded the areas where they were manufacturing all sorts of wartime things, so that worked out, but they lost a lot of planes and men unfortunately.

Anyway, that guy was actually with us, and he took us to his home where he had worked everything out and we were able to film there. So we went everywhere he went when he was testing it, out on the lakes of England, trying it all out until he got it right. So that was quite an interesting film. I didn't work on all of the films on this list, but I wrote them down, because there was a certain connection with them that I wanted to remember, but 90% of them I worked on.

[We end up talking about *The Jungle Book*] I had to teach Sabu English. They got him from India, because he was so good with the elephants on location, so they brought him back to England and he was great. He was a bright young lad, and it was my job while I was making him up to try and bring him up a little bit so I would speak to him all the time and try to teach him English. We used to get in Italian actresses sometimes who didn't speak a lot of English so they would say to me, 'How do you say this?' so I found quite often I was teaching them some English grammar.

[Stuart starts talking about his early film days]. That's when I got involved in aging and realizing there was a lot of room for improvement. Korda said, 'Forget about the existing English crews, they're not very good!' because at the time we were only making 'quickie quotas'. All the theaters were in America and the major films were American films, so the second picture was always a cheap English film, because we hadn't reached the stage they had in Hollywood in those days.

Somehow or another, they got Guy Pearce over and said to him, 'We want you to interview young people that you think are likely to be successful as makeup artists, and train them the Hollywood way,' so I was so incredibly lucky to get in. I don't know why he took a fancy to me, but he would get me on to anything like that to help him with it and eventually do it. In 1937, I was doing all the aging because what was being done at the time wasn't good enough so I thought we needed different methods and different materials which would also be much easier to take off and not do as much damage to the skin, which I did on my own. Guy Pearce liked that, so he used to put me on all of these things and away we went.

[Richard Attenborough] I had worked with Dickie as an actor and did all sorts of makeups on him, including the one before where he was playing Christie the mass murderer of all these girls, which was based on a true story. So I had to make him up as Christie, and he said, 'Stu, I want to direct from now on. I want to ask you a question, because you've been in the business for a while now: there's a part in the film I want to direct, that I would very much like to play myself as well as direct; do you think that's a good idea?'

I said, 'Well, I think I've got the answer and it's no,' because I had been working with Larry Olivier on many films and he started to direct including a couple in which he acted and directed and he suffered very much, so he regretted it and never did it again. He just directed or he went back to acting. So I said, 'You asked me and I told you why, because that was my experience,' and he said, 'I'm glad you said that, because I had a feeling that perhaps that's the way it should be.' So we did the film, which was *Oh, What a Lovely War*.

[Peter Ustinov] He had a great sense of humor. He played Nero, so he used to come in and he had all his robes on so I would be making up Deborah Kerr and some of the characters with beards and things, so there was a lot of that work to do, and the other guy was making up Peter Ustinov, and he would come in with all his robes, almost looking a bit feminine in those robes, but even though he was Russian, he had the perfect accent, so he did a takeoff of a Brighton boarding house lady and he did it perfectly and it fitted what he was wearing, so he did this whole routine as though he was a Brighton boarding house lady in these robes and we all fell apart laughing, which was really difficult when we were trying to make everybody up.

And later on, Mervyn LeRoy the director was starting to get very unpopular, because he used to shout and scream at all the artists and was not a very good director. He made a name for himself, but he was disliked by the artists, so there was going to be this big scene on the back lot out in the open air and Mervyn LeRoy was yelling at them all, and these were all big artists, and he kept on and on and on, and suddenly, as I think I've told you before, Peter Ustinov suddenly did Mervyn LeRoy, a perfect imitation of him and saying all the things that he had just said, and he was shouting them out, one after the other and for quite a long while and Mervyn LeRoy just had to stand there and listen to it, and the rest of the artists clapped like mad when he was finished. He was a fantastic man, with the guts and the nerve to do it, but it made a lot of difference, because he behaved himself after that, because we were just over six months filming *Quo Vadis*.

Part VII: 10/9/97

When Sheelagh and I retuned to finish our conversation the following day, we had a long list of loose ends that I was determined to tie up. That included a bunch of questions about David Lean and specifically Stuart's near-fatal accident during production of 'River Kwai,' although I had no idea the story would end up meandering into so many new and interesting directions.

I also took another crack at resolving the Star Wars cantina question, but again that sadly went nowhere. But having compiled all of Stuart's bits and pieces, there was no shortage of other names and topics to cover...

[We're looking at Stuart's photo albums again, talking about the various people he worked with over the years]

The last time we talked, you had started telling me about Guy Pearce and how he got you in as a makeup artist.

The thing was, I don't know if I mentioned this to you before, Guy Pearce was quite a handsome sort of guy, tall and good-looking, and his wife who was Max Factor's chief hairdresser in Hollywood, came over with him as chief hairdresser doing the same thing; taking on young hairdressers the same as Guy Pearce was doing, and training us all the Hollywood way.

Whenever we got a leading actress, especially a very attractive one, not only Americans but German and French and British; if they happened to be good-looking, Guy Pearce had a hell of a time, because she was so intensely jealous that she would start to make it really difficult for him, so he'd perhaps just do a quick makeup on them and then hand it over to me for some reason. I don't know why, maybe he thought I happened to be better than the others who were doing that kind of thing I suppose, I don't know, it just happened to be, but I was taking over all the leading actresses right from the word go, which I couldn't understand.

That was pretty unheard of at your age.

It was, I just couldn't believe it. I was making up all these leading actors and actresses for the films we did then. [Looking at picture] She had a few little wrinkles, and what I did with her to lose them, I said, 'I think I can lose your wrinkles,' and she was getting worried. This was Gracie Fields. She's dead now of course, but she was very famous in the early days, and then she met an Italian guy and lived out in Capri and died out there. A lovely lady, and a very popular singer. She was basically a singer, who started doing musicals, and I used to do her makeup. To lose some of this here, she had a big wig fortunately, so what I did was put tapes here, pulled it back and hid it under the wig. She said, 'Oh, no one has ever done that before,' so the first thing she'd do was come in and say, 'Have you got my sticky tapes ready for me?' I'd say yes, of course and it was quite a gag between us.

Robert Taylor, who we talked about before?

I used to make him up- I think it was two films he came over and did during that period, and Vivian Leigh on many occasions. I got to know her very well.

You worked with her on films that Olivier was on with her and some he wasn't.

Oh yes, of course. Olivier was on one film and I was making him up, and also making *her* up on a different film. He was married to someone else, and she was married, and it happened to be the time that she came in to me, so I'd finish her makeup, and the next one on my list was Larry Olivier on a different film.

Of course it wasn't long before I realized that there was something going on between them. I would be finishing up, and she'd sit there patiently while I perfected it. The last thing I'd do is the lips, and I'd do as perfect lips as I can, and then Olivier would come in early and stand there watching, which was a bit annoying, but I put up with it, and as soon as I finished, he'd bend down and kiss her, spreading lipstick all over, and he did that not once but two or three mornings where he'd come in and do the same thing. In the end, I was saying, 'Get out of here!' and throwing him out.

This photo is labeled 1937, which is early in your career, isn't it?

I started in April, 1936. He was in every other film that was being made there. Merle Oberon, I made her up quite a lot, and she married Korda in the end, so she became a lady because he became a knight and she became a lady, and she was in the crowd. She was a crowd artist in the early days, but somebody took a fancy to her and gave her a little part, and she was a keen actress and did it well, and they began giving her leading parts. And then Korda took a fancy to her and married her.

When did you work with Edward G. Robertson?
On several films. That was in the early days, round about the late thirties. I think it was '38 or something like that. I can't believe it was after the war. I'm sure it was at Denham, because this I kind of did while I was at Denham.

Here's Sabu, signing it 'To Stu.' You *did Elephant Boy* with him, *Black Narcissus*, and *Thief of Baghdad*.

That's me, eating our lunch. I had a little bit of hair in those days. And here's Charles Laughton, I did so many films with Charles Laughton.

What was Laughton like to work with?
He was a lovely guy, very easy to work with. I liked him, nice fella… These were some of the old makeups we did in those days. I worked with Guy Pearce on all these disguises. Robert Donat of course. I worked with him on so many films, right from the very beginning to when he died. At that point, he was one of the biggest English leading men in films. I had him and Marlene

Dietrich to make up. Guy Pearce came to me and said, 'Marlene Dietrich won't be too much trouble, I want you to look after her on set, but I understand that she likes to do her own makeup, so I said I wouldn't interfere, but I'd like you to look after her and watch what she does so you can check it on the set.'

So I checked a few things on set and did her lipstick for her because she couldn't really do it on the set, and I watched her and she said, 'You know, I think you could do this for me. You've seen me and you know what I've been doing; why don't you try?' so I actually made her up for the rest of the film. I thought that would never happen, and I didn't dare tell Guy Pearce that I made her up.

She was in this bath scene, and in the last shot they were actually filming, as she gets up, she puts a towel around her, and they'd done it successfully two or three times, and then somehow or other, the soap got dropped and she slipped, and the towel went flying, so they got all of her and there was a big thing about the processor, it wouldn't be in the film, but they were keeping it to 'check' it every now and again!

Valerie Hobson. She was a character. A lovely lady, a bit on the wild side, but very nice. Flora Robson, she was hopping from England to Hollywood, did quite a few backwards and forwards. There's Patricia Ellis, in *Paradise for Two*; that's one I haven't written down, another one I've got to add to the list. That was the best studio of all in England. I worked there for three years before the war, and another five years after the war, and then they knocked it all down. It broke my heart, it really did.

Knight without Armor- we had talked about making up animals, and there was something about having to make up horses for some reason. There was some tricky makeup I had to do. On this sort of picture, there were supposed to be these African fuzzy-wuzzies with long straw-like hair and weird makeups with stripes that they put on, but the actors playing the fuzzy-wuzzies were born and bred in London and came down to the studio by train. When they took their clothes off and put a bit of straw around their necks, and I had to extend their ears with a little stick, a bit of a branch stuck in. But then they said, 'Stop!' because they all had vaccination marks.

In those days, and especially on Negroes, those marks come up much bigger than English and nobody ever thought of that. So they just yelled 'Makeup!' and said, 'Fix that!' I thought, what the hell am I going to do, get some scissors and cut them off?

I got my box out, and took out the non-flex collodion for scars which dries out quickly and it sinks in. I've used it for scars as we did in those days, because there was nothing else, and it works very well on the soft parts of the face, and this was soft, so I thought, I'll use that and sink it in until it goes a bit beyond and then I can put hard wax- I had various consistencies of wax- and I put the firmer one on top and put flexible collodion over the top and smoothed it over and then put makeup over that, and it worked fine.

I'd never heard of doing that before, but that's the thing about makeup: you're doing things on the spot and you might never do them again. It's so interesting when you think back about the problems that come up suddenly, and somehow or another, you've got to do it. You know that you've done all these odd things before, perhaps even more impossible and you've done them, so you know you're going to do them somehow, but you don't know how. It's a matter of seconds you've got to think of it, and they're all waiting and getting agitated because they're losing £10,000 a minute.

You worked with Ralph Richardson in some of those early films?

The last thing we did was with all the knights as they were then, they'd all become knights, was the one in Brighton, the Dickie Attenborough one- Sir John Mills, Sir Larry Olivier- *Oh, What a Lovely War*. That was '69. They had all the knights in that, all of Dickie's friends but Dickie didn't become one until after all that, but he's a Sir now. Sir Richard Attenborough, but we just knew him as Dickie.

Sir Lawrence Olivier- I used to swear at him and chuck him out of my room, but it's extraordinary what he went on and became. I worked with him on many films, so many different makeups. I was very fond of him because I got to know him, but I had to finish my makeups by a certain time, and I had other artists after him, so I had to get all of my artists out, on the minute I could, so the others would come in and there was no hold up, because they're not just sitting there in-between. They're either in the hairdressing department or wardrobe department, and we would work it out between us, so the wardrobe department would say, 'We've got to have these people first for a fitting, and you can have them while they're doing that.' The hairdressers will say, 'We've got to do a shampoo first on this actress, and then you can do what you want; when you've done that, their hair should be dry enough,' and then we would finish it off, so the three departments used to sit down together when everybody else had gone home, and work out in what order we wanted our artists, so they were never waiting around doing nothing and they would go from one to the other, so we worked it all out. There wasn't any time to play around, because they had all those responsibilities. They've got to finish him and get him off, because the other departments were waiting for him.

Olivier was a perfectionist, wasn't he?

Oh yes. But you get to know them and how to handle them in that particular way, and they're all slightly different in some way or another. Peter Sellers was fantastic most of the time, and other times he would just be impossible, but you knew his background and you knew the reasons why, so you kind of forgave him and just put up with it. But there were times when he got impossible.

The same with Alec Guinness. I probably told you the story about when we did *Oliver Twist*, he still wasn't very well known. He had only done a little part as Herbert Pocket in the previous film with David Lean [*Great Expectations*] so nobody had seen him, and most of the crew on *Oliver Twist* hadn't met him before. He would come in at half past five and I made him up, and then he went on set, completely covered in this makeup, because he never appears without it all the way through.

When they finished shooting, the crew would go home and Alec would come back to me and I spent some time cleaning him up and taking the pieces off, some of which I was going to use again, so I had to carefully clean him up. And when he went home, there was usually nobody there, because everybody had already gone. We had been doing this for a few months, and one day I started to make him up, and the assistant came in and said, 'Stuart, the director said stop making up Alec Guinness, because certain things have happened, and we can't shoot on Alec today, so whatever you've done, you can take it off and clean him up; he's finished for the day!'

So I cleaned him up and Alec said, 'Oh, I'll just go down on the set and say hello to my chums I've been working with!' So he went on set to say hi and nobody took any notice of him! He didn't know why and kept saying, 'What have I done?' but they didn't recognize him, because they had never seen him without his makeup. He came back to me so upset, and said, 'Nobody knows me!' I said, 'Alec, it's simple, they've never seen you without your makeup!' and he said, 'Oh… of course!'

Speaking of Lean, is it true when they had a big screening of *Bridge on the River Kwai* and Lean attended, where he didn't thank you, he thanked your wife?

Yes, that's true, I had forgotten that. Have I told you the story of what really happened at the end, when they were going to blow up the bridge? They left it to the very end of course, and we were doing it in Ceylon, so they had to get an actual train from where it all happened with the railway lines.

They brought the engine and carriages over from there to Ceylon and they had to build the railway, because they got similar mountings and the river and everything was similar, which is why they chose it, because it was a pretty near match to where it all happened, but a month before, they had to dig out four miles of track, and at the end, there was the bridge and it carried on, but of course it only went on far enough so that the train could stop and they weren't shooting beyond that. So you could see it go over the bridge and it was finished, and after that it was all rocks they had dug out, with the river at the bottom.

They brought in two engine drivers from the area, so one driver drove the train up, and another was on the other side. We did lots of rehearsals, and of course the driver was not going to stay on the engine as it goes over the bridge, because it's going to blow up, so he's got to jump off on the other side without the cameras picking it up.

And when the train comes across the bridge, they would lose it if it shot across too fast, so the driver slowed it down enough so he could jump off and the other driver could jump on and stop it, and there was sufficient distance for it to pull up on the other side before it goes off the edge and into the river and smashes up.

Anyway, I had to make lots of bodies to put in the carriages, which was another little sideline job that nobody ever mentions, which was creating all these bodies sitting in the train. You hardly see them, actually, but they were there just in case. The thing was, to figure all of this out and make it work right, they had five cameras shooting from different positions so when Lean came to edit it, he had a choice of how to build up the tension right up to the last moment, but he needed lots of material to get the timing right and have plenty to choose from.

So they've got the driver, and the train is still way down over the mountains and trees, and as he's driving along, there's a big white cross painted on one tree for him to see, so he knew what to do when he got to it. In order to build the tension, David Lean wanted to hear the engine coming and before you actually see it, you see all the smoke shooting up and the train making noise, and then it comes around. The driver needed to get it up to top speed and there are three gears, so he's got to go one, two, three speeds to the top gear. Before he shoots all the smoke out, he's got to be going at top speed, but after that, he turns it down to second gear so it's slow enough for him to jump out and the other driver to jump on.

They had rehearsed it many times, day after day but they still weren't ready to shoot it yet because they hadn't got it quite right. The timing had to perfect, so David Lean said, 'I will do the timing, and I'll push the button to blow up the bridge, because I don't want the bridge to blow up if something goes wrong,' so it was going to be his responsibility. He didn't want somebody else blowing up the damn bridge if he changed his mind because something wasn't quite right with the timing.

Lean was sufficiently far away from the bridge, so he couldn't really see what was happening but he had it all timed so he could see the engine come out and see the smoke, and he had five little lights in front of him, so if one camera wasn't working, he wouldn't push the plunger to blow up the bridge. He wanted all five cameras working, so if the timing and speed were right and everything was going according to plan and all five lights came up, boom, he was going to blow it up.

We rehearsed it many times and Lean says, 'Action!' The train comes around, and you can see it in the distance from where I'm standing, halfway up this little mountain. The smoke is coming up as the train comes around the corner, but something has gone wrong, and he's going at a high speed, which is going to make it all wrong for David Lean's timing, because the train is going to be over the other side of the bridge before it blows up, so they'll lose the train *and* the bridge and he still hasn't got the shot.

It was a tricky situation, and all the technicians could see what was happening, but nobody knew what was going on inside the engine driver's mind when he had been told that the bridge was going to blow up this time. Only he knew how to get off the train in time, but he had got so nervous that he forgot to bring the train down to second gear. It kept going, and we were thinking, 'This is it, the bridge is going to go any second while the train is going across!' but neither happened. The bridge *didn't* blow up, and the reason was, the cameras were working fine, but in the excitement, one cameraman forgot to put his finger on the button, so only four lights came up and David Lean didn't push the plunger to blow the bridge up.

So the bridge was okay, but what was happening to the train? The generator just happened to be near the rail line just out of sight of the camera, so the genny operator saw the train coming much too fast and realized something had gone wrong, so he backed the generator over the line so the train hit the generator which flew over the edge, and it was a write-off, and the engine zigzagged off the tracks, half-on, half-off and right up to the edge, but didn't go over.

We had two weeks off while they mended the lines and put new wheels on the engine, because they had cracked the wheels, and then backed it up again and then we had to do it again. This time, we used the other engine driver and kept our fingers crossed and I can't tell you the tension, but all the lights came up, the timing was perfect and he pushed the plunger down, and we blew up the train and the bridge. It took months and months to build that bridge.

I didn't realize until I read the David Lean book that you had been in a serious accident on that film, getting thrown from a jeep and nearly getting killed.

Oh yes, I was completely paralyzed for a long time, but I went back to work in a plaster jacket from head to foot, because they wanted to see the bodies lying on the beach and they couldn't get the actors to be lying down there all that time, so they came to me and said, 'Will you make the bodies for us?' so I did life casts of their faces and modeled the bodies and put costumes on them. I used the hotel kitchen oven to cook the foam rubber- I got foam rubber from somewhere and managed to get the right chemicals, and I did foam rubber faces to match the actors, putting hair on them and laid the bodies in there.

This was *after* the accident?

This was after the accident. I could just move around then. At first, I was totally paralyzed and couldn't move at all, and it was hot as well. I was head to foot in solid plaster, and members of the crew would sometimes get time off to see me, because they were working a fair distance away now. They were doing most of the prison scenes with the principal artists, but they would come in and I would be perspiring and irritated because I couldn't scratch or anything. I could speak at that point, but I couldn't move at all at first, and gradually my movement came back. I was still lying there, but I couldn't get up or anything.

I had this terrible Indian barber who would come in and shave me every day, but his mouth was always wide open and his nose was half an inch from my face and his breath was diabolical and his teeth were green and yellow and some were missing and I finally said to the nurse, 'Do you have to shave me?' She said, 'I'm sorry, it's the rules!'

Anyway, members of the crew would come up to me and say, 'Hi, Stinker!' which made me think, 'I can't smell anything, but

I guess you can,' because of all this perspiration underneath the plaster. I couldn't have a bath or anything like that, but at least I got shaved, although I wish I wasn't. They eventually took the plaster off, and made a leathery jacket with steel bars in it, which was wrapped tightly around me, because three of my vertebrae were totally squished. I'm now an inch and a quarter shorter than I used to be, so they never came up again. My neck was nearly broken but not quite.

There was a swimming pool in this hotel, and they said, 'You've got to get in the swimming pool and swim, because you need all the exercise you can to build up your muscles which you've lost,' so I did that, but I wasn't to do anything other than that, until I was able to do lightweight things, which was good.

How long were you hospitalized?

We're talking about weeks. It was towards the end of filming, so I had done most of the tricky stuff and it was getting near the end. But while I was in this jacket and having done some swimming, I was on crutches to start with for a few days and then I managed to lose them because I had learned how to walk again with crutches, so I could walk to the swimming pool and get in and swim, and then I got the use of my arms again. At that point, I had to take up the job again and make those dummies when I was finally able to get back on set.

It must have been scary, spending that time in a hospital so far from home.

It was.

But you persuaded them to put you in a British hospital?

At first, we were taken to an Indian hospital, and that was a terrible experience. I don't even want to think about it, it was so dreadful, and then our first assistant came to see us and he looked around and said, 'Oh my God, I've got to get you out of this!'

From there they took us to more of a nursing home than a hospital. It was an English tea plantation, because there were many

British tea planters out there fortunately, so it was an English tea planter's nursing home; half-Indian nurses and half-English nurses and they were great. The only problem was, I was in a bed upstairs with quite a few stairs, and the cameras for taking x-rays were down below, so they had four Indian guys, a couple of little guys and a couple of big guys who would come in, pick me up and put me on a stretcher but instead of having the tall guy on the bottom, they did it the other way around, so I would scream at them from this stretcher, 'For God's sake, I'm sliding off!'

And when we went up again, it was the same, so they put the tall guys on the bottom and the little guys at the top, but I couldn't get through to them, because they didn't speak any English. So there I was, trying to hang on with nothing to hang on with. I couldn't use my arms, so I just felt myself sliding down, and they just managed to get me up in time. I'll never forget that. But other than that, they were pretty damn good.

Anyway, I rested up for a while when I came back, and then Peter Sellers heard about it, so after about months of being home and resting and exercising, I got a call from him saying, 'I'm doing a film, but I haven't got anything too difficult for you; I would love you to come back and do my makeup if you feel you can, but I promise, I understand your situation, so you'll only have me to do, and you can rest for the rest of the day. It's a straight makeup, nothing too complicated, so you don't have to come to set and look after me. You can just come in and do my makeup.'

I said, 'That would be great, it would help me get my confidence,' so I did that film and they were wonderful and didn't put me through any physical strain at all. After I had done that, I never had long enough between films, because you usually finish one film and go on to another almost immediately or they would overlap, so I would have Kath with me, and after we finished the principal photography, I would say, 'Kath, you finish and I'll start the next one and you can join me when you finish this one.'

We did that several times, so she would go on to the next one and start it off, and if the principal artists went to the end, I would join her. I had my three sons as well, so I thought it was time to take them for a holiday. I thought it should be somewhere interesting, so we went to Zermatt, a little town in Switzerland where the Matterhorn was, so we saw the Matterhorn and all the little mountains where people were practice climbing before they could climb the Matterhorn, so that was interesting.

We were there for a week, and then got on the train and went through Southern France and came home again. But after we left, Kath said, 'I left my dress in the hotel!' We were already on the train so I said, 'Well, I guess you can forget that now!' Anyway, we came home and there was a pile of mail on the floor, and a package. I opened it up, and it was her dress with a note from the hotel. There was a youngish couple at the hotel who we got to know quite well, and she spoke some English, but the husband didn't speak any English at all. Anyway, she said we had forgotten the dress, so here it was. I didn't expect to see it again.

And then I opened a letter that said 'Where the hell are you? We've been trying to get you- will you please answer this immediately? We're going to a place called Zermatt to do a film called *Third Man from the Mountain* and several artists have asked for you, but if you don't answer within two days, we'll have to get somebody else!' I hadn't even opened my bags yet, but I phoned them immediately and said, 'As a matter of fact, I've just come from Zermatt!' so I went right back. This was a year after the accident in Ceylon, and I thought, 'Surely, I'm not going to have to climb the mountain!' but I had to climb to the very top of the Matterhorn!'

I had one assistant with me, and they said, 'You're going to have your own guide, who's going to be with you all the time, and he's going to train you for two or three weeks while we're in pre-production, so you're going to go out and do so many hours of climbing each day, and we'll see how you get on with it.' It was mostly on the glacier to start with, which was a thousand feet deep in the ice and of course the bottom is not absolutely flat. It's got bumps in it, and when it gets to a certain distance, sometimes it will bend around according to where the weight is on this thousand foot-thick ice, so you get crevasses that are sometimes quite wide. Sometimes they're just little ones, but they can close up again as the ice goes up the hill a little bit.

So this had also happened in the real story. What happens is, overnight you get a lot of snow and maybe it just cracks a little bit, so you get this thick snow that packs down a bit when the sun hits it for a little bit. There's more snow on top, and then the ice opens up quite wide while the snow stays quite solid across it so you just can't walk across it; you've got to be very careful where you walk.

We went to the top of the mountain by helicopter, 12,000 feet high, where the air is so rarefied that it has to drop a bit until the propeller can get a grip in the air once it's gone down a bit. It could only take two people at a time, and we had an entire crew, so to get there, it could only take two crew members and a certain amount of gear, goes down and comes back again and then picks up two more, so we would take it in turns as to who was going to be first and last in that order.

We were there for nearly five months, so at the end of the day, if you're on the end, it could well be that the helicopter is not coming back, because the weather has clamped down on it and he could only fly in certain conditions. You might find that half a dozen of us were still there and no helicopter so they would call us on our little walkie- talkies and say, 'Sorry, you've got to walk!' We had these sticks that we would use to poke the crevasses to see if there was a big gap underneath it before you walk on it, so it was very tricky as you had to climb your way home.

So that was the situation, and in the first week, when we got 2,000 feet up and it was nothing but solid ice underneath, I could do the fingers and toes climbing, and then it bent back, so you had to actually bend back a bit, so you were really depending on your fingers now because there was nothing to hold you at all and you were aware of that, and I must say, I was pretty scared looking down, and a lot of people would have given up after two or three days and said, 'I can't do it!' They would have to give up and find somebody else to take over. I only had my assistant who said, 'No way!' knowing there was that 2,000-foot drop, so he would be on his hands and knees crossing, and I said, 'Sydney, what the hell are you doing down there?'

I finally said, 'Look, get up this far and I'll leave all the gear and you can sit here all day looking after it, but I've got to go up there and do your work as well as mine. If I'm short of something, I'll send somebody back, but I can't get all that stuff up there!' so that's what he did and it was entirely me now.

But after a week, this fear suddenly disappeared and I said, 'I'm not scared anymore; it's gone!' When I first saw people climbing, I could barely look, but I was suddenly doing it myself and it was incredible. I hadn't gone to the very top; we were shooting a little bit below on a big ledge, and then we very nearly got to the end of filming, and we had some other shots to do down below, so you come halfway up by train and you go to the next place in little huts before you do the big bit, so I thought, this is it now, I've got to go to the top!

By then, the entire crew was going down in a long, thin line climbing down and guide had gone down with them, so I thought, 'They're a bit slow, I can get down there and catch them up before they get to the little railway station!' so I went along the ledge until I saw what was called a 'chimney,' which is a hole going right up, and then there's this 2,000-foot drop and it meant standing on the edge, putting your foot out, putting both hands out and then your other foot and walking up the chimney, but if you slip, there's nothing to slip on to because it goes straight down. So I looked at it and thought I would do it, but then, oh my god, perhaps I might get to the top, but when I come down, how am I going to get back? It could be worse, and I could be absolutely exhausted by now, so that scared the daylights out of me, so I said forget it.

And then I saw some of the strata, all the lines of the rocks going up and I thought, 'That's the way up, I can do that, I can go up that way!' but it was split quite wide, like a V cut into it, so I thought I would reach across and get my fingers in and then put my foot across and then let go and swing my body over, so it was a bit tricky, but I've got to do it, so I went over and did it and went up to the top and there were clear skies still, so I go to the top and it was fantastic, and this one white cloud came up and hit me and it was full of ice. So I came down and got to this V, but I had made a mistake: in my hurry, I had gone a bit too high, and this time the V cut was wider there and I thought, 'I can't reach it, what am I going to do?' So I went up to the top again and came back down, but this time it was really full of ice and it was all I could do to get myself over.

At one point I thought, 'I'm never going to do it!' because I couldn't get a grip enough to let go on the other side, so my mind went blank. I thought, 'I can't stay here, but I can't get across!' so I blanked out for a moment, until a minute later, I found I was climbing again and I was on the other side- I had done it without knowing. Something had taken over, and I can't remember ever doing it. I remember trying it and getting so scared that my mind went blank on it, but my subconscious mind took over and took me across, so I was doing it and I'll never forget that, even though I can't remember doing it myself. I don't know if my eyes were still closed or not, but I went along and I just couldn't believe it, and I climbed down as quickly as I could, until I saw the little trail of people and my guide was walking back towards me, so he came up to me and said, 'I vas watching you; you vas in big trouble, vasn't you?' I said no, I wasn't, and he said, 'Oh yes, you vere!' so we rejoined with the rest of the group and quite rightly, they gave me quite a ticking off when I got back to the hotel, because they had seen me too and said, 'You should never have done that!'

I said, well, I had to, because only a year ago, I was totally paralyzed with all my bones broken, so I had to prove to myself that I could do something a bit more out of the ordinary. That's all I wanted to do, to know I was back in this world again.

You mentioned a movie with Peter Sellers, but you also did *The Naked Truth, The Mouse That Roared*, and *Tom Thumb*, which all took place in that period.

I think *The Naked Truth* was the one. With *Tom Thumb*, Charles Parker got the credit for that one, because he started it while I was on something else and then I joined him because Peter wanted me. I didn't get a credit, but I made up Peter Sellers and few others as well. My niece was a dancer and would occasionally dance in a film, so she happened to be on that one. It was the first time we had ever been on the same film, but she had danced across Italy and Europe and would occasionally do the odd film.

Changing the subject completely, I recently saw *The Importance of Being Earnest*.

Edith Evans, my goodness. After that film, she had problems with her eyelashes and I invented a special eyelash glue that didn't have any effect and was much easier to use. She liked to put on her eyelashes for the theatre and whatnot, and forever afterwards she would write to me and say, 'Can you please send me another bottle of that special eyelash glue?' so I would send her bottles of that glue. I also used to send false noses to other young ladies who had nose jobs done that had gone wrong so I would quickly do a cast and make a nose for them, and years later, I was still sending them noses, even to Australia.

I think I told you about one girl who was a swimmer and a dancer, who did a lot of high diving, and she thought she would have a nose job. She was very attractive, but her nose was a bit big, and people were all having nose jobs back then, so it was all going fine, but they said, 'You mustn't dive for four months!'

After about two and a half months, she was one the top of the diving board and she couldn't resist it; she had to dive, and it all ripped off and became scar tissue, so they said, 'There's nothing we can do, we did tell you, and we can't do anything for you!' So she had this horrible mess, and arrived one morning and they sat her in my chair and I thought, 'Oh my God!' She had some wax over it, so she explained what had happened, and I had to make a nose there and then for the rest of filming. And then I made her some proper noses that she could put on herself and gave her a big box full to take away and she loved them.

I also had a French girl who had done the same thing, where something had gone wrong and her nose was scarlet, but they wanted to shoot with her that day. It was all greasy, but she said, 'That's special ointment and I mustn't take it off!' so she had this terribly scarlet nose with all this grease on it and I mustn't touch it, but now I've got to make her up to look right, so I did another quick 'nose job,' doing a little cast over the grease with some special material I had to go over it, so when I took it off, it still left some of the ointment on it.

And then I made a little skin nose which took about a quarter of an hour to make. I put that on top of the grease, painted it around the edges and it worked fine. We shot the rest of the film with her and she went back to Paris and I had a letter from her saying, 'Just to let you know, my nose is perfectly all right now. It's all healed up, and thank you for what you did; allowing me to work without any more damage to it!' So that was another success, and I didn't have to keep sending her noses!

Changing the subject again, I was surprised that you worked on *Things to Come*.

The Shape of Things to Come, that's right. The film had already been made, because I saw it before I ever got into film, but there was something a bit missing about it. They had somehow cut a big chunk of it out, so something wasn't quite right. As soon as I got to Denham Studios, they decided to redo it or at least that section of it, which was quite a big bit and perhaps blend it in with what they had already done. I thought, 'This is extraordinary, it's a film I've already seen and now I'm working on it!' That was just a few months after I got into the studio.

Do you remember *The Man Who Could Work Miracles*?

That was early on too. We had a special Hollywood special effects man who came in to work on that, because we didn't have much in the way of people at Denham who did those sorts of jobs. Up until then, it was just 'kitchen sink' films, where you didn't need anything. They avoided films that needed any special work done on them, but Korda changed all that. If he didn't have the right specialists, he would get them from Hollywood, so I met a lot of interesting people and got to know them, and saw them many times since when I was over in Hollywood.

I assume all of that came to a head with *Thief of Baghdad*.

Oh yes, everything was in that film. For the time, it was pretty big stuff. That one was extremely interesting, because they were doing things that had never been attempted in England before.

We had guys, some American, some English who came in and had an opportunity to really go into all of those things, which was extremely interesting. It fascinated me, although I wasn't doing any of it, but I could understand what they were trying to do, so I got very interested in how they were doing these special things.

I did get on set quite a bit, but during the day you get artists who come in later on, because they're not in the first scene so you've got to go back to the makeup room and make them up throughout the day, so you miss quite a bit. We were also working on quite a number of other films at that point, so there were a lot of principal actors that had to be made up, and I would often be in the makeup room rather than on set. We would have assistants that would be on set while I was up in the makeup room nearly all the time in those days. There were times at night where we might be standing by on set, because we didn't have all the actors working. (Oh, before I forget, Kath left instructions for how to make a good cup of coffee, so if you decide you want a cup of coffee, let me know!)

What did you have to do with Rex Ingram as the genie? I remember working with Guy Pearce on him. Whenever he had to do a bald cap, I was always with him doing it, because it took two people to get it in place right, so I did a lot of that. I remember working on Queen Victoria, from a young woman right the way up to when she was 60-odd years old or more.

I find it interesting to look at some of the trends you were involved in, because there were a lot of war movies at one point, and suddenly nobody was making war movies.

They didn't want to know about it anymore. There were a lot of post-war films about the war, but they quickly packed them up, because people had enough of the war, and that's when we changed to musicals. It was a good time for musicals that cheered people up a bit, because they'd had enough of the war.

Let's go back to David Lean. You worked with him at the very beginning of your career, didn't you?

As I said, we worked on a lot of films in those days. David Lean didn't really start until the end of that period at Denham, maybe 1938. I have a feeling that David Lean didn't appear on the scene until '38. I'm not aware of him being around before that. I worked with him a lot just after that, from 1947 on.

You did one of the Muppet films, *The Great Muppet Caper*?

They were coming to me a lot in the early days, because they didn't know how to do foam rubber, which they started to use in making creatures. Before that, they would have a chunk of foam and they would shape it by scissoring it and cutting it up, but of course it would wear out after a while, or things would happen to it, so they had to have a new one and somebody had to sit down and scissor it and make it look the same. They found it was very difficult doing it that way.

I was working at Elstree Studios at the time, and Henson had a big section of it, so I was introduced to everybody because I heard about them so much. So they said, 'We know what you've done with foam rubber; will you please teach us how to use foam rubber?' They explained that when they did their creatures like Miss Piggy, they used them so much that they had to keep making new ones, which was difficult. Dick Smith wrote and told me about it, because they weren't too far from where he lived, so he said he went along and tried to explain foam rubber to them, but somehow they never really got into it. Maybe they did some, but this group didn't really know how to do it.

So I said, 'I thought Dick Smith had already advised you on all of this!' They said, 'Well, no, it hadn't got to us; that was a different section of the company!' I didn't know they were split up like that, but anyway, I was working on something else at the time, but in-between, they said, 'We'd like you to work on our next film and do some makeups for us, and also at the same time, give us some more know-how to creature-making! That was fun to do, because they were a nice bunch and Jim was a great guy. I loved working with him, and fortunately I got to know him, and his buddy Frank Oz, so when Gary Kurtz, who was one of George Lucas' producers, we were talking about Yoda and how they were going to operate it.

As we talked about before, I said, 'I'm not going to have time to operate it myself, because I've already got so much to do; I'd like to get somebody to operate it.' He asked who I would suggest, and I said, 'Well, I only know one person who's really good and that's Frank Oz, but whether or not we can steal him from Hensons, I don't know,' but Kurtz said he would give it a try and we got him. I created the mechanisms and taught him how to use it and Frank Oz provided the voice as well, so that solved two problems: the voice and somebody I could rely on who was experienced in puppeteering.

Are they going to follow those principles when they do the new Yoda?

I should think so, because I don't see any other way they can do it. They had the original head and analyzed all the mechanisms, and I went through it all with them a few times, but I don't think you'll be getting Frank Oz interested in doing it, because he's directing his own films now.

Did you have to explain to Irvin Kershner on '*Empire*' how Yoda worked?

I had to have little sessions with him, so he knew what it could do and couldn't do. I explained the movements to him so he didn't have to spend a lot of time asking me to change things, if there's another area he felt we needed, perhaps we could add something to it, but we basically left it as it was because there was going to be time to do much more anyway.

The idea of doing a puppet character was unheard of at the time, wasn't it?

I think Yoda was the first time. They said it would normally be considered makeup because there was an actor inside it, and I could understand that, but Yoda was only two feet high and all you've got is a human hand, so is that still a makeup job'

They said, 'Yes, because you know anatomy, not only of humans but creatures as well, see you would know how to model it, the same way you've been doing mechanical masks on humans, so this is the same thing. It's basically a mechanical mask, and even though it's got a hand inside it, it's still makeup!' so that's how it happened. I did query it, but nobody else wanted to know about.

So you were a one-man effects house for a while.

I was for a while, because there was nobody else doing those things, and because of that, they settled on me.

Was there anybody doing animatronics in England at the time?

Not that much, no. Sometimes when you're forced to do something, you think, 'My God, this is impossible!' but you find a way of doing it, and then you can use it many times after that because you now know how it's done. But there are other things that are so outrageous that you don't ever want do them again, but you sort of know that situation won't arise again. I remember there was a situation with Charlie Chaplin, where he wanted to look much younger and lose this big wodge under his neck, so instead of doing some of the things you do with an old age makeup, you're actually doing it in reverse so you're youth-ifying him instead of creating an old age makeup. That's something you don't do very often, but I later found it very useful when I was working with Peter Sellers, where I was able to take his big double chin away.

When I finished that film and was getting ready to start another one I got this call, 'Stuart, I'm going to a very special do tonight; can you come up to my place and fix my chin for me?' I've had to do a special makeup on an actress many times for special dos, but going to the north of London where he lived was a long way, so I had to say, 'I'm sorry, Peter but I'm starting a new film tomorrow!'

During the '70s and '80s, you trained a lot of new people, didn't you?

I had to, because there was now so much of that specialty work, it was coming up in every film I did, so I had to have a sufficient crew and train them to do certain things. They all had different abilities to do different things, which I got to know, so I would give them special jobs I knew they were good at, and I would select a crew I knew could handle so much. It went on for picture after picture; nearly every film we did called for that kind of work from there on. Eventually of course, the better ones would go off and do it themselves on their own.

Is there anybody that you are particularly proud of, who you gave a start to?

Well, it's difficult to say, because different people were good at certain things.

Do people become more specialized? I know Nick Dudman fell into special effects makeup for example, and that became his area.

I was about to mention him, but I can't really recommend him as a makeup man, because he never seemed to be interested in doing makeup. But I had recommended him for other films where he did some of that specialized work because that's what he knew about. Even now, I was surprised that he wasn't doing any makeup on the new *Star Wars*; he's not even making anything, he's just got a big crew, and he's supervising and that's all.

There's another makeup man I trained, one of my other boys, Paul Engelen, who is doing the makeup. He's a specialist in straight makeup; he doesn't really do effects stuff, but Nick Dudman has quite a big crew up there where they're all modeling away and making creatures, with cables and that sort of thing, and they don't really do anything else. They don't do makeup, and he's sort of supervising them, but I'm sort of surprised that he didn't take over the makeup, because I did try and teach him makeup but he didn't seem to get into that very much and now he's got Paul Engelen to do it for him.

When you got started, it was just makeup and nothing else really.

It was just pure makeup, and I always felt that I was a makeup man. My principal thing was making up the artists and I still do, or I did up to the end, but in addition to that I found that nearly every picture I did ever since *2001* and then *Star Wars*, it was all that kind of thing. I even had to do quite a lot of that on *Superman*. There were lots of little things they came up with that needed that kind of work, which people wouldn't even have dreamed of getting involved with, like the flying and making different size doubles they needed to fit the size of set there were going to make, so I had to make bodies that were the right proportions.

I don't think people are aware of just how much work you did on those films.

I had plenty of work to do on Superman in those films. Chris was marvelous, but I also had to create two different characters that people would know was the same man but at the same time, there had to be sufficient difference that the leading actress in the story wasn't sure and didn't know at first because they were sufficiently different. Only after a while she connects the two as the same person, so I had to make it sufficiently different that in her mind it was believable that she wouldn't know but at the same time, you knew that it was the same man, so how far do you go?

So it was mostly hair?

Highlights and shadows. On Superman himself, I did a nice clean makeup but highlighting his bone structure to make it all stand out. On the other one, I shaded it but not so far that you couldn't see it, because there's a limit on how far you can go but I went as far as I could go in both directions with highlights and then the shading to where I thought I could get away with it, so I did a lot of that on the two different characters. And then of course there was different, strengthening on Superman and softening on eyebrows and other features and things like that on Clark Kent, making subtle changes wherever I could, but physically it could be the same man. People don't realize all of that, and we also the time when Superman got drunk and funny and made a few mistakes and I had to make it look like he had gone off a bit.

Did you work with Richard Donner because you had done *The Omen* together?

I liked him very much. Some people thought he was difficult, but I found him to be marvelous. He had a good brain and he was a strong man with a lot of power and good intentions.

Will a director asked for a specific makeup artist they want on a film?

Yes they do, quite often when they've worked with certain make-up people. Dicky Attenborough was one of them.

But you had already made him up as an actor.

Oh yes, I had made him up on many films, and since then of course, he chose me to do some of his films. He wanted to me to do *Gandhi* in India and I've still got all the drawings I did for the different artists they suggested so I had them all printed up over a period of a couple of years and then the money ran out. And then it suddenly happened and I had already started on *Star Wars*.

Did you hate to lose that one?

I would have loved to do that one, because I had already spent so much time thinking about it and working on it, but I couldn't, so. Tom Smith ended up doing it, who was one of my better boys. Once again, he didn't really get too much into prosthetics. All he ever used was BBC foam which was good up to a point but not the best. He wouldn't ever go into foam rubber for some reason, so if he had to do a false nose, it was BBC in the same thing with eye bags. He was a good artist and he painted beautiful pictures and things like that but he never wanted to get into chemistry at all.

Everybody seems to specialize nowadays.

That's true, but I had to do everything. My main job was make-up, but at times they knew there was going to be a bit more to it than just foundation, lipstick, eyelashes and the odd mustache or two; maybe a bit of aging, so that was all considered makeup, but there was much more to it in actual fact, so I ended up getting into creatures. I never thought I would be making creatures, but once I had done it, I was into creatures. George Lucas was going to do the first *Star Wars* in Hollywood but he didn't like the creatures they were making and then he saw the monkeys in *2001* and wasn't sure if they were real monkeys or not, so he said, 'Are they real monkeys or are they actors made up?' and was told, 'No, they are actors made up as monkeys.'

Lucas asked who did them, and he quickly came over here and he's been over here ever since. But for me, my major job is still making up the actors and actresses. I will occasionally do the special effects on top of that, so you would consider them special effects makeup in creatures and whatnot and all these extra things, because I love doing them, but I haven't gone over to creature-making as though that is what I am going to do from now on. It's just something that happened to be asked for in addition to makeup jobs, so I still think that way. If I went back into doing films now, I would go back as a makeup artist and if they wanted a creature or two, I would throw that in as well. I don't think I've ever changed in the way I thought about it.

I think *Return of the Jedi* was the first time you were referred to a creature designer as opposed to a makeup artist, at least by title.

I suppose it was, but I was making up the artists as well. I think when we were on *Star Wars* it was chief makeup artist, Stuart Freeborn and special creature designer or something like that. That was added on so they had the two different things.

I seem to recall you fell ill at one point on the first *Star Wars* and Rick Baker put together some of the Cantina creatures. How did that make you feel?

Well, they used all of my creatures in the Cantina sequence anyway. They used Rick Baker's creatures out in the street for all of that street stuff where you saw the odd creatures in the street. He did make a set of creatures for the Cantina, but they also had the original ones that I had already made. There were one or two odd creatures but it wasn't entirely Rick Baker's stuff.

I think they wanted to pack as many creatures as possible, so they already had your stuff but wanted more.

In the big scene where they had Jabba the Hutt. I still did Jabba, as well as Chewbacca, Yoda and the Cantina creatures, but there were one of two little creatures that the Hollywood boys did for that scene when they had Jabba the Hutt. That was a complete mixture of my stuff and the Hollywood stuff, but they did use my stuff for the actual Cantina scene. Phil Tippett is a lovely guy and I spent a lot of time with him and his workshop over there and it was fascinating to see what he was doing.

Going back to the names on your list, what was Sean Connery like to work with?

I've done quite a few films with Sean Connery, in the very early days. I found him a very nice chap indeed, very pleasant.

If you get a young actor and train him as a professional, does that help later on?

Kath: It shouldn't be up to the makeup artists to them. It should be the assistants who train them up.

But they do, quite a lot of them, they ask you about people and how to go about this and that. It's amazing what they have faith in you knowing. All the time, you're aware that they're thinking about the part and worrying about whether they're going to make a success of it, they've all got a little tension because they don't know if they're going to get on with the director or the other artists; it's all going on in their minds, because of the things they ask you about and say to you. They get a bit nervous, so you quickly become aware of what's going through their minds, and although there are those who after a while get used to it and don't worry about it anymore; they've made up their minds that they're going to do it this way and that way, and they probably know the director very well and just get on with it, but in the first year or two, they're very apprehensive and they rely on you because you're with them at the time that they're thinking about it most, and part of your job is not just making them up but making them feel good, better than when they first came in. That happened many times.

Did you have actors you knew were going to be big?

That had the potential to become quite a big star? Oh yes, you could sense it somehow. I did that with Sean because he wasn't even known when I first met him. I worked on the second film he ever did, and I thought, 'This guy is going places!' He was kind of direct about everything he did, but pretty positive too, and I felt that he'd got a lot going for him, and by Jove he did. Of course it was the 007 films that really put him on the map; he fitted into that world perfectly and that really made him, but he could change all that and be whatever he was when he did other, completely different films, and he fitted in nicely to almost everything he did.

I was surprised you didn't work on Bond with Sean and Terrence Young.

I had had calls to do them, but I was already tied up. It got to the point where I more or less knew what I was going to do for the next two years over quite a long span. From 1960 on, I got to the stage where I was getting calls not only from England but from the States as well, so I more or less knew what I was going to do, fitting them in, because there might be six of them that I had offers from and I'd say, 'Well, I finish this film approximately such and such a date.'

Anyway, I usually had six films that I could work into, but there were others popping up every now and again, and I'd say, 'Sorry, no, I won't be available.' You never knew whether they were going to be made or not, but they were there, so I kind of had enough to know that I could be working. If some of them didn't happen, I still had others, and I had offers of jobs for two solid years. That went on as the years went by, and I'd be adding to them all the time.

Would you hold yourself open for a really good film, or could you not wait?

There were times when there were certain films that I would dearly love to have done, some I did and some I wasn't able to do because they started early before we finished, but I'd never say, 'I want to turn this picture in now, I've got another one!' Whatever it was, even if it was just two more weeks to go, I would always see it through. You don't do that sort of thing, because there's a little book up there where it all gets written in, and they all know about it. A lot of people have done that I've noticed, and I thought that's one thing I'm never going to do. I'd rather give up the possibility of working on a good picture but still have my name in that book as being reliable right up to the very end, so that's a principle I always worked on.

I always knew the company I had just worked with would ask me again, and they would also tell other people. A lot of that goes on, where people say, 'Who did you use for that particular job, and were they any good?' It goes on all the time, so apart from doing a good makeup job and making the artist happy, you've got to make a good impression with the production company, because they're going to be asked by other people.

Over the space of ten years, at a certain point in time every year, we worked on an American film in Italy, because American companies were interested in coming over to Europe and the cheapest place in those days was Italy. Money was the big thing, and apparently it was getting to be very expensive in Hollywood, so I would then get phone calls from American companies saying, 'We're going to make a film in Italy, and would you be available to come over as chief makeup artist? We'll pick up an Italian crew, and you can select your crew.' I had done several films before that, but I didn't know there was going to be ten years of it, and then that company would go back and another company would know about it because they wanted to go to Italy, so they would say, 'We hear you went to Europe; we want to do a film there, so who do you recommend?' They would take one or two people from England as heads of department and pick up their crew over there, so every year for ten years running, we had this happen, where we worked in Italy and it was all because one company would pass the word. And then very suddenly, it all ended the same way that France did, because it was too expensive.

The studios are going to a lot of ex-Iron Curtain countries now.

Our last film was in Hungary, wasn't it? Once again, an American company; it was a television film for TNT, a wartime true story, *Max and Helen*. It was a mixture of American and English artists and one or two Hungarian. It was for television. But yes, Sean Connery was a great guy, because he had nothing when I first worked with them and he said, 'Stu, I bought a car, the first car I've ever bought; it's in the car park, come down and see it!' so I went down with him, and he said what you think?' and I had never seen such an old banger, but I said, 'It's great, what a nice car!' But more recently, I was talking to him and he has his own bank to handle his money, because he's made a lot of money, so it was a bit different from buying those old bankers.

Kath: He used to say, 'You must always study the small print of your contract. That's the most important part of your contract!' He just goes about everything in a very businesslike manner.

Did I tell you the story of when I worked with him in Oslo? Before that, we had gone off to South Africa for holiday for a few weeks but I had a call to go to Elstree Studios to do *Orient Express*, so I said okay, and when I got back they said there was a delay money-wise, so 'We'll let you know but it could be weeks yet or even months maybe.' In- between that time, I had a call from Sean Connery saying, '*Thunderball* is going off to Oslo to make the film, and would I be available to go with him, just to make him up? He was probably the only English actor there, so I said fine.

Everything was going okay and towards the end, I got a call from Sean saying, 'Stu, you might be interested to know that I had a call from Elstree Studios for this film,' and they wanted him to work on *Orient Express*. I said, 'Oh, that's strange, I went up and saw them about it and it was delayed, so I came here with you, so they've obviously got somebody else now.'

He said, 'What I wanted to tell you was, there are lots of artists in it, and I put it in my contract that I want to take my own makeup man, and I'd like you to work with me on that picture.' I said, 'Fine, I wasn't able to do the picture, so I'll come with you instead and just make you up!' but when I got there, they told me about how Charlie Parker had failed miserably on it and asked if I would forget Sean Connery because he was only a straight makeup. I said, 'Well, you'd better ask Sean about it, because he asked me to come in and do it with him!' So they talked to Sean who said, 'I understand the situation, so okay,' so I never made up Sean at all on that film, because I was tied up with all the other characters. I ended up taking over some of the tricky makeup jobs and principal artists, while somebody else handled Sean which was a fairly straight makeup. But he's such a nice guy to work with; sometimes it's nice to just do a straight makeup for a change. It was going to be a holiday for me.

One of your last films was *Haunted Honeymoon* with Gene Wilder?

That one was fun to do and he's lovely guy. I wanted to go see him in this show he was doing in the West End [a Neil Simon play] and knock on his dressing room door. He was a lovely man, but he had personal problems all his life; well, not in the beginning, but once he separated from his first wife.

Kath: He made most of them himself.

Yes, he did actually. He did a few things wrong here and there, so I suppose you could say he brought it on himself, but other than that, he was a great guy.

Did you do the Dom DeLuise character?

That was wonderful, because I knew Dom DeLuise from other films, and on this one we made him up as a fat lady, and he was just great. He was so funny and so nice. He was in most of Gene Wilder's movies, like *Sherlock Holmes Smarter Brother*.

Is that the one where Christopher Lee played his brother?

Kath: They were making a straight Sherlock Holmes at Elstree while we were making *'Smarter Brother.'*

I didn't know until we talked about it that you did a Dracula film with Christopher Lee.

I did a Dracula *and* a Fu Manchu. We did Dracula in Barcelona with Christopher Lee and Fu Manchu in Rio.

Kath: I wasn't working, so I spent my time on the beach. I came out for holiday.

She needed it, because it was just after *2001* and we'd been working very hard, something like 12-18 hours a day, seven days a week, with one day off in three, for over two years. We were totally exhausted, so we were going to Granada for a three or four-month holiday and forget all about films. And then Christopher Lee himself phoned me because I had made him up before on other things and he said, 'Stu, I'm going to Rio to make a Fu Manchu film, and I've asked for you!'

I said, 'I'm sorry, Chris, but we just had a terrible experience for the past two years with Stanley Kubrick, and we decided we can't survive if we don't take a long holiday.' He said, 'Well, this would be a holiday for you, because I set it up so you'll only be making me up and you won't have to worry about the whole film, and I am fairly straight, and I'm only going to work half a day,' so this was going to be a holiday in Rio and we had never been to Rio, so I said, 'Well, I still can't, because Kath has been working with me and she needs a holiday same as I do.'

He said, 'That's all right, bring her too, they'll pay all your expenses so bring her along!' I thought, well, it's Rio, half a day's work on one straight makeup; what the hell?' so we went along and thoroughly enjoyed it. I only made him up for half a day and it was great. And when it time to go home, I always say, 'I'm going to hang on to my return ticket.' I never do a film unless I can hang on to my return ticket, because I had big trouble before, so I wasn't going to experience that again.

They said, 'Okay, fine,' so I had my return air ticket in my pocket and they never got their grubby hands on it. And then the production said, 'We would like you to stay here; we're going back to England now, because we finished the film, but we want to come back here and do another film, not with Christopher Lee but with Shirley Eaton, the *Goldfinger* girl, We went to China and used a Chinese makeup man, and she had a terrible experience so we want her to do it but she said no way, unless she could choose her own makeup man. It happened that she knew me, because I'd worked with her on several films before, so when they said, 'Okay, who would you choose?' she said, 'Well, I've worked with Stuart Freeborn before so if it's possible to get him.'

They said, 'As a matter of fact, we've got him and he's already out there! But it will be five weeks,' so they told me, 'We'll keep paying you for those five weeks and give you your full allowance and everything, because it's going to save us fares back and forth, so you can enjoy yourself in Rio and see it for five weeks!'

So we stayed, and Kath had come out by then, but the thing was, I said, 'How about the allowance, who's going to give us our allowance and pay for our hotel bill?' They said, 'Oh, the accountant will be staying too,' but unfortunately the accountant had other ideas so by the end of the following week, he had disappeared back to England, and the hotel people came to me and said, 'Nobody has been paid; what's happening?'

I said, 'The accountant, Mr. So and So-' and they said, 'No, he's gone back to England!' I said, 'Well, that means we can't stay here; I'm sorry, but if nobody's paying us, we won't be able to stay!' We had a certain amount of money but that was it, so I just had a bit of money to stay on with and I thought I would be getting another allowance any day but I hadn't got it.

So I said, 'Okay, Kath, we've got a car,' so we went to the airport and booked tickets to come back to England and the hell with them; you can't pull tricks like that on us and fortunately, I already got my return ticket.

I had enough money from my previous allowance so that we could stay on for a few more days and it was a few days before I could get this plane trip anyway, so we thought we would stick around for a bit and then we packed up. I did manage to settle with the hotel, but we couldn't stay any longer, so we got in the hire car and we were nearly at the airport, it was a Sunday and absolutely everybody disappears on a Sunday. We were just a couple minutes from the airport, and as I was driving through this big square, a car came up behind us at high-speed. We saw a hand come out the window waving a pile of money, so we pulled up and they said, 'Here's your money, we're very sorry, but please don't go!' The accountant had just come back again, so it was just a matter of minutes and they would've lost us.

I had already settled with the hotel so I said, 'Look, pay them for the rest of our time here' so we had a bit of an argument, but we went back and it was fine, and Shirley Eaton came over and they all came back and we finished the other film, with a five-week paid vacation in-between, which worked out fine. Sometimes if we had a long weekend, we would go to the bus station and the buses had names on them of where they were going and we would look at the names and say, 'That sounds like an interesting place, so we'll go on that one today!' We would just get on the bus and go, and it was nice to be driven all along the coast, so we found a lot of interesting places.

There was one place we went to one day, which was a lovely beach. It was Ipanima like the song, and when I went on the beach, it was Christmas time, and there were all these groups of people, and they all had these little altars and they were putting buckets of wine all around the beach.

Kath: I don't know what they had been drinking, but it put them in a trance, so they were wandering around the beach and walking into the sea, which would usually bring them around most the time.

And then they would take a young girl and dunk her as though they were purifying her, as well as two other guys we saw them dunk, so it must've been some religious thing that was purifying them, and they were all half-drunk anyway.

The next day, I went swimming, and I swim out quite a long way and something hit me in the side. I thought it must be a log or something but I couldn't see it because there was nothing floating on the top. If it was wood, part of it would be on the top.

There were lifeguards on the beach, but I was a long way out, but I went under and I could see this body; it was a man, drowned obviously, and you could see he was dead and not breathing at all. He was one of the people from the day before when they got drunk and there he was, so that's what I hit without knowing it because the water was little bit misty and you couldn't see through it.

I swam like hell to the beach and got the lifeguards out and said, 'There's a dead guy out there!' so they went out there but they couldn't find him. I don't think they ever found him, because there were strong currents, or maybe they thought I was drunk as well, but I knew he was there.

So all of this happened because Christopher Lee promised you a free vacation.

Exactly that. It was immediately after *2001*.

With your Dracula, were you trying to match the look from the Hammer films?

Phil Leakey did all the Hammer films with him, and I did the Spanish one. I think I just read the script to see what he was supposed to look like and carried on the way I thought. We had the opportunity to do a lot of those films but I wasn't really into that area, so we turned most of them down. But it was different when I got a call from Christopher Lee himself, because he was such a lovely guy. I made him up for one of his first tests in a studio, which became Bray Studios.

You worked with Peter Cushing again on *Top Secret*, near the end of his career.

Peter Cushing was very nice. He was never quite the same after his wife died, but that happens to a lot of people, like Gene Wilder who we were talking about before.

Kath: After that, he didn't care if he worked or not.

What was that film where I had been to Australia? I was always fond of swimming; I was born and bred by the seaside, and always thought I could swim; I was thrown in the sea when I was two years old, so I don't even being taught because I could always swim, and whenever possible whenever we went anywhere, I would always go swimming and try to teach our sons.

I went to Australia for a film; no, it was Fiji, on *His Majesty O'Keefe*. I got a makeup girl from Sydney, because unfortunately the American crew were upset and obviously we would've been upset if it had been the other way around… We were going to Fiji because we were British, but none of the American crew wanted to come, so I said, 'Right, I need assistants!' They said, 'Well, we don't want to get anyone from England because it's too expensive, so we'll get three or four people from Australia.'

Well, they got three over and one was an old boy who was good at making things and I had to do lots of ear things, so I had him sitting down all day putting sticks through the noses for all these Maori characters where I had to put little things in their ears and sticks through their nostrils. There were lots of balsa trees, so I would get him to carve up little sticks and we would trick it by putting them on the outside and putting plugs inside so it widened it so it looked like it went right through.

There was a fairly elderly lady, and we had lots of rough locations to go on and she couldn't manage that, so I had to send her back, and then there was a young girl and a young boy, who actually knew nothing. I happened to see him sitting in the lounge one day, which was the only place we could go to in this little bungalow place built out of bamboo where we lived; no bars or anything like that, and we saw him reading the newspaper, and he said he was the chief makeup artist, but he was useless, so they got rid of him. I was pleased about that, because I really didn't want to cause problems, so I was stuck with the old man who sat there and saved me a lot of time by carving things that he was good at; and this girl, who was the only one who could come out with me to do things.

We had to jump on these little boats to go from one location to another so it was tough. We worked six days a week on location with Sunday off, and as I said, there were no bars or anything like that, just the trees and the sand, so we would go swimming every night, and this girl would come with me. She was Australian, so of course they're all great swimmers, and she would try to teach me the Australian crawl, which went on for Sunday after Sunday as I tried to learn.

On the Sunday, the whole crew would come down and we would go out swimming, so everybody was on the beach, while I was practicing this Australian crawl for all I was worth thinking, 'I've got to get this!' I could see this girl standing on the beach, but I had gone way out, further than anybody else, when I suddenly heard a lot of shouting. I turned around in the water looking back, and most of the crew was on the beach, standing there, waving their arms and shouting. A few people were swimming back as fast as they could, and I suddenly heard, 'Shark! Shark!'

I looked around and saw this fin not very far from me, and I remember somebody saying, if you're ever near a shark, don't swim, keep very still, but I guarantee nobody could ever do that! Even though I was thinking 'That's what I had to do!' I went away, as fast as I could go, despite what was in my mind. When I got in, there she was standing there and said, 'Well done, I've never seen you do it so well; that was the perfect Australian crawl!' so it takes a shark to do it right! I don't know if anybody could just remain still, because your instinct is to go, so that's what I did, but anyway, she approved of it.

The next Sunday, nobody was in the sea, so I thought, 'I've got to go in for my swim!' There were all the coral reefs around, and they said the sharks didn't really come in there very often, so I thought, I'll walk along the beach and I saw this lovely pond, where there were a lot of leaves and things maybe a foot under the water, so I thought, 'I can just swim on the top!' There was a little river coming into it from the mountains and running out of it again into the sea by the coral reefs, so I thought, 'This looks great, I'll swim here!'

One side was a bit deeper than the other with all this leaf stuff, so I dove in, but I suddenly got a terrific fear: get out, get out quick! I don't know why, so I thought, 'Don't be ridiculous!' I kept swimming, but this terrible fear came over me that told me to get out, so I got out thinking, 'How weird, because everything was peaceful, but why doesn't anybody come here? You would think a lot of people would've seen me swimming; there's got to be something!'

I walked all the way back to this small hut, where they had a little bar so I went up to the bar where I knew this guy Joe who was a Fijian behind the bar and said, 'Give me a whiskey, please.

Tell me, I walked along the beach, and saw a pond out there and I took a dive in it and I went swimming but I suddenly got a terrible fear come over me and I don't know why. Why aren't there any other people swimming there?'

He said, 'Oh, that's known as [something] in Fiji.' I said, 'What does that mean in English?' He spoke pretty good English but he had to think about, and he finally said, 'That would be 'Shark's Nest.'That's what it was: the sharks would go in through the coral reefs and that's where they would breed. Nobody had ever talked about it or mentioned it, but I can understand this natural instinctive fear. Something just didn't add up for me and my conscious mind, and thank goodness it didn't, because little did I know that the sharks were all in there, just under where I couldn't see. There's a lot more to us as human beings then we realize, and we have a subconscious mind that does things that you have no control over. It does a lot of things that you can't consciously work out for yourself but something guides you, and it had a number of experiences like that, like the one up the mountain that we talked about before, as well as this one and a few others like that, that I can't account for, but my conscious mind didn't have anything to do with it.

Part VIII: 5/19/04

In January of 2002, the first annual Makeup Artist Trade Show (better known as IMATS) was held in London, where Stuart appeared as one of the main speakers. His talk was memorable, particularly when one of the audience members asking questions turned out to be none other than fellow makeup legend Dick Smith, who approached the stage so the two could talk face to face.

In the months that followed, I heard from a number of people who were unhappy that they missed the show and Stuart's appearance. When the next IMATS was confirmed for the following January, Sheelagh and I approached the show's organizers with the idea of bringing Stuart back as an unbilled guest. We would sit him down in a foyer outside the main hall, I would ask him a question or two to get things started, and once he was rolling, I could just walk away, leaving him surrounded by a small crowd of fascinated attendees, who would sit on the floor around him, hanging on every word. Sheelagh and I would pop in every once in a while to make sure he was happy and see if he needed lunch or a break, and at the end of the day, we would put him in a cab for home, still telling stories as he got into the car. The informal round-table proved to be so popular that we asked Stuart if he would do it again, and this time, his storytelling circle was twice as big.

This last conversation is a strange footnote, as it took place several years after our string of previous conversations, and I honestly don't recall the reason why it happened. I think it might have been because

Sheelagh and I got a call that Stuart was packing up his workshop, because he and Kath were selling off the house and property in order to move to a smaller and much more manageable cottage nearby. Within minutes, we had jumped in the car and rocketed off to Esher. And while I hadn't planned on doing an interview, I carried my tape recorder as I always do, so when Stuart started telling stories, I was able to record them.

As it turned out, we got there a bit too late to rescue most of Stuart's most valuable pieces, which had already been sold off to auctioneers for pennies on the dollar I'm sure, but we did spend the rest of the day finding tons of smaller treasures, including old call sheets with notes and recipes written on the back, a couple of dramatically thinned-out photo albums and a bunch of original head casts, which were carefully wrapped in bubble wrap and stowed in the trunk. There was a set of Christopher Lee's red-rimmed contact lenses (incorrectly filed in a drawer marked 'false teeth'), a box of Stuart's engineering tools and a mint copy of Dick Smith's Monster Make-Up Handbook from 1965, now one of my most precious possessions.

I can't recall if this was the last day we spent with Stuart and Kath, but I think it was. Time has a way of vanishing when you're not paying attention, and when you suddenly look up to discover that several years have somehow passed. But one thing I'm sure of: this was our last interview...

Before I forget, you wanted to tell me the story about a human head.

There was a studio doing a real-life wartime film in Prague, where they needed a human head to be chopped off. They said [in the story], 'The Germans have got this boy and they're trying to make him tell them something they know he knows but he won't tell them. They know he lived just up there and his mother is up there now, so if we shock the life out of him, that might make him talk,' so apparently the story was true. It did happen, so they found this woman, his mother and chopped her head off, and then they held the head out to scare him stiff, and this really happened.

So they said to me, 'We want somebody to do this, and we've heard that you could possibly make a head like that for us. We contacted a certain actress, who asked if we knew Stuart Freeborn and he could do the cast and make the head for you. She said, 'I've worked with Stuart Freeborn on several films,' and since the actress didn't live too far away, she came around and I made the head.

That was all straightforward stuff, and then they said, 'We'll let you know when we want you to take a plane to Prague Airport, where we'll have a man there who speaks a little English, so he'll meet you at the airport. You're going to be staying with us for quite a few weeks, because we want you to be there while we're filming just in case we need to do something with it.'

I said that was fine, so I got to the airport and looked around, but I couldn't see anybody who recognized me, so I went through customs and put my luggage up and suddenly realized, 'My God, the head is in the bag!' I dared not it put it on a luggage truck, so when she was looking at the other bags, I quickly put it down on the floor.

She went through the bags and went like this [doing a double-take] and I thought, 'Oh Christ, she's seen me put it down, what am I going to do?' so I had to pick it up. There was nothing I could do, I had to show it to her; and where's that guy? I didn't speak a word of Czechoslovakian and she didn't speak any English, but she wanted to see inside the bag. I get a lot of problems like that in my life where I think, 'Why does this happen to me?'

[Sheelagh comes in and Stuart picks up the story again]   When I made this head, it was translucent and looked very realistic and I knew I could get it to the point where it looked believable, so I packed it up, and the blood I put on it was sort of shiny and wet, so I put it in a bag. The head had to be strong and solid, because the actors had to hold it out to frighten this boy who knew things they wanted to know and to scare him, because he wouldn't tell them otherwise.

Anyway, when I got to the airport and the customs lady started going through everything, I had to pick the bag up, and when I took the head out, they all looked like this [Stuart makes a freaked-out look] because it looked so realistic that they wouldn't know otherwise. So she was yelling to the people around her and they're getting on the telephone to get the police, while I'm thinking, 'Oh my God, what am I going to do now?' And this chap who spoke a bit of English and was supposed to meet me, *still* hadn't come, so all of this was going on for quite some time.

I was wondering how I was going to get out of it, when suddenly this chap came in and saw me there, and said, 'Is your name Stuart Freeborn?' I said, 'Thank God you're here, they think it's real and they're calling the police! Can you explain it to them?' so he explained that it was only for a film, but there were a few strange moments.

You had another story you meant to finish from a previous conversation?

That was from *Top Secret*. Only a week ago, they took the horse away in two bits. I don't know if you remember the film, with Val Kilmer, but you see them in the room as the picture starts, so he and his wife are in the very first scene and the phone goes. He picks up the phone and he says, 'Yes, okay, I'll be ready!' and he puts it down.

She says, 'Who's that?' and it's a big thing that you know who the goodies and baddies are, and that her father is being taken away and put somewhere and captured, so they're going to Paris or wherever they can find him. You see a lot of other action going on, and then you're back in the flat and he gets in the car and it's now getting dark and he's going to this posh hotel that he knows well and he says, 'I would never have gone to this hotel this way; where the hell is he going?'

He carries on, and the car suddenly stops, and you get a long shot of it and it's in a big car dump, where a big magnet suddenly comes down and takes the car up. The side bits come in and squash it, so that's the finish of him, and the rest of the story goes on from there, and you're back in the flat and she's sitting there and there's a knock on the door and she goes a few steps down to the door and opens the door and there he is, this high, it's still him and I had to make the broken car and fit it all around him [Note: this is supposed to be Omar Sharif that Stuart is talking about]. So I made the car with the cracked glass and the metal, fitting it all together, so he's standing there, about this high. I did the cast of his face and I got one of our dwarves from *Star Wars* and fitted it on him, so you could see it's the character but a miniature of him and she says, 'Oh, what happened to you?' In real life that never would have happened!

I believe you also had a story from *His Majesty O'Keefe*?

I got this call from America, and they said, 'You've worked with Burt Lancaster before, and he liked what you did. He's going to do our next film, so it's eight months in the Fiji Islands. I said, 'Yes, I like Burt Lancaster, so I'll certainly do it!' so we all went off to the Fiji Islands.

We were getting close to the end, and there were only a couple of weeks to go, when I got a cable from Orson Welles saying, 'I found out where you are, and I'm going to make a film in Rome, at Cinecitta,' which was the big studio in Rome. I've done 12 films all over Italy, and Welles would be acting in it as well, so he said, 'I'll meet you in Rome on a certain date!'

I wrote it all down, so we were supposed to have finished this film but they said, 'Sorry, we're not quite finished; we have another week or so to shoot,' so I had to re-plan it all and re-book the plane. Anyway, I finally got there and I knew exactly where his offices were, because I had worked in Rome many times, so I knew it better than I knew London. They asked if they could get me a car from the airport, so we went to this hotel and it was quite late now, maybe four in the morning and I hadn't eaten very much so I was very hungry and very tired.

So I got to the hotel, and I remembered that in Rome, they have little restaurants that stay open all night long, so they showed me the room and there was no girl at the front desk, but I came down again, and there was this guy lying on a divan asleep, so I had to wake him up. He told me where to go, so I went out and walked in to a restaurant, which was empty but for one man at the table. He saw me come in, and I must have looked English because he said, 'Come and join me!' He was actually American, and he said, 'I've just been making a film in the Mediterranean and I've got to see Rome before I go back to America!'

I said, 'I'm actually in the film business too, and I'm here to meet Orson Welles.' Anyway, we had a meal and I went back to the hotel for a bit of sleep. I had some very good friends in Rome and their family would pick us up on a Sunday and take us to the coast, which was a regular thing, because everybody in Rome goes to the coast on a Sunday.

I went to sleep and woke up and it was still dark, and I thought, 'That's strange, I must have woke up too early, maybe I only got half an hour's sleep!' so I walked over to the wash basin and looked in the mirror and I had a beard, so I must have slept all the way through the next day!

After a little while, one of the girls came in and they remembered me because I had stayed there before and she said, 'We didn't want to disturb you because you were fast asleep!' They had come in to clean the room during the daytime and I had slept all the way through the day, so they said, 'We were very quiet, we didn't want to wake you up!'

I went to Welles' office, and was nearly there when a woman came towards me and I recognized her and it was his wife. She says, 'Oh Stuart, we've been waiting for you, but I have some bad news for you; something has happened and there's a big disagreement about running the film and Orson Welles is not at all happy with how they've rearranged it, so he's had to call it off, so I'm sorry we've dragged you all the way here!' So I got to Rome, had a midnight meal, got some sleep and that was it, I had to get on the plane back to England!

Afterword

I was sitting at my desk here in New Jersey one morning when I heard that Stuart Freeborn had passed away, not all that long before his 100th birthday. Despite his advanced age, it was still a shock; I suppose we assume some people will be around forever. One would think Stuart's death would have been a motivating factor for finally putting this book together, but the sad truth is, the countless interview tapes took forever to track down after so many years. In fact, I only came across the final tape of Sheelagh's solo visit while cleaning out our London flat just a few weeks before writing this.

The other reality I had to deal with was that Stuart had loaned out the bulk of his photos for various interviews over the years, and most of those journalists weren't very good about returning them. In those pre-digital/Internet days, it pretty much meant they were gone forever. Sheelagh and I were able to rescue one photo album of remaining images, as well as a small trove of bits and pieces- call sheets, makeup notes, etc- when we visited the Freeborn house together for the last time.

All of that material has finally been put together here in as coherent form as I could manage. The interviews have been put in chronological order with most of the redundancies edited out, with the exception of an occasional supplicate story I left in for context. It's as close as you can get to the flavor of those original conversations. I do hope you enjoy them. - Joe